WORLD HISTORY
DATES

Jane Chisholm
Designed by **Iain Ashman**
Illustrated by **Ian Jackson** and **Richard Draper**

Consultants
Anne Millard BA, Dip.Ed., Dip.Arch., Ph.D.
Malcolm Falkus B.Sc.(Econ), F.R.Hist.S.
Senior Lecturer in Economic History,
London School of Economics.

Map illustrations by **Guy Smith**

Additional illustrations by
**Joseph McEwan, Gillian Hurry, Chris Lyon, Martin Newton,
Roger Phillips** and **Sara Silcock**

Contents

About this book

This illustrated book of world history dates covers the span of history from about **9000BC** to the present day. The book is divided into eight periods. These can be identified by the dates at the top left-hand side of each double page and a coloured triangle at the bottom right-hand side.

 c.9000BC-AD499

 500-1199

 1200-1499

16th CENTURY

Each section contains features on important topics, as well as date charts which are arranged in columns according to geographical area. This means that you can follow what was happening in different parts of the world during the same period. The periods are shown below.

 17th CENTURY

 18th CENTURY

 19th CENTURY

20th CENTURY

Using this book

This book can be read cover to cover, or used for reference.

The following abbreviations have been used:

c. stands for *circa*, the **Latin** for "about". Many early dates begin with a **c.** as historians have only been able to discover an approximate date.

BC stands for "**Before Christ**", although many historians now believe that, due to a miscalculation, the birth of Christ was probably **c.5BC**, rather than the year **0**, as was once thought.

AD stands for *Anno Domini* and applies to all the years after the birth of **Jesus Christ**. It means "Year of the Lord".

In the first section of the book, to avoid confusion, **AD** and **BC** have been used throughout the features, in the first entry of each column of the date charts and where the dates in the charts change from being **BC** to **AD**. They have not been used in subsequent sections, as the dates concerned are all **AD**.

The dating system used today is called the **Gregorian calendar**, and was introduced in **1582** (in **Catholic** countries only) by **Pope Gregory XIII**. It is a revised version of the **Julian calendar**, introduced by

Julius Caesar in **46BC**. His calendar was identical to ours, except that the year did not begin on the **1st January** and he used a different system for leap years.

Dates that appear in brackets after a person's name, such as **Isaac Newton (1642-1727)**, refer to his or her life. In the case of kings, queens and emperors, such as **Maria Theresa of Austria (1740-1780)**, the dates of the reign are shown instead. There are one or two exceptions to this, such as **Charles V** and **Frederick II of Hohenstaufen**, who ruled over different territories at different times.

All dates and key words, such as the names of countries and people, are highlighted in bold type. If a word in bold type is followed by an asterisk (for example **Renaissance***), it will appear in a footnote at the bottom of the page. This will refer you either to a feature where you will find a fuller explanation of the subject, or to its first appearance in a date chart. Some of the words are referred to a glossary on pages 113-114. If the word is familiar to you, there is no need to interrupt your reading. For reasons of space, we have simplified the footnotes, so that **Hittite Empire** and **Hittite Kingdom** appear as just **Hittites** and words such as **Judah**, **Judaism** and **Jewish** appear under one entry, **Judaism**.

The first farmers

The earliest people lived as **nomads***, hunting animals and gathering wild plants. The change to a settled, agricultural way of life was a gradual one, occurring in different places at different times. Farming probably began in the **Middle East** in about **9000BC**, in an area known as the **Fertile Crescent**.

Jericho consisted of densely packed mud brick houses, built behind a strong defensive wall with a huge watchtower.

As people adopted farming, they began to build permanent settlements. One of the best known is **Jericho**, which had about 2000 people by **8000BC**. It was destroyed in **7000BC** and later rebuilt.

Çatal Hüyük, Anatolia.

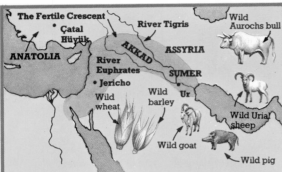

The Fertile Crescent
• Çatal Hüyük
ANATOLIA
River Tigris
River Euphrates
• Jericho
AKKAD
ASSYRIA
SUMER
Ur
Wild Aurochs bull
Wild wheat
Wild barley
Wild goat
Wild Urial sheep
Wild pig

The wild ancestors of wheat, barley, lentils and peas, goats, pigs, sheep and cattle were native to this region. People had probably been living off them for centuries before they started to select, domesticate and cultivate them.

In **Çatal Hüyük** they had elaborately decorated shrines for their gods and goddesses.

By **6000BC**, **Çatal Hüyük** was a flourishing town of 5000-6000 farmers and traders. They made pottery and textiles. We know little about how this way of life developed, as such sites are few and scattered.

Europe

c.6000BC Groups of farmers, possibly from **Anatolia***, reach **Greece**, **Crete*** and the **Aegean islands**.

c.5200-2000 Farming spreads through **northern** and **western Europe**.

c.4000-1500 Building of **megaliths**, large stone monuments, such as tombs and **henges**, in **Malta**, **Brittany**, the **Iberian peninsula** and the **British Isles**.

Stonehenge, Britain c.2000BC

Henges are circular areas, often made from stones.

c.4000 Copper is being worked in the **Balkans**.

c.3000 Olives, vines and cereals cultivated in the **Aegean**. Some trading contacts abroad.

c.2500 Bronze begins to be used in **Europe**.

c.2500-2000 Corded Ware (or Battle-axe) and Beaker cultures spread in **Northern Europe**.

Beaker pots **Corded Ware** pots

Wessex gold cup

c.2000-1700 First Palace Period on **Crete***.

c.2000-1500 Wessex culture in southern Britain.

The Middle East

c.9000BC Agriculture is underway in the **Fertile Crescent** (see map above).

c.8000 Jericho is a flourishing town of about 2000 people.

c.7000 Pottery, spinning, weaving and hammering of copper are all in use.

c.6000 Çatal Hüyük has 5000-6000 people.

c.5000-2000 Civilization of **Sumer***.

Sumerian panel known as the **Royal Standard of Ur**.

c.4000 The technique of copper and gold smelting is discovered.

c.3400 The wheel is invented in **Sumer***.

c.3300 Writing develops in **Sumer***.

Stone tablet with **Sumerian** writing.

c.2371-2230 Kingdom of **Akkad*** is established.

c.2000 Hittites* set up states in **Anatolia***.

c.2000 Rise of **Babylon***.

In **c.1000BC**, the **Urnfield** people began spreading into neighbouring areas as **Celts, Slavs, Italics** and **Illyrians**.

Germans

Balts

Wessex

Brittany

Extent of **Urnfield** culture

La Tène

Celts

Hallstatt

Cimmerians
Scythians
Sarmatians

Hittites

Extent of **Hallstatt** culture

Illyrians

Kassites

Italics

Aryans

Thracians

Area of **Beaker** culture

Greeks

Mitanni

Between **1000-1BC**, the **Celts** expanded all over **Europe**, reaching **Spain, Britain, Ireland** and the **Low Countries** by **200BC**.

Sea Peoples

Phoenicians

Aramaeans
Hebrews
Nabataeans

Area of **Corded Ware** culture

The migration of peoples

Egyptians

Akkadians
Southern Semites (Arabs)

Between **3000-2000BC**, there were movements of peoples across **Asia** and **Europe**. Many belonged to one of two main language groups - **Semitic** and **Indo-European**. By **c.3000BC** the **Semites** began to spread out all over the **Middle East**. Semitic languages include **Arabic** and **Hebrew**, as well as languages that

have died out, such as **Babylonian***. The **Indo-Europeans** may have come from **southern Russia**. From **2000BC** many of them began to colonize new areas. Most **modern European** languages, as well as **Armenian, Latin, Sanskrit** and some **Hindu** dialects, are descended from a common Indo-European language.

Africa

c.5000BC The **Sahara**, which had once been green, is still fertile in parts and there is evidence of cattle herders.

Rock paintings from this period, found in the **Sahara** region.

c.5000 Farming begins in **Egypt***. The Egyptians also develop pottery, linen-making and, later, metal-working.

Farming scene from an **Egyptian** tomb-painting.

c.3300 Hieroglyphic* writing develops in **Egypt***.

c.3118 King **Menes** unites **Egypt***.

The Far East

c.5000BC Gradual adoption of agriculture in **China**.

c.4000 Farming communities settle in the **Indus Valley** in **India**.

c.3000 Hunter/gatherers living in **Japanese islands**. Use of pottery.

c.2500-1500 The **Indus Valley Civilization** in **India**, based on agriculture, with contacts as far as **Mesopotamia***. It centres around large cities, with public buildings, good sanitation and houses set out on a grid system. They also have a form of writing. The best known sites are **Mohenjo-Daro** and **Harappa**.

c.1800-1500 Legendary **Hsia** dynasty rules in **China**.

Stone statue and bronze figure from the **Indus Valley Civilization**.

The Americas

c.6000BC Farming gradually develops in **Central America**.

c.3200 Introduction of pottery in **Ecuador**.

c.3000 Pottery is in use in **Colombia**.

c.3000 Gradual change to an agricultural way of life in **Mexico** and **Peru**.

c.3000 North America: hunter-gatherers, known as **Cochise**, living in the south-west.

c.2300 Mexico: the agricultural way of life leads to settlement in permanent villages.

c.2300 Use of pottery spreads to **Mexico** and **Guatemala**.

c.2000-1500 Pottery spreads among farmers in **Peru**.

North America

Hopewell people

Adena people

River Mississippi

Cochise hunters

Hohokam people

Babylonia, 7; Egypt, 10-11; hieroglyphics, 10; Mesopotamia, 6-7.

5

Mesopotamia and Anatolia c.5000BC-AD200

One of the earliest known centres of civilization was in **Mesopotamia**, the area between the **Rivers Tigris** and **Euphrates**.

From **c.4000BC**, societies grew up there, with cities, public architecture, writing and political, religious and legal systems.

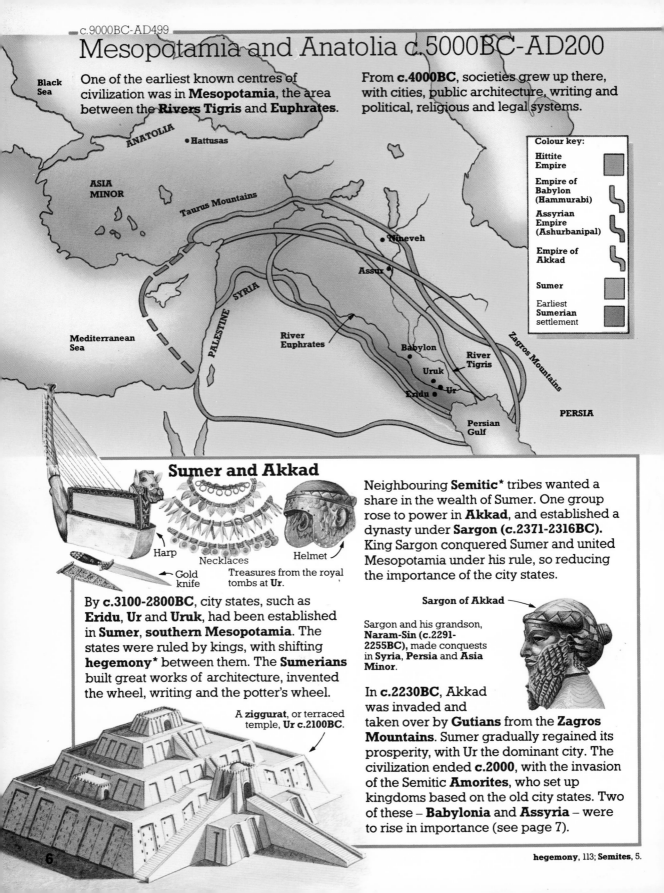

Black Sea

ANATOLIA

• Hattusas

ASIA MINOR

Taurus Mountains

• Nineveh

Assur

Mediterranean Sea

SYRIA

PALESTINE

River Euphrates

Babylon

Uruk

Eridu • • Ur

River Tigris

Zagros Mountains

PERSIA

Persian Gulf

Colour key:

Hittite Empire	
Empire of Babylon (Hammurabi)	
Assyrian Empire (Ashurbanipal)	
Empire of Akkad	
Sumer	
Earliest Sumerian settlement	

Sumer and Akkad

Harp

Necklaces

Helmet

Gold knife

Treasures from the royal tombs at **Ur**.

By **c.3100-2800BC**, city states, such as **Eridu**, **Ur** and **Uruk**, had been established in **Sumer**, **southern Mesopotamia**. The states were ruled by kings, with shifting **hegemony*** between them. The **Sumerians** built great works of architecture, invented the wheel, writing and the potter's wheel.

A **ziggurat**, or terraced temple, **Ur c.2100BC**.

Neighbouring **Semitic*** tribes wanted a share in the wealth of Sumer. One group rose to power in **Akkad**, and established a dynasty under **Sargon (c.2371-2316BC)**. King Sargon conquered Sumer and united Mesopotamia under his rule, so reducing the importance of the city states.

Sargon of Akkad

Sargon and his grandson, **Naram-Sin (c.2291-2255BC)**, made conquests in **Syria**, **Persia** and **Asia Minor**.

In **c.2230BC**, Akkad was invaded and taken over by **Gutians** from the **Zagros Mountains**. Sumer gradually regained its prosperity, with Ur the dominant city. The civilization ended **c.2000**, with the invasion of the Semitic **Amorites**, who set up kingdoms based on the old city states. Two of these – **Babylonia** and **Assyria** – were to rise in importance (see page 7).

hegemony, 113; **Semites**, 5.

Babylonia

One of the **Amorite** kingdoms, with its capital at **Babylon**, gradually expanded and conquered **Akkad** (c.1894BC). Later all **Mesopotamia** was absorbed into the **Babylonian kingdom**.

This stone slab records the code of laws of King **Hammurabi (1792-1750BC)**, conqueror of **Mesopotamia**.

Unrest followed **Hammurabi**'s death, and parts of the kingdom broke away. In **c.1595BC** Babylonia was invaded by **Kassites** from the **Zagros Mountains**. They were in turn ousted by the **Elamites** (c.1174BC), who ruled briefly. In **1170BC**, Babylonian rule was re-established by **Nebuchadnezzar I**. The kingdom eventually fell to the **Assyrians** in **689BC**.

The Neo-Babylonian empire

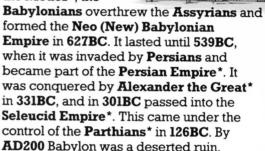

The **Ishtar Gate, Babylon**, built by **Nebuchadnezzar II (605-562BC)**. He established control over **Western Mesopotamia, Syria, Palestine** and **Elam**.

With the help of the **Medes***, the **Babylonians** overthrew the **Assyrians** and formed the **Neo (New) Babylonian Empire** in **627BC**. It lasted until **539BC**, when it was invaded by **Persians** and became part of the **Persian Empire***. It was conquered by **Alexander the Great*** in **331BC**, and in **301BC** passed into the **Seleucid Empire***. This came under the control of the **Parthians*** in **126BC**. By **AD200** Babylon was a deserted ruin.

The Assyrians

Assyrian stone relief from the palace of **Sargon II** at **Khorsabad**.

The Assyrians were great builders and decorated their palaces with huge stone reliefs, which was their main art form.

The **Assyrians** were **Semites*** who had settled in **Mesopotamia** around the cities **Assur** and **Nineveh**. They became an aggressive, militaristic people. The **First Assyrian Empire (1814-1754BC)**, was conquered by **Shamshi-Adad** and his son, **Ishme-Dagan**. It was smashed by the **Babylonians** and passed under the control of the **Mitanni*** (c.1450BC).

Inside an **Assyrian** palace.

The king is shown receiving prisoners after a battle.

The Assyrians gained their independence to form the **Middle Assyrian Empire (c.1375-1047BC)**. Under **Tiglathpileser I (1115-1077BC)**, they conquered more territory, exacting **tribute*** from subject peoples. The empire fell apart with the arrival of the **Aramaeans*** (c.1047BC).

The **New Assyrian Empire (c.911-609BC)** grew to dominate the **Middle East**. At its height it included all Mesopotamia, much of the highlands to the east, **Syria**, **Levant**, **Palestine** and **Lower Egypt**. However, there were frequent rebellions. An alliance formed against Assyria in **614BC** by the **Medes*** and the Babylonians led to the overthrow of the Empire.

The Hittites

Hittite war chariot

The Hittites were skilled in the use of iron.

The **Hittites**, an **Indo-European*** people, arrived in **Anatolia c.2000BC** and set up small rival states. The country was united by **King Labernas**, who founded the **Old Kingdom (c.1650-1450BC)** at **Hattusas**. The Hittites expanded into **north Syria** and overran **Babylon c.1595BC**. For a while during the **Empire Period (c.1450-1200BC)** they ruled an area from the **Mediterranean** to the **Persian Gulf**. The Empire collapsed with the advance of the **Sea Peoples*** c.1200BC.

Europe

c.2000 BC Horses and wheeled vehicles are in use in **eastern Europe**.

Bronze chariot, **Denmark, 1500BC**.

c.1900-1200 Civilization of **Mycenae***.

c.1700-1450 Second Palace Period on **Crete***. Writing, known as **Linear A**, is in use. **Linear B**, an early form of **Greek*** writing is introduced c.1400.

Cretan disc showing **Linear A**.

c.1400-1200 Mycenae* is at its height.

c.1380 Fall of **Knossos** in **Crete***.

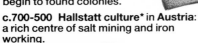

Village settlement from the **Urnfield culture**.

c.1300 Urnfield culture* in **central Europe**.

c.1250 The **Trojan Wars**, fought between the **Mycenaeans*** and the **Trojans** (from **Troy** in **Asia Minor**), lead to the destruction of Troy.

c.1050-750 Dark Age in **Greece***.

c.900 Etruscans (metal-workers from **Asia Minor**) are established in **northern Italy**.

c.800 Homer composes the *Iliad* and the *Odyssey*, **Greek** epic poems describing the **Trojan Wars**.

776 First **Olympic Games** in **Greece***.

Etruscan bronze warrior.

Hallstatt bronze axe.

753 Traditional date of the founding of **Rome***.

c.750 Greek city states* begin to found colonies.

c.700-500 Hallstatt culture* in **Austria**: a rich centre of salt mining and iron working.

Scythian gold ware from **Russia**.

c.700 An **Indo-European*** people called **Scythians** spread from **central Asia** to **eastern Europe**.

683 Athens* replaces its hereditary kings with nine **archons** (chief magistrates), chosen yearly by the nobles.

c.600-500 The **Archaic Period** in **Greek** art.

594 Solon is made sole **archon** of **Athens***. He introduces government reforms.

510-509 In **Rome***, the **monarchy** is replaced by a **republic***.

509-507 Cleisthenes introduces reforms which lead to **democracy*** in **Athens***.

c.500 Celts* begin migrating from **west** and **central Europe** to **Spain, Britain, Ireland** and the **Low Countries**.

The Middle East

c.1814-1754 BC First Assyrian Empire*.

c.1792-1750 Reign of **Hammurabi**, King of the **Babylonian Empire***.

c.1650-1450 Hittite Old Kingdom*.

c.1595 Hittites* sack and burn **Babylon***.

c.1450-1200 Hittite Empire* (New Kingdom) is founded by **King Telepinus**.

c.1450 Assyrian Empire* passes under the control of a **Semitic*** people called the **Mitanni**.

c.1400 First mention in **Egyptian*** records of raiders known as the **Sea Peoples**. They comprise several groups of peoples from the **Mediterranean islands**, the **Anatolian coast** and **Greece***.

1380-1340 Shuppiluliumash, King of the **Hittites***, destroys the **Mitanni** kingdom and causes the break-up of the northern part of the **Egyptian Empire***.

c.1375-1047 Middle Assyrian Empire*.

c.1269 Treaty between **King Hattusilis II** of the **Hittites*** and **Ramesses II** of **Egypt***.

c.1200 Migration of the **Sea Peoples**, who overwhelm **Cyprus** and many Middle Eastern cities and destroy most of the **Hittite Empire***.

c.1200 Arrival of the **Hebrews*** in **Canaan**, led by **Moses** and **Joshua**.

c.1200-1000 Rise to power of the **Phoenicians** (in what is now the **Lebanon**). They found colonies around the southern and western shores of the **Mediterranean**, with leading cities at **Byblos, Sidon, Beirut** and **Tyre**. Their alphabet forms the basis for **Greek, Latin** and modern **Roman** scripts.

Phoenician port

c.1190 Ramesses III of **Egypt*** defeats the **Sea Peoples**. One group, the **Peleset** (whom we call **Philistines**), settle in part of **Canaan**, which becomes known as **Palestine** after them.

1115-1077 Reign of **Tiglathpileser I** of **Assyria***.

c.1010-926 United Jewish* Kingdom of **Israel***.

926 Israel* splits into two kingdoms: **Israel** and **Judah***.

c.911-609 New Assyrian Empire*.

Solomon's temple, **Jerusalem**

847 First mention of people called **Nabataeans** in **Arabia**. They settle south of the **Dead Sea**.

835-825 Sarduri I founds the kingdom of **Urartu** (or **Ararat**) in the area of **Lake Van**. An important trading centre, based on iron and copper production, it is conquered by the **Assyrians*** (721-705), then the **Scythians** and becomes part of the **Median Empire*** in 610.

Africa

Statue of **Prince Rahotep** and **Princess Nofret** c.2660BC.

c.2686-2181 BC **Old Kingdom** in **Egypt***: dynasties III-VI.

c.2181-2040 **First Intermediate Period** in **Egypt***: dynasties VII-X. Collapse of central government. Order is partly restored by the kings of dynasties IX-X, who rule at **Heracleopolis**.

Jewellery belonging to a **Middle Kingdom** princess.

c.2133-1633 **Middle Kingdom** in **Egypt***: dynasties XI-XIII.

c.1674-1567 **Second Intermediate Period** in **Egypt***: dynasties XIV-XVII.

1567-1085 **New Kingdom** in **Egypt***: dynasties XVIII-XX.

Bust of **Queen Nefertiti**, wife of **Akhenaten** (see below).

1503-1482 Reign of **Hatshepsut**, woman **pharaoh** (ruler) of **Egypt**.

c.1500 Cattle and goats become domesticated in **West Africa**.

c.1450 The **Egyptian Empire*** now stretches from the fourth cataract of the **River Nile** to the **River Euphrates**.

1379-1362 Reign of **Akhenaten** of **Egypt***. He attempts to impose the worship of one god only, but fails.

1190 **Ramesses III** of **Egypt*** defeats the **Sea Peoples***.

c.1085 **Nubia** and **Kush** have regained independence from **Egypt***.

1085-656 **Third Intermediate Period** in **Egypt***: dynasties XXI-XXV. Egypt begins to decline.

900BC-AD400 **Kingdom of Meroë** is established.

814 Founding of **Carthage** in **North Africa** by the **Phoenician*** princess, **Elissa of Tyre**.

The Far East

c.1500BC Collapse of the **Indus Valley Civilization***, partly due to arrival of **Indo-Europeans*** (or **Aryans**) from the north west, and to the flooding of the **River Indus** which destroys cities already in decline. Aryan control spreads as far as the **River Ganges**.

c.1500-1028 **Shang dynasty** in **China**: a feudal state, with walled cities and temples, ruled by priest-kings.

Shang dynasty bronze vessels.

Chinese writing on bone.

c.1500-600 **Vedic Period** in **India**. The **Hindu** religion is gradually established. The **Vedas** (scriptures) are composed and the Hindu caste system develops.

c.1028 **Shang dynasty** in **China** is overthrown by the **Chou dynasty** (1028-771).

c.800 **Indo-Europeans*** expand south in **India** spreading the **Hindu** religion.

660 Legendary date of founding of **Japan** under **Emperor Jimmu**. (Japan was probably founded c.120.)

c.650 Introduction of iron-making in **China**.

c.600 Probable date for the introduction of the religion and philosophy of **Taoism**, by the **Chinese** philosopher, **Lao-tze**.

After **Buddha**'s death, parts of his body were buried under domed buildings, called **stupas**, in various parts of **India**.

Great Stupa at **Sanchi c.150BC.**

c.560-483 Life of **Gautama Siddhartha**, known as the **Buddha**, **Indian** founder of the **Buddhist** religion.

551-479 Life of **Kung Fu-tze**, also known as **Confucius**, the **Chinese** philosopher.

512 **Indian** provinces of **Gandhara** and **Sind** become part of the **Persian Empire***.

The Americas

c.2000-1000BC The beginning of the **Mayan culture** in **Mesoamerica** (Central America – see map below). This is known as the **Early Pre-Classical Period**. Farmers begin to settle in villages.

2000 First evidence of metal-working in **Peru**.

c.1800-900 The **Initial Period** in **Peru**. People settle in permanent villages. Evidence of social and religious organization. Pottery spreads.

Peruvian temple platform

c.1500 **North America**: agriculture reaches the south-east and, rather later, reaches the mid-west.

c.1500BC-AD200 Spread of the **Olmec culture** in **Mexico**. The Olmecs use **hieroglyphics** (picture writing) and calendars. They build ceremonial centres and carve huge stone (basalt) heads and small "baby-faced" jade figures.

Giant basalt head.

c.1000-300 The **Middle Pre-Classical Period** of the **Mayans**. They build mound platforms for temples and palaces.

c.900 **Mexico**. The **Olmecs** build the first ball court at **La Venta**, for use during religious festivals.

Mesoamerica

	Mayan culture
	Olmec culture
	Zapotec culture

El Tajín · Teotihuacán · Valley of Mexico · Oaxaca · La Venta · Monte Albán

c.900-200 The **Chavin culture** flourishes in **Peru**, producing work in gold and silver. This period is known as the **Early Horizon**.

Chavin goldwork

Ancient Egypt

One of the greatest civilizations of the Ancient World was that of **Ancient Egypt**. The Egyptians produced art and architecture, studies of mathematics, astronomy and medicine and invented a form of picture writing (**hieroglyphics**).

Palette showing **King Menes**.

Farming communities grew up along the **River Nile** before **5000BC**. By **c.3300BC** these were organized into two kingdoms. They were united **c.3118BC** by **King Menes**, who established a capital at **Memphis**.

Under the **Old Kingdom (c. 2686-2181BC)** there was a great flowering of Egyptian culture, including the building of **pyramids** and temples. By the end of the period the power of **nomarchs** (provincial governors) was growing and central government collapsed. There followed a time of internal strife, famine and invasions.

Later pyramids, such as the **Great Pyramid** at **Giza**, were straight-sided.

Step pyramid at **Sakkara**, built for **King Zoser (2667-2648)** and designed by **Imhotep**.

Egypt

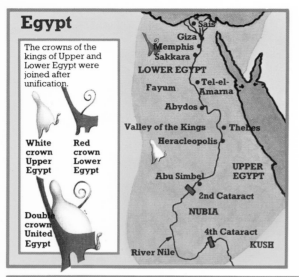

The crowns of the kings of Upper and Lower Egypt were joined after unification.

White crown Upper Egypt

Red crown Lower Egypt

Double crown United Egypt

Sais
Giza
Memphis
Sakkara
LOWER EGYPT
Fayum
Tel-el-Amarna
Abydos
Valley of the Kings · Thebes
Heracleopolis
Abu Simbel
2nd Cataract
NUBIA
4th Cataract
UPPER EGYPT
KUSH
River Nile

Europe

c.500-338BC Classical period in Greek art.

490 and 480-479 Persian campaigns against **Greece***.

Classical Greek architecture.

461-429 Pericles plays a leading role in **Athenian*** politics.

Examples of **Celtic** design from the **La Tène** period. The shield is from **England**.

c.450 Start of **Celtic*** culture, based at **La Tène, France**.

450 Roman* laws are codified.

431-404 Peloponnesian War in **Greece***.

395-387 Corinthian War: Athens*, Thebes, Corinth and Argos unite against **Sparta***.

387 Celtic* tribe of **Gauls** sack **Rome***.

359-336 Reign of **Philip II*** of **Macedonia**.

340 Hellenic League of **Greek** cities is formed against **Philip II***.

338 Philip II* conquers the **Hellenic League** at the **Battle of Chaeronea**.

336-323 Empire of **Alexander the Great***.

280-168 Antigonid dynasty rules **Macedonia**.

The Middle East

835BC Rise of the kingdom of the **Medes***.

800 Kingdom of **Phrygia** is established.

c.745 Assyria* conquers small **Hittite*** states in **Syria**.

722-705 Reign of **Sargon II of Assyria**: the height of Assyria's military power. They conquer **Judah*** and sack **Babylon***.

7th century Phrygia falls under the domination of the **Cimmerians**. The kingdom of **Lydia** rises to prominence.

680-652 King Gyges extends the kingdom of **Lydia**.

668-631 Reign of **King Ashurbanipal** of **Assyria**.

653-583 Reign of **Cyaxeres** of **Media***. Media becomes a major power.

627-539 The **Neo-Babylonian Empire***.

615-609 Medes* and **Babylonians*** ally against **Assyrians***, resulting in the collapse of the Assyrian Empire.

586-538 The **Babylonian Captivity**: King **Nebuchadnezzar II** of **Babylonia*** (605-561) destroys **Jerusalem** and takes many **Jews*** captive.

The **Hanging Gardens of Babylon**.

Egyptian fortress

During the **Middle Kingdom (c.2133-1633BC)**, princes of **Thebes** rose to power **c.2040BC** and reunited the country. Egypt conquered part of **Nubia** and built large forts to defend its frontier. Then came invasions of **Hyksos**, who conquered the **Nile Delta** and **Lower Egypt** and subjected much of **Middle Egypt** to **vassal***status.

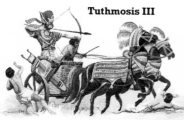
Tuthmosis III

The **Egyptian Empire** reached its greatest extent during the reign of **Tuthmosis III** (1504-1425BC).

Theban princes drove out the Hyksos and reunited Egypt under the **New Kingdom (1567-1085BC)**. Egyptian power was at its height and a vast empire was conquered, from the **Fourth Cataract** of the Nile to the **River Euphrates**.

Many great works of architecture were built during the **New Kingdom**. Egyptian kings, now called **pharaohs**, were buried in rock-cut tombs in the **Valley of Kings**.

Treasures from the tomb of **King Tutankhamun (1361-1352BC)**.

From **1085BC** Egyptian power declined. The country was conquered and occupied by **Persia** (525-404BC) and (343-332BC) and by **Greeks** and **Macedonians** from 332-30BC. In **30BC** Egypt became a province of the **Roman Empire***.

Temple at **Abu Simbel**, built by **Ramses II (1290-1224BC)**.

Africa

750-656BC Egypt is ruled by kings from **Kush** (dynasty XXV), who are later driven back south.

c.700 Cattle and sheep are domesticated in **West Africa**.

671 Egypt is conquered by **Assyrians***.

664-332 Late Period in **Egypt** (dynasties XXVI/XXX). The country is reunited by the princes of **Sais** and **Egypt** regains prestige.

663 Introduction of iron tools and weapons in **north Africa** from **Asia**. They reach **Nigeria** by c.450 and the south by c.AD100.

c.650 Carthage* has built up a fleet and armies to protect the **Phoenician** colonies.

Phoenician warship

525-404 Egypt is conquered and occupied by **Persia***.

The Far East

327-325BC Campaign of **Alexander the Great*** in **India**.

321-185 Maurya dynasty is founded in **India**.

300BC-AD300 The **Yayoi culture** in **Japan** is influenced by travellers from **China** and **Korea**, bringing bronze-making skills.

272-231 Reign of **King Asoka** of the **Maurya** dynasty. He builds an empire uniting **north** and **central India** and becomes a **Buddhist***.

Capital of a column erected by **Asoka**.

221-206 Ch'in dynasty in **China**. The **Great Wall of China** (214) is built to keep out the **Hsiung-Nu***.

An army of lifesize terracotta warriors was buried inside a **Ch'in** emperor's tomb.

The Americas

c.700BC Founding of **Monte Albán**, the sacred city of the **Olmecs*** in **Oaxaca, Mexico**.

c.600 Oaxaca becomes the main centre of **Olmec*** culture.

c.600-200 The **Adena** people in **North America** farm and construct earth works for ceremonial buildings and burial mounds.

Adenan mound

c.300 Gradual decline of the **Olmec culture*** in **Mexico**. Rise of **Zapotec** culture in **Oaxaca**.

c.300BC-250AD The rise of the **Maya*** in **Mesoamerica**: the **Late Pre-Classical Period**. Large political and religious centres develop, such as **Monte Albán**, **Teotihuacán** and **El Tajín**.

c.300 North America: the **Hopewell** people displace the **Adenas**. They are great mound builders and traders.

Greece

Crete c.3000-c.1100BC

The earliest known **European** civilization developed in **Crete** between **c.3000-2000BC**. It had well-planned towns, skilled craftsmen, a form of writing (known as **Linear A**) and flourishing trade. It became known as the **Minoan civilization**, after a legendary king, **Minos**.

The greatest of the palaces was at **Knossos** (shown above). At its peak, the city had 100,000 inhabitants.

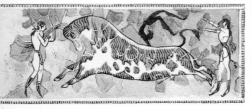

Minoan palaces had sophisticated plumbing and fine wall-paintings. This one shows **bull-leaping**, a mysterious sport that may have had religious significance.

Pottery snake goddess

The eruption of a volcano on **Thera** (c.1500-1450BC) is thought to have caused widespread destruction on Crete. At about the same time, **Mycenaeans** from Greece arrived and took over the island. Knossos fell **c.1380BC**. This may have been due to an earthquake, a Cretan rebellion or an attack by rival Mycenaeans. By **c.1100BC** the island had declined.

Crete's golden age (known as the **First** and **Second Palace Periods**) lasted **c.2000-1450BC**. The Minoans built a series of large and splendid palaces – including **Knossos**, **Phaistos** and **Mallia** – and developed trading links with **Greece**, **Egypt*** and **the Levant**.

Mycenae c.1900-1050BC

From **c.2500-1900BC**, groups of **Indo-Europeans*** speaking an early form of Greek arrived in **Greece** and mixed with the native population. They built a series of strongholds, each ruled by a king, the most important of which was at **Mycenae**. A period of increasing wealth followed, influenced by contacts with **Crete** and elsewhere.

Gold mask of a **Mycenaean** king or prince.

Homer's *Iliad* and *Odyssey*, written down in the **8th century BC**, tells legends of the **Mycenaeans**.

From **c.1600-1200BC** the Mycenaeans were the leading mainland power. They invaded Crete, **Rhodes** and **Cyprus**, taking over Cretan trade, and developed **Linear B**, an early form of Greek writing. However, **c.1250BC**, Mycenaean society was disrupted by inter-state warfare and by **1050BC** the civilization had collapsed.

The Dark Age c.1085-750BC

Between **c.1085-750BC**, the old centres were destroyed, the art of writing forgotten and people dispersed. Trade was taken over by the **Phoenicians***.

Map of Greece

Macedonia

ASIA MINOR

GREECE

Aegean Sea

Thermopylae

Chaeronea Delphi

Thebes

Plataea Marathon

Leuctra

Mycenae Athens

Salamis

Corinth

The Peloponnese Sparta

Thera

Mediterranean Sea

Rhodes

Knossos Mallia

CRETE

Phaistos

Greek pottery

Greece 750-338BC

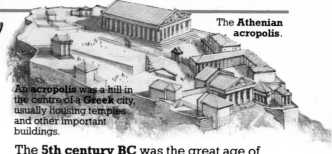

The **Athenian acropolis**.

Gradually trade revived and a new, simplified alphabet was adopted (**c.725BC**), based on the **Phoenician*** one. Small city states grew up around the old strongholds – the most important ones at **Corinth**, **Sparta** and **Athens**. Colonies were founded in **Anatolia** and the **Aegean islands**. In many states kings were replaced by an **aristocracy** (a group of nobles), an **oligarchy** (a small group) or a **tyrant***, followed sometimes by a **democracy** (the rule of the people).

An **acropolis** was a hill in the centre of a **Greek** city, usually housing temples and other important buildings.

The **5th century BC** was the great age of Greek civilization, especially in Athens, which became a great commercial and cultural centre. The foundations of European civilization are based on ideas about art, architecture, literature, drama, politics, philosophy, science and history which developed at this time.

Sea battle between **Greeks** and **Persians**.

Athens became a great naval power in the **5th century BC**.

Greek theatre

Masks worn by actors.

At the start of the **5th century BC**, **Greece** was threatened by the **Persian Empire***, who had taken over the Greek colonies in **Asia Minor** in **546BC**. In **500-494BC** these colonies rebelled unsuccessfully. Athens, Sparta and other states together defeated the Persians, after several major battles (**Marathon 490BC**, **Salamis 480BC** and **Plataea 479BC**).

Rivalry between Sparta and Athens, and resentment by many states of Athenian power, led to the **Peloponnesian War (431-404BC)**, which tore the Greek world apart. Sparta won, but was later defeated by Thebes at **Leuctra** in **371BC**.

The rise of Macedonia

Taking advantage of the weakness of the city states, **Philip II of Macedonia (359-336BC)** set out to unite **Greece** under his rule. Having unified Macedonia and reorganized his government and army, he defeated the Greek cities at **Chaeronea** in **338BC**. All except **Sparta** agreed to accept his leadership.

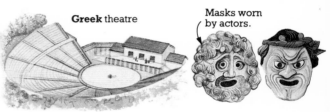

Macedonian soldiers in a **phalanx** (battle formation).

Alexander the Great

Under **Philip's** son, **Alexander (336-323BC)**, **Macedonia** became a major world power. A brilliant soldier and conqueror, he defeated the **Persians*** at **Issus** in **333BC** and marched across their empire as far as **India**, making conquests and founding cities along the way. After his death his empire was broken up by his generals, the **diadochi**, who fought over the succession. Although the empire was short-lived, it was responsible for the spread of **Greek** language and culture. The period following Alexander's death is called the **Hellenistic Age (323-30BC)**.

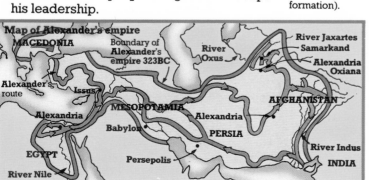

Map of Alexander's empire
MACEDONIA
Boundary of **Alexander's** empire 323BC
River Oxus
River Jaxartes
Samarkand
Alexandria Oxiana
Alexander's route
Issus
AFGHANISTAN
Alexandria
MESOPOTAMIA
Alexandria
Babylon
PERSIA
EGYPT
Persepolis
River Indus
INDIA
River Nile

Europe

Hannibal and his army crossing the Italian Alps.

218-201BC Second Punic War*. Hannibal of **Carthage*** invades **Italy.**

215-205 First Macedonian War between **Rome*** and **Macedonia.** Further wars (200-197 and 171-163) end in the defeat and partition of Macedonia.

149-146 Third Punic War* ends in the defeat of **Carthage*.** The **Roman Empire*** expands to include Carthaginian lands.

91-89 War between **Rome*** and her **Italian** allies ends with their being given Roman citizenship.

82-79 Sulla is **dictator*** of **Rome*.**

73-71 An unsuccessful slave revolt is led by the slave, **Spartacus.**

60 Julius Caesar, Pompey and **Crassus** rule **Rome*** jointly, as a **triumvirate*.**

58-51 Julius Caesar conquers **Gaul (France).**

49-45 Civil war between **Julius Caesar** and **Pompey.** Caesar becomes **dictator*.**

46 Julius Caesar introduces the reformed **Julian** calendar.

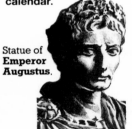

Statue of **Emperor Augustus.**

44 Julius Caesar is assassinated and civil war follows.

31 Octavian wins the **Battle of Actium** and establishes leadership of **Rome*.**

27BC End of **Roman Republic*.** Octavian becomes Emperor, taking the title **Augustus,** and rules until **AD14.**

AD

AD43 Romans* conquer **Britain.**

61 Queen Boudicca of the **Iceni,** a **British** tribe, leads a revolt against the **Romans*** in East Anglia.

98-117 Roman Empire* reaches its greatest extent during the reign of **Emperor Trajan.**

Trajan's column, built in **AD113** to commemorate his victories.

122-127 Hadrian's Wall is built to mark the northern frontier of the **Roman Empire*** in **Britain.**

c.200 Germanic tribes* begin attacking the frontiers of the **Roman Empire*.**

c.370 Huns* invade **Europe.**

378 Battle of Adrianople. Roman* emperor, **Valens,** is defeated and killed by the **Goths*.**

391 Roman* emperor, **Theodosius,** makes **Christianity*** the state religion.

395 Roman Empire* becomes permanently split.

401-413 Visigoths* invade **Italy.** The **Roman*** capital is moved to **Ravenna.** Power in Rome is taken over by the Bishop of Rome (the **Pope**).

406-436 Burgundian kingdom of the **Rhône.**

The Middle East

605-560BC Lydia becomes a major power under King **Alyattes.**

560-546 Croesus of Lydia (famous for his wealth) subdues all the **Greek*** colonies, except **Miletus.**

550 The **Persian Empire*** is founded by **Cyrus II.** Persia conquers **Assyria* (550), Lydia** and **Greek*** cities in **Asia Minor** in 546 and **Babylonia*** in 539.

Carved head of a **Persian** king.

4th century The **Nabataeans*** build a city in rock at **Petra.** They dominate the rich **Arabian** trade in incense and goods from as far away as **India.**

Ruins of the city of **Petra.**

336-323 Empire of **Alexander the Great*.**

304-64 Seleucid Empire. At first it controls **Asia Minor, Persia*, Mesopotamia*** and **India,** but is gradually reduced in size.

c.280-47 The kingdom of **Pontus** on the **Black Sea** is founded by **Mithridates I.**

279 Celts* establish the kingdom of **Galatia.**

279-74 The kingdom of **Bithynia** is established.

263-133 Kingdom of **Pergamum** founded by **Eumenes I.**

247BC-AD277 The **Parthian** kingdom is established.

BITHYNIA **PONTUS** **GALATIA** Independent Greek states. **PERGAMUM** **SELEUCID KINGDOM** **PARTHIAN KINGDOM** **BACTRIA**

Hellenistic world c.200BC

171-138 Reign of **Mithriades I** of the **Parthians,** who extends control over **Persia** and **Mesopotamia*.**

168 Judas Maccabeus leads a **Jewish*** revolt against the **Romans*.**

133 Last king of **Pergamum** bequeathes his kingdom to **Rome*.**

88-64 Wars with **Rome*** reduce the size of the kingdom of **Pontus.**

74 Kingdom of **Bithynia** passes under **Roman*** rule.

64 Spread of the **Roman Empire*** in **Middle East. Palestine** becomes the Roman province of **Judea.**

47 Battle of Zela: the kingdom of **Pontus** is conquered by **Julius Caesar.**

37-4 Rule of **Herod the Great,** King of **Judea.**

c.5 Birth of **Jesus Christ*** in **Bethlehem, Judea.**

AD

AD26-36 Pontius Pilate is governor of **Judea.**

c.29 Crucifixion of **Jesus Christ*.**

73 Romans* destroy **Jewish*** stronghold of **Masada.**

Africa

510BC First of a series of treaties between **Carthage*** and **Rome*** (the others are in **348** and **306**), safeguarding Carthage's trade **monopoly*** in the **western Mediterranean** and allowing her free trade with **Sicily**.

c.500BC-AD400 **Nubian** kings move their capital south to **Meroë**. A new phase of cultural development follows, with the building of towns, temples, palaces and pyramids, all showing **Egyptian*** influence.

Pyramids at Meroë

c.500BC-AD200 **Nok** civilization in **Nigeria**.

343-332 **Egypt*** is again conquered and occupied by **Persia***.

Nok carving

332 **Egypt*** is conquered by **Alexander the Great***.

323-30 The **Ptolemaic** dynasty (descended from **Ptolemy**, one of **Alexander's*** generals) rules **Egypt*** from **Alexandria**. Alexandria becomes an important centre of invention and the largest city in the **Greek*** world.

Alexandrian lighthouse, built **c.285BC**.

203 **Romans*** defeat the **Carthaginians*** at **Tunis**.

202 **Romans*** destroy the **Carthaginian*** army at **Zama**.

146 **Carthage*** is destroyed by **Rome***, and becomes the **Roman** province of North Africa.

Ruins of **Leptis Magna**, a **Roman** town in **North Africa**.

30 **Egypt*** falls to the **Roman Empire*** after the defeat of the **Egyptian** queen, **Cleopatra**, at **Actium**.

AD

AD44 **Mauretania** (Morocco) is conquered by **Rome***.

The Far East

Jade burial suit made for a **Han** princess.

206BC-AD222 **Han dynasty** rules **China**. China grows in size and prosperity.

c.200 Three kingdoms are established in **South India**.

200 **India** is invaded by **Greek Bactrians** and **Parthians***. Small Greek states are established in the **Punjab** from **c.170**.

c.150BC-AD50 Bronze age culture in **North Vietnam**, named after the village of **Dong-son**.

140-87 **China** expands under **Emperor Wu-ti** to include **Korea** and **North Vietnam**. He develops an efficient civil service, reduces the powers of the nobles and builds a network of roads and canals.

c.100s **North India** is invaded by **Greeks*** and **nomadic*** tribes, including the **Kushans**.

Emperor Wu-ti

AD

AD9 **Wang Mang** seizes power and sets up the **Hsin dynasty** in **China**.

25-222 **Han dynasty** is restored. New age of **Chinese** culture.

Carving of **Buddha** from the **Kushan Period** in **India**.

c.50 **India** is invaded by **nomadic*** **Bactrians**, who establish the **Kushan Empire** in northern **India**.

91 **Chinese** defeat the **Huns*** in **Mongolia**.

c.100 Paper is invented in **China**.

c.100 **Buddhism*** is introduced into **China** from **India**.

c.180 Tribal groups begin to unite in **Japan**.

c.195-405 **Parthians*** control northern **India**.

The Americas

c.200BC-AD200 **Paracas Necropolis** culture in **Peru**. Brilliantly coloured, embroidered textiles have been found in a cemetery from this period.

c.200BC-AD600 **Peru**: regional development and technological experiments among the **Mochica** people of the north coast and the **Nazca** people of the south coast.

Nazca pottery

c.200BC-AD700 The rise of the culture of **Teotihuacan*** in **Mexico**.

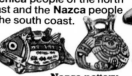

West coast of South America — **Mochica** people — **Chavin** culture — **PERU** — **Paracas Necropolis** — **Nazca** people — **Lake Titicaca**

Pyramid of the Sun, Teotihuacán.

c.100BC **North America**: **Hohokam** people in the south east are building ditches and dykes to irrigate their crops. **Pyramid mounds** and **ball courts** are also built.

AD

c.AD250-600 Early Classical Period of the **Mayan** civilization*: their artistic and intellectual peak. They use **hieroglyphics** (picture writing) and erect **stelae** (stone slabs). Astonomers develop advanced mathematical skills.

Mayan ball court.

c.250-750 Classical Period of the **Zapotec** culture*.

Zapotec burial urn.

c.400 **Incas*** start to establish themselves on the **South American Pacific coast.**

Europe

AD 409 **Vandals***, **Alans** and **Suevi*** overrun **Spain**.

410 **Visigoths*** sack **Rome***.

415 **Visigoths*** establish the kingdom of **Toulouse**.

416-711 **Visigoth*** kingdom in **Spain**.

443-534 **Burgundian*** kingdom of the **Rhône-Saône** is established in **France**.

449 **Angles***, **Saxons*** and **Jutes** invade **England**. Many **Britons** flee to **Wales**, **Cornwall** and **Brittany**.

451 **Battle of Chalons**. **Romans*** and **Franks*** halt the invasion of **Gaul (France)** by **Huns***.

451 **Merovingian dynasty*** established in **France**.

455 **Vandals*** sack **Rome***.

457 **Anglo-Saxons*** establish seven kingdoms in **Britain**: **Kent**, **Northumberland**, **Mercia**, **East Anglia**, **Wessex**, **Essex** and **Sussex**.

476 **Western Roman Empire*** comes to an end.

481-511 Reign of **Clovis***, King of the **Franks***.

493 **Theodoric** of the **Ostrogoths*** establishes a kingdom in **Italy**.

495 **Cerdic**, later King of **Wessex**, lands in **Britain**.

496 **Clovis the Frank*** converts to **Christianity***.

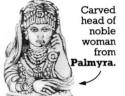

Ostrogoth jewellery, from the time of **Theodoric**, found at **Cesena**, near **Ravenna**.

The Middle East

AD 106 The **Nabataean*** kingdom is reduced to a **Roman*** province by **Emperor Trajan (98-117)** and trade declines.

115-117 Uprisings of **Jews*** in **Egypt***, **Cyrenaica** and **Cyprus**.

131-135 Unsuccessful **Jewish*** revolt, led by **Bar Cochba**. **Jerusalem** is destroyed and rebuilt as **Aelia Capitolina** and many **Jews** are exiled. This leads to the **Diaspora**, the dispersal of **Jews** around the **Mediterranean**.

227 **Sassanid dynasty** is established in **Persia** by **Ardashir I**.

260 **Shapur I** of **Persia** defeats the **Romans*** and captures **Emperor Valerian**.

Carved head of noble woman from **Palmyra**.

268-273 **Queen Zenobia** of **Palmyra** conquers **Syria**, **Mesopotamia*** and parts of **Egypt***.

310-379 Reign of **Shapur II** of **Persia**.

325 First **Council of the Christian* Church** meets at **Nicaea**.

4th century mosaic of loaves and fishes, early **Christian** symbols.

484 The **Persian Empire** is attacked by **Huns*** and the emperor is killed.

The Persian Empire

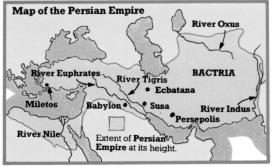

The palace had giant columns, far higher than those of the **Greeks**, topped with animal carvings.

The **Palace of Persepolis**, begun by **Darius I** in **516BC**. It was destroyed by **Alexander the Great** in **330BC**.

In **c.1500BC**, **Indo-Europeans*** began moving into the area now called **Iran**. By **c.700BC** two groups, the **Medes** and the **Persians**, had established rival kingdoms (**Media** and **Parsa**, or Persia). In **550BC**, **Cyrus II** of Persia **(559-529BC)** defeated his grandfather, **Astyages** of Media, and united the two kingdoms under the **Achaemenid dynasty**. He conquered **Lydia** in **547BC**, **Babylon** and the **Greek*** cities in **Asia Minor** in **535BC**. His son, **Cambysus (529-522BC)**, conquered **Egypt* (525BC)**. The empire was greatly extended by **Darius I (522-485BC)**, who reorganized it into 20 provinces, called **satrapies** and established a fair and efficient code of laws.

In the **5th century BC,** Persia came up against the rising power of **Greece*** and failed in attempts to invade the Greek mainland **(490-479BC)**. In **331BC**, Persia was defeated by **Alexander the Great***, and absorbed into his empire in **330BC**.

Map of the Persian Empire

River Oxus

River Euphrates

River Tigris

BACTRIA

Ecbatana

Miletos

Babylon

Susa

Persepolis

River Indus

River Nile

Extent of **Persian Empire** at its height.

Africa

c.AD 70 Christianity* reaches **Alexandria**. It starts spreading south from c.180.

100-1000 Civilization of **Axum (Ethiopia)**: a trading state which derives its wealth from maritime trade and export of ivory.

c.300 Axum conquers **Nubia*** and becomes the dominant power in the **Red Sea**.

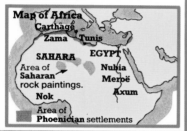

Obelisk (a tall stone monument with a pyramid top) at **Axum**.

400 Axum converts to **Christianity***.

429 Vandal* kingdom of **North Africa** is set up.

Map of Africa
Carthage, Zama, Tunis, SAHARA, EGYPT, Area of Saharan rock paintings, Nubia, Meroë, Nok, Axum, Area of Phoenician settlements

The Far East

AD 222-265 Han dynasty* in **China** is replaced by three independent regional states. This is known as the **Period of the Three Kingdoms**.

265-316 Succession of small states in **China**.

c.285 Traditional date for the introduction of writing to **Japan**. (It is probably nearer 450.)

c.300 Yamato government is established in **Japan**. Society is organized into clans, who practise the **Shinto** religion.

304 Huns* break through the **Great Wall*** in **northern China**, followed by **Turks**.

316 Empress **Jingo** of **Japan** invades **Korea**.

316-589 Rival dynasties in north and south **China**.

320-535 Gupta Empire in **India** is founded by **Chandragupta II**. The **Classical Age** in **India**.

430-470 Invasions by **Huns*** cause the decline of the **Gupta Empire**.

Buddha from the **Gupta** period

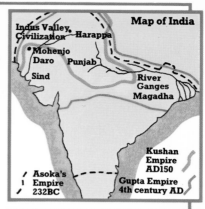

Map of India
Indus Valley Civilization, Harappa, Mohenjo Daro, Punjab, Sind, River Ganges, Magadha, Kushan Empire AD150, Asoka's Empire 232BC, Gupta Empire 4th century AD

Map of China
MONGOLIA, Great Wall, Peking, Ch'ang-an, KOREA, River Huang Ho (Yellow River), Area of Shang influence, Han Empire, Ch'in Empire, VIETNAM

Judaism

The **Hebrews** (later known as **Jews**) were **Semitic*** tribes, united by a belief in one God. They were led by **Moses** from **Egypt*** to **Canaan** (in **Palestine**) **c.1200BC**. Under pressure from the **Philistines*** and the **Ammonites**, they united under one king, **Saul, c.1010BC**. Under **King David (c.1000-966BC)**, they defeated the Philistines and set up the kingdom of **Israel**, with their capital at **Jerusalem**.

Semitic tribes from an **Egyptian** wall painting. According to the Old Testament, the **Hebrews** were driven to Egypt by a great famine in **Canaan c.1600BC**.

Israel reached its peak under David's son, **Solomon (c.966-926BC)**, who built a temple in Jerusalem. After his death, the kingdom was split into Israel and **Judah**. Israel was destroyed by the **Assyrians*** in **722BC**, and Judah by **Babylonians*** in **587BC**. Thousands of Jews were held captive in **Babylon** between **586-538BC**. This is known as the **Babylonian Captivity**. When **Persia*** conquered Babylon in **516BC**, the Jews were allowed to return and rebuild Jerusalem. But in **332BC**, they were conquered by **Alexander the Great*** and then passed under the control of the **Ptolemies*** **(301BC)** and **Seleucids*** **(198BC)**.

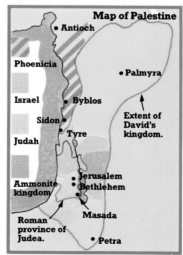

Map of Palestine
Antioch, Phoenicia, Palmyra, Israel, Byblos, Sidon, Extent of David's kingdom, Judah, Tyre, Ammonite kingdom, Jerusalem, Bethlehem, Masada, Roman province of Judea, Petra

In **63BC**, Palestine became the **Roman*** province of **Judea**. Religious and nationalistic tensions grew and there were unsuccessful Jewish uprisings in **AD66-70** and **AD132**. Jerusalem was destroyed and many Jews went into exile.

The Roman Empire

From **c.1000BC**, a new wave of **Indo-Europeans***, with iron-using skills, settled in **Italy** among the **Bronze Age*** farmers. One group, the **Latins**, built a cluster of villages on the edges of the **River Tiber**, which eventually grew into the city of **Rome**. The traditional date for the founding of Rome is

Roman senators

753BC, but it may have developed earlier, or later under the influence of **Etruscan** metal-workers from **Asia Minor**.

Rome was ruled by kings until **510-509BC**, when a **republic*** was established. It slowly expanded until by **c.250BC**, most of Italy was under Roman control. Clashes with **Carthage*** led to the **Punic Wars (264-241BC, 218-201BC** and **149-146BC)**. As a result, Carthage was destroyed and Rome acquired an overseas empire. By **44BC** Rome controlled most of the **Mediterranean**.

Sea battle between the **Romans** and **Carthaginians**.

The expansion of the overseas empire and the political ambitions of the military leaders put the constitution under strain. There was a period of civil war and dictatorships (**Sulla 82-79BC, Pompey 52-46BC** and **Caesar 45-44BC**), ending with the victory of **Octavian** in **31BC**. He was given the title **Augustus** and became the first Roman emperor **(27BC-AD14)**. This began the **Empire Period**.

Rome c.4th century AD

The **Pantheon**, a temple built in **27BC**, and rebuilt by **Emperor Hadrian AD120-124**.

Roman architecture was modelled on that of the **Greeks**, but the **dome** was a Roman invention.

The **Roman Empire** eventually covered most of **Europe** and parts of the **Middle East** and **North Africa**. It achieved its greatest extent under **Emperors Trajan (98-117)** and **Hadrian (117-138)**. From **c.200** there were serious attacks on the frontiers by a number of **barbarian tribes** (see opposite). This, with economic recession, civil wars and a succession of weak and corrupt emperors, led to the temporary collapse of government in **235**.

Roads, bridges and **aqueducts** (structures for carrying water) were built all over the **Empire**, and the frontiers were guarded by permanent armies.

Diocletian (284-305) tried to improve government by dividing it between himself and a co-emperor. **Emperor Constantine (306-337)** moved the capital to **Byzantium** (renamed **Constantinople**) and reunited the Empire. However, by **395** it had become permanently split – into an **Eastern Empire**, based in Constantinople, and a **Western Empire**, based in Rome. Outlying provinces fell to barbarians (see page opposite) and Rome itself was sacked by **Goths (410)** and **Vandals (455)**. In **476** the Western Empire came to an end.

Barbarian invasions

In the **4th** and **5th centuries AD**, the civilizations of **India** and **Rome** were undermined by the invasions of mounted **nomadic*** tribes from the **Steppes**, grassy plains in **central Asia**. They had been driven west by the **Huns** of the **Altai** region of **Mongolia**.

As early as **230-200BC** nomadic tribes of **Indo-European*** origin, later known as **Germani**, began migrating south from **Scandinavia** and the **Baltic** to the north eastern borders of the **Roman Empire**. Some were allowed to settle on the frontiers as *foedorati* (confederate states)

The **Hsiung-Nu**, a tribe related to the **Huns**, broke through the **Great Wall of China** in **AD304**.

or were recruited into the Roman army. However, the arrival of the Huns in **eastern Europe c.AD370** pushed many of them west, into conflict with the Romans. The **Western Empire** was gradually overrun and when it fell in **AD476**, it was replaced by **Germanic kingdoms**.

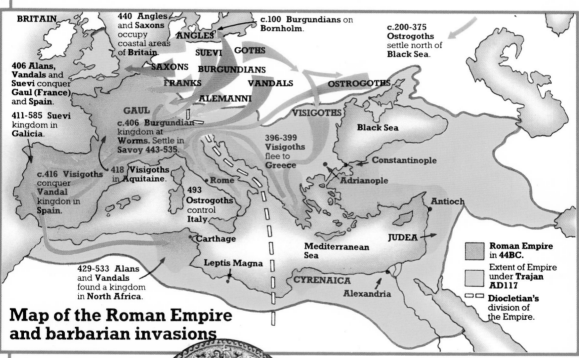

BRITAIN

440 Angles and **Saxons** occupy coastal areas of **Britain**.

ANGLES

c.100 Burgundians on **Bornholm**.

c.200-375 Ostrogoths settle north of **Black Sea**.

SUEVI **GOTHS**

406 Alans, Vandals and **Suevi** conquer **Gaul (France)** and **Spain**.

SAXONS **BURGUNDIANS**

FRANKS **VANDALS** **OSTROGOTHS**

411-585 Suevi kingdom in **Galicia**.

ALEMANNI

GAUL

c.406 Burgundian kingdom at **Worms**. Settle in **Savoy 443-535**.

VISIGOTHS

Black Sea

396-399 Visigoths flee to **Greece**

Constantinople

418 Visigoths in **Aquitaine**.

c.416 Visigoths conquer **Vandal kingdom** in **Spain**.

Rome

493 Ostrogoths control **Italy**.

Adrianople

Antioch

Carthage

JUDEA

Leptis Magna

Mediterranean Sea

429-533 Alans and **Vandals** found a kingdom in **North Africa**.

CYRENAICA

Alexandria

Roman Empire in 44BC.

Extent of Empire under **Trajan AD117**

Diocletian's division of the Empire.

Map of the Roman Empire and barbarian invasions

Christianity

5th century Christian mosaic from **Ravenna**.

Christianity was founded in **Palestine** by **Jesus of Nazareth (c.5BC-AD29)**, later known as **Jesus Christ**. He was arrested and crucified for his teachings. After his death, the faith was spread by his followers, or **disciples**, especially **Paul of Tarsus**, who made missionary journeys throughout the **eastern Mediterranean** in **45-48**, **49-52** and **54-58**.

At first the teachings were aimed mainly at **Jews***, but as few converted, it was preached to **gentiles** (non-Jews). Despite repression and persecution, Christianity spread rapidly throughout the **Roman Empire***, especially among the poor. By the **4th century**, the Church was organized into **dioceses** (areas), each under a bishop. The most important were **Antioch**, **Rome** and **Alexandria**. **Constantine*** became a **Christian** in **312**, and in **391** Christianity became the official religion of the Empire.

Justinian and the Byzantine Empire

The **Eastern Roman Empire**, also called the **Byzantine Empire**, survived for a thousand years after the fall of **Rome*** Based in **Constantinople**, it was an important political power and helped to preserve classical learning and **Christianity***, through the **Eastern (Greek Orthodox) Church**. Its religious and cultural traditions were inherited by the **Greeks** and **Slavs***.

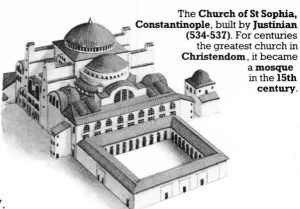

The **Church of St Sophia, Constantinople**, built by **Justinian (534-537)**. For centuries the greatest church in **Christendom**, it became a **mosque** in the **15th century**.

Mosaics showing **Justinian** and his wife **Theodora**, from the **Church of San Vitale, Ravenna**.

Emperor Justinian (527-565) struggled to reunite the Roman Empire by restoring the old **Western Empire**. He succeeded in retaking the **Vandal*** kingdom in **North Africa (535)**, the **Ostrogoth*** kingdom in **Italy (553)** and part of the **Visigoth*** kingdom in **Spain (554)**.

Justinian's most lasting achievement was to organize the Roman legal system into the **Code of Justinian (528-534)**, which became the basis of **western European** law. He also launched a great building programme. However his reconquests were lost after his death. In **568** the **Lombards** took north Italy and ties with the West were largely severed. **Greek** replaced **Latin** as the official language and the Eastern and **Western (Catholic) Churches** began to move apart.

Southern and Western Europe

507-711 Visigoth* kingdom in Spain.

535-555 Justinian reconquers the Ostrogoth* kingdom in Italy.

c.537 Death of King Arthur of the Britons, at the Battle of Camlan.

Visigoth crown, belonging to **King Recceswinth**.

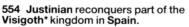

Celtic cross from **Iona**.

554 Justinian reconquers part of the Visigoth* kingdom in Spain.

563 St Columba, an Irish monk, founds a monastery on Iona. His followers begin missionary work in England and Scotland.

568-774 Lombard kingdom in north Italy.

596 St Augustine is sent to Britain by Pope Gregory the Great to convert the Saxons* to Christianity*.

Treasures from **Sutton Hoo (c.625)** – part of a memorial to one of the last **pagan Anglo-Saxon** kings.

Northern and Eastern Europe

c.500-700 Slavs* migrate from **central Europe** to the forest zone of **Russia**.

527-565 Reign of **Emperor Justinian**, of the **Eastern Roman**, or **Byzantine Empire**.

The **Church of San Vitale, Ravenna**, built in the **6th century**. During **Justinian's** reign, Ravenna was the capital of the **Eastern Church** in **Italy**.

540-561 War between Persia and the Byzantine Empire.

603-628 The final war between Persia and the Byzantine Empire, ending in Persian defeat.

610 Accession of **Emperor Heraclius** of the **Byzantine Empire**. Links with the **West** are neglected and the official language changes to **Greek**.

632 Arabs* begin attacking the **Byzantine Empire**. They defeat **Heraclius** in **Syria (634-638)**, occupy **Egypt (639-642)** and take **Carthage (698)**.

Icons, religious images often painted on wood, were common in Byzantine art. Between **724-843** they were banned as idolatrous and many were destroyed. This movement was known as **iconoclasm**.

Byzantine mosaic of **Christ** as **pantocrator** (creator of the Universe).

Ravenna

Rome

Constantinople

Cordoba

Carthage

Sicily

Alexandria

Empire inherited by **Justinian**.

Justinian's reconquests

Justinian's empire

The conquests of the **Persians (611-616)** and the **Arabs* (632-750)** cost the empire its territories in the **Middle East**, North Africa, Spain and **Sicily**. The frontiers were pushed back considerably during the **Macedonian dynasty (867-1056)**, especially under **Basil II (976-1025)**, but constant warfare imposed a heavy strain. In **1071** the **Seljuk Turks*** won a crushing victory at **Manzikert** and took over much of the Byzantine territory in **Asia Minor**.

The Turkish victory led to the **Crusades***, which ended in disaster for the Byzantine Empire. The **Fourth Crusade (1202-1204)** resulted in the conquest and pillage of Constantinople by Crusaders and the establishment of a short-lived **Latin Empire**. A Greek emperor was restored in **1261**, but the Empire was fatally weakened. It was unable to resist a new threat, that of the **Ottoman Turks***, who took Constantinople in **1453**.

Middle East and Africa

531 The monk **Julian** is sent by **Justinian** to **Axum**, with a group of monks. They convert **Ethiopia** to **Christianity***.

531-579 Chrosroes I rules the **Persian Sassanid Empire***. The Empire is at its greatest extent.

Sassanid Empire

543 Julian moves from **Ethiopia** and converts **Nubia**. **Nubia** is divided into three **Christian*** kingdoms – **Nobatia**, **Makuria** and **Alodia** – each with their own king and bishops. They are cut off from the rest of **Christendom*** by the **Arab** conquest of **Egypt** (639-642).

Egyptian wall-painting showing a **Nubian** queen.

The Far East

535 The **Gupta Empire*** collapses. **India** divides into warring kingdoms.

552 Buddhism* is introduced into **Japan** from **China**.

581 General Yang Chien founds the **Sui dynasty**. He unites **China** in 589.

594 Japan adopts **Buddhism*** as the state religion.

605-610 Millions of people are drafted to build the **Imperial Canal**, linking **Rivers Yangtze** and **Huang Ho** in **China**.

606 First written examination is introduced in **China** for entry into the civil service.

607 Tibet becomes politically unified.

618-907 T'ang dynasty in **China**.

624 Buddhism* becomes the official religion in **China**.

627-649 Reign of **T'ai Tsung the Great**, Emperor of **China**.

645 Buddhism* reaches **Tibet**.

Glazed **T'ang dynasty** camel.

The Americas

c.500 North America: the prosperity of the **Hopewellian mound-builders*** begins to decline. **Mississippi mound-builders** appear on the lower reaches of the **Mississippi River**. They trade in marine shells and extend their influence over a wide area.

Pottery bottles made by **Mississippi mound builders**.

500-900 Golden age of the **Zapotec culture*** in Oaxaca, Mexico.

Pyramid at **El Tajín**.

500-1200 Culture of the **Central Gulf coast** of Mexico, also known as **Totonac**, based around **El Tajín**.

c.600 High point of **Mayan civilization***. There is evidence of intensive agriculture, based on elaborate irrigation techniques.

The rise of the Franks

The most successful of the **barbarian*** kingdoms was that of **Clovis the Frank (481-511)**, a **Christian** and founder of the **Merovingian dynasty**. He conquered the **Visigoths*** in 507. His successors defeated the **Thuringians (531)**, the **Burgundians* (532-534)** and the **Alemanni (535)** and in 537 took **Provence**.

In accordance with Frankish tradition, the kingdom was divided between the king's sons. But this weakened the dynasty and power fell into the hands of leading families. A powerful line of officials, known as **Mayors of the Palace**, emerged with **Pepin I (580-640)**. **Pepin II (640-714)** defeated his rivals at the **Battle of Tertry (687)** and virtually ruled the Frankish kingdom.

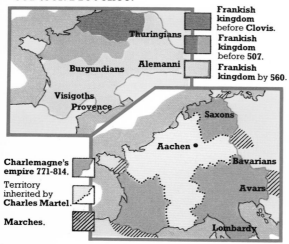

Frankish kingdom before **Clovis**.
Frankish kingdom before 507.
Frankish kingdom by 560.

Thuringians
Burgundians
Alemanni
Visigoths
Provence
Saxons
Aachen •
Bavarians
Avars
Lombardy

Charlemagne's empire 771-814.
Territory inherited by **Charles Martel**.
Marches.

Bust of **Charlemagne**.

Pepin II's son, **Charles Martel (714-741)**, defeated the **Arabs* (732)** and drove them out of **France**. In 751, **Pepin III** deposed the Merovingian king and founded the **Carolingian dynasty**. The kingdom was inherited by his sons, **Carloman** and **Charles (Charlemagne)**. Charlemagne became sole ruler on his brother's death in 771.

Southern and Western Europe

c.695 *Lindisfarne Gospels* are produced: the first book of psalms in **Anglo-Saxon**.

711 **Arabs*** conquer Spain, except the Asturias.

Inside the **Great Mosque, Cordoba**, built 788.

732 Battle of Poitiers: advancing **Arabs*** are defeated in **southern France** by **Charles Martel** (see above) and forced to turn back.

751 **Childeric III**, the last **Merovingian** king, is deposed. **Pepin III (751-768)** becomes first **Carolingian** king of **France** (see above).

751 **Lombards** conquer Ravenna, the last **Byzantine*** possession in **north Italy**.

756-1031 The **Omayyads*** set up a **caliphate*** at Cordoba, Spain.

757 **Offa of Mercia (757-796)** builds a dyke to keep out the **Welsh**. He becomes ruler of all **England** in 779.

768-814 Rule of **Charlemagne** (see above).

773-774 **Charlemagne** conquers **Lombardy, north Italy**.

793-794 First **Viking*** raids. Vikings plunder **Lindisfarne** and **Jarrow** in England.

800 **Charlemagne** is crowned **Emperor of the Romans**.

806 **Vikings*** raid **Iona***, a **Scottish** island, and the monks flee to **Ireland**.

Northern and Eastern Europe

674-678 **Arabs*** unsuccessfully besiege **Constantinople**.

c.680 **Bulgars*** invade the **Balkans**, intermarry with **Slavs*** and establish a **Bulgar** state.

716 The **Bulgar state*** is recognized by the **Byzantine Empire*** and lasts until 1018.

717 **Byzantine*** emperor, **Leo III** allies with **Bulgars*** and **Khazars***.

718 **Arabs*** unsuccessfully besiege **Constantinople**.

Byzantine icons

726-843 **Iconoclasm*** in the **Byzantine Empire***. **Leo III** and successive emperors prohibit the use of **icons*** in churches and many are destroyed.

787 **Church Council of Nicaea** orders the restoration of **icons*** in churches.

c.793-794 **Vikings*** begin raiding **Europe**.

A **Viking** settlement.

Under Charlemagne **(771-814)** the Frankish empire reached its greatest extent. He conquered **Lombardy (773-774)**, the **Bavarians (788)**, the **Avars (796)** and the **Saxons (804)**. He also set up **marches** (or border zones) to protect the kingdom.

The chapel at **Aachen (Aix-la-Chappelle)**, one of **Charlemagne's** capitals. The chapel was closely modelled on **San Vitale, Ravenna**.

Charlemagne encouraged scholars at his court at **Aachen**. Texts from the **Bible** and classical authors were copied and sent to the libraries of **monasteries**.

Charlemagne's son, **Louis the Pious (814-840)** shared his inheritance with his three sons. Internal conflict led to the partition of the empire at **Verdun (843)**, into the **Western**, **Middle** and **Eastern Kingdoms**. At the **Treaty of Mersen (870)** most of the Middle Kingdom was split between the Eastern and Western Kingdoms and the outlines of **modern France** and **Germany** began to take shape.

Charlemagne's campaigns against the Arabs and the pagan **Magyars*** and Avars, and his enforced conversion of the Saxons earned him the role of defender of **Christendom***. In **800** he was crowned **Emperor of the Romans** by the **Pope**, despite the protests of the **Byzantines***, who saw themselves as the heirs of **Rome***.

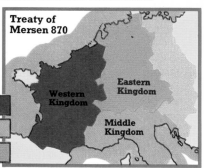

Treaty of Mersen 870

Kingdom of **Charles II the Bald**.

Kingdom of **Louis II**.

Kingdom of **Louis the German**.

Western Kingdom

Eastern Kingdom

Middle Kingdom

Middle East and Africa

611-614 The **Persians** take Antioch, Damascus and Jerusalem from the **Byzantines*** and overrun **Asia Minor**.

618-619 Persians conquer Egypt.

622 Mohammed* flees to Medina.

629 Byzantine Emperor Heraclius (575-641), allies with Ethiopia, defeats Persia and wins back the lost provinces.

632 Death of Mohammed*. Abu Bakr takes over as **caliph***. **Arab*** expansion begins. Arabs overrun Syria and Iraq (637) and Jerusalem (638).

639-642 Arabs* defeat the Byzantine* fleet and occupy Egypt.

642 Arabs* conquer Persia and overthrow the Sassanids*. Persia adopts the Shi'ite* branch of the Muslim* religion.

661-750 The Omayyad dynasty* rules from Damascus.

698-700 Arabs* conquer Carthage and Tunis. The north African coast converts to Islam*.

The Far East

657 The **Chinese** defeat armies of **Turks*** and extend their power in **central Asia**.

665 Tibetans expand into Turkestan.

690-713 Empress Wu usurps the throne in China.

Buddhist temple, near **Nara, Japan**.

718-784 Nara Period in Japan.

745-840 Uighur Empire in Mongolia

c.750 Three empires in **India** wage war against each other: **Rajputana** (north west), **Rashtrakuta** (south), and **Bengal** (north west). **Arabs*** begin invading the **Indus** region.

751 The **Abbasids*** defeat **T'ang*** armies at **Talas River**, ending **China's** influence in **central Asia**.

794-1185 Heian Period in Japan. The emperor rules from Heian (Kyoto). Power is increasingly in the hands of the nobles.

The Americas

c.600 Teotihuacán* is now a large city, about 20 km (8 miles) square and laid out on a grid plan. The Teotihuacán culture is at its peak, extending from the city to surrounding highlands. Its wealth comes from agriculture, crafts and trade.

600-1000 The Middle Horizon Period in South America. Large urban centres are built. Local cultures are merged together under two great empires, based around **Tiahuanaco**, an important religious centre, and **Huari**, a militaristic capital which spreads the religion of Tiahuanaco over a wide area.

650-900 Huastecan culture on Gulf coast of Mexico.

c.650-850 Teotihuacán culture slowly declines in highland areas.

700-1000 North America: Hohokam* farming communities in the south west (Arizona) reach their most developed stage. They build platform mounds and play ball games, demonstrating close links with Mexico.

c.700-1000 Anasazi farmers emerge in North America.

Mohammed and the rise of Islam

The **Great Mosque** at **Kairouan, North Africa**

Mohammed's teachings were written down by his followers in the *Koran*, the **Muslim** Holy Book.

Mohammed (c.570-632), the founder of **Islam**, was born in **Mecca** – a centre of pilgrimage for **Arabs**, who came to worship at the **Kaaba**, a black meteoric stone. In **610**, he began preaching that there was only one God. He gained many converts and aroused the hostility of the local **aristocracy**＊.

Mohammed's followers, later known as **Muslims**, met in **mosques** to pray.

In **622**, Mohammed was forced to flee to **Medina**, where he organized his followers into a community. He defeated the Meccans at **al Badr (624)** and in **630** captured Mecca, making it the centre of the new religion. By his death, Islam extended over most of **Arabia**.

Arab warriors

In **661**, **Ali**, the fourth caliph, was murdered and replaced by the **Omayyad dynasty**, who ruled from **Damascus (661-750)**. At this time a breakaway sect emerged, called the **Shi'ites**. They believed Ali to be Mohammed's legitimate successor and were oppposed to the official interpretation of the *Koran*. This had been compiled in the reign of **Othman**, the previous caliph and a member of the Omayyad family.

Arab astronomers from the **Abbasid** period, taken from an **Islamic** illustration.

Mohammed was succeeded by a series of **caliphs** (elected successors), who conquered the tribes of **southern Arabia** and then expanded their empire. They defeated the **Byzantine**＊ army in **636** and by **643** had overrun the **Persian Empire**＊. By **711** they had conquered **north Africa** and **Spain** and occupied **Transoxiana** and the **Indus region**. In **751** they defeated the **Chinese** at **Talas River**.

In **750** the Omayyads were massacred and overthrown by the **Abbasid dynasty (750-1258)**, who moved the capital to **Baghdad**. Arab civilization reached its peak under the Abbasids, although the Islamic world soon lost its political unity, as several areas broke away and formed their own local dynasties. It was a time of prosperity and cultural and intellectual achievement, particularly in medicine, mathematics and astronomy.

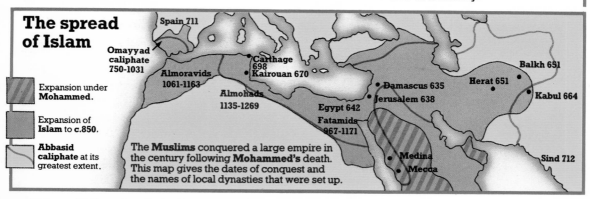

The spread of Islam

Spain 711
Omayyad caliphate 750-1031
Carthage 698
Kairouan 670
Almoravids 1061-1163
Almohads 1135-1269
Balkh 651
Damascus 635
Herat 651
Jerusalem 638
Kabul 664
Egypt 642
Fatimids 967-1171
Medina
Mecca
Sind 712

Expansion under **Mohammed**.

Expansion of **Islam** to c.850.

Abbasid caliphate at its greatest extent.

The **Muslims** conquered a large empire in the century following **Mohammed's** death. This map gives the dates of conquest and the names of local dynasties that were set up.

The migrations of the peoples of the Steppes

The **Steppes** are plains, stretching from **eastern Europe** to **Asia**. During this period they were inhabited by mounted **nomadic*** peoples of **Asiatic** origin, many of whom began migrating west. They lived in tribes, which grouped together in **hordes**. Each horde was led by a **khan**, who ruled over a region called a **khanate**.

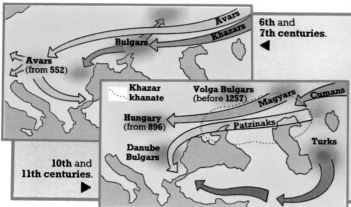

6th and 7th centuries.

10th and 11th centuries.

Map of migrations

The **Avars** migrated west in **552**, drove the **Slavs*** from their homeland and established a large **khanate c.600**, destroyed by the **Byzantines*** in **803**.

The **Patzinaks** set up a state in the **Balkans** in the **10th century**, which was wiped out by the **Byzantines** in **1091**.

The Bulgars

The **Bulgars** were remnants of the **Huns***, who retreated to **south Russia (c.400s)**. They were driven out by the **Khazars (c.500s)** and one group established a state on the **River Volga** (until **1257**).

Gold engraving of a **Bulgar** horseman.

Another group settled on the **River Danube**, intermarried with **Slavs*** and founded a **Bulgarian kingdom (c.680)**, which was conquered by the **Byzantines* (1018)**.

The Polovtsy (or Cumans)

The **Polovtsy** were pushed from **central Asia (c.400s-700s)** and occupied the lands of the **Khazars (c.900s)**. They were defeated by the **Mongols* (1237)** and their survivors merged with the **Golden Horde***.

The Khazars

The **Khazars** established a **khanate** in the **Ukraine (c.500s)** and expanded west. The state disintegrated **(c.1000s)** under attacks from **Russians*** and **Polovtsy**.

Tribesmen of the **Steppes** on horseback.

The Magyars

The **Magyars** moved into the **Hungarian plain (c.800s)**, after **Charlemagne*** destroyed **Avar** power. They raided across the **German** frontier **(862)** and fought the **Bulgars**. In **896** they set up a **Hungarian state** under the **Arpad dynasty (896-1301)**.

Crown of **Stephen I** ("the **Saint**") **(997-1038)**, recognized by the **Pope** as King of **Hungary** in **1001**.

The Turks

The **Turks** began moving west in about the **9th century**. Many converted to **Islam*** and one group founded an empire under **Mahmud of Ghazni (997-1030)**.

Turkish tribesmen with **yurts** (tents).

During the **11th century**, a group of tribes known as the **Seljuks** spread rapidly until they dominated the **Middle East**. They captured **Baghdad (1055)** and their leader was proclaimed **sultan***, ruling on behalf of the **Abbasids***. Their victory at **Manzikert* (1071)** established Turkish control in **Anatolia**, which became known as **Turkey**. Their empire was not long-lived, but it strengthened the Islamic world.

Southern and Western Europe

832-847 Vikings* raid and settle in **Ireland**.

835 Danes* begin raiding **England**.

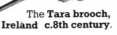

The **Tara brooch, Ireland c.8th century**.

843 Treaty of Verdun: partition of the **Carolingian empire***.

865-874 Danes* conquer **Mercia**, **Northumbria** and **East Anglia**.

871-899 Reign of **Alfred the Great**, King of **Wessex**. He resists the advance of the **Danes***. **England** is divided into **Wessex** and the **Danelaw**.

917-921 Edward of Wessex conquers the southern half of the **Danelaw**.

919 End of **Carolingian dynasty***. **Henry (the Fowler) of Saxony** is elected king of **Germany**.

936-973 Reign of **Otto I of Germany**. He establishes control over the German duchies, conquers the kingdom of **Italy** and stops the westward advance of the **Magyars*** at the **Battle of Lechfeld (955)**. In 962 he is crowned **Holy Roman Emperor of the German nation** and becomes founder of the **Holy Roman Empire**.

Crown of **Otto I**.

Otto's empire emerges as the leading power in the West, claiming equal status with the **Byzantines**.

987-1328 Capetian dynasty rules **France**.

991 The **Danes*** defeat the **English** at the **Battle of Malden**. English pay **Danegeld***.

1008-1028 Civil wars cause the break-up of the kingdom of **Cordoba***. This leads to the **reconquista***.

1016-1035 Canute of Denmark rules **England**.

1016 Normans* invade **south Italy**, led by **Robert** and **Roger Guiscard**.

1042-1066 Reign of **St Edward the Confessor**, King of **England**.

1046-1075 The **papacy*** initiates reform of abuses such as **simony** (sale of **ecclesiastical*** offices) and the marriage of priests.

1054 Schism (split) between the **Eastern** and **Western Churches**, caused by the **Pope's** claim to supremacy over the whole **Christian Church**.

1054 Robert Guiscard is created **Duke of Apulia** and **Calabria** by the **Pope** and invited to take **Sicily** from the **Arabs***.

1061-1091 Conquest of **Sicily** by Robert Guiscard's brother, **Roger**, who is made **Count of Sicily**.

1066 Battle of Hastings*: **William of Normandy** conquers **England** and becomes **King William I** (1066-1087).

1071 Normans* conquer **Bari**, the last **Byzantine*** possession in **Italy**.

1075-1122 The **Investiture Controversy**: a quarrel between the **Pope** and the **Holy Roman Emperor** over who has the right to **invest** (confer authority on) bishops and abbots. Settled at the **Concordat of Worms (1122)**. Part of a wider, longer-lasting power struggle between the **Empire** and **papacy***.

Northern and Eastern Europe

812 Battle of Adrianople: Khan Krum of Bulgaria defeats the **Byzantines*** and kills their emperor.

Battle between the **Byzantines** and the **Bulgarians**.

830 Establishment of the independent **Slav*** kingdom of **Moravia**. Destroyed by **Magyars* (906)**.

860 Varangians* unsuccessfully besiege **Constantinople**.

861 Vikings* discover **Iceland** and settle there (874).

862 St Cyril (826-869) and **St Methodius (815-885)** work as **Christian** missionaries in **Moravia**. Cyril develops the **Cyrillic alphabet**.

c.862 Rurik* settles in **Novgorod** and establishes the principality of **Russia***.

866 Conversion of **Russia*** to **Christianity*** begins.

867-1056 Macedonian dynasty rules the **Byzantine Empire***.

Mosaic showing **Emperor Constantine IX** and his wife **Zoë**, of the **Macedonian dynasty**.

882 Oleg the Wise conquers **Kiev** and moves the **Russian*** capital there.

889 Magyars* invade **Hungary** and set up a state under the **Arpad dynasty (896-1301)**.

c.890s-930s Norway is first organized as a single kingdom, under **Harald Finehair**.

929-967 Bohemia emerges as a stable political unit under **Boleslav I**.

960 Mieszko I (960-992) unites the tribes of **northern Poland** and founds a **Polish state**. He becomes a **Christian*** in 966.

965 Harald Bluetooth, King of Denmark (c.950-986) becomes a **Christian***.

965 Destruction of the **Khazar empire*** by **Svyatoslav of Russia**.

976-1025 Reign of **Basil II**, a great warrior emperor of the **Byzantine Empire***. He wins a series of victories against the **Arabs***, **Russians***, **Bulgarians***, **Armenians** and **Normans*** and extends the frontiers of the Empire.

980-1015 Vladimir*, Grand Prince of **Kiev**, becomes sole ruler of **Kievan Russia***. He marries a **Byzantine*** princess (986), becomes a **Christian*** (989) and introduces the **Eastern (Greek Orthodox)** religion.

Vladimir of Kiev

Middle East and Africa

c.700s **Arab** merchants and travellers develop a flourishing trade with rich Saharan trading cities. The Arabs bring horses, copper, tools and weapons in exchange for gold, ivory, skins and slaves. This encourages the growth of strong **African kingdoms** and trading empires, such as **Ghana** and **Kanem-Bornu**.

Arab traders crossing the **Sahara**.

c.700-1200 Kingdom of **Ghana**, the first **West African** trading empire, rich in gold.

750-1258 The **Abbasid dynasty*** rules from **Baghdad**: the golden age of **Islamic*** culture.

Inside a **Baghdad** library, a scene from an **Islamic** painting.

786-809 Reign of **Caliph Harun al Rashid**, of the *Thousand and One Nights* stories.

c.800 Three small, independent **Arab** kingdoms are set up in **north Africa**.

800-1800 Kingdom of **Kanem-Bornu**, a great trading empire in **West Africa**.

Mounted warriors from **Kanem-Bornu**.

868-905 The **Tulunid dynasty** rules in **Egypt** and **Syria**.

902-1004 The **Samanid dynasty** rules in **Persia**.

909-972 The **Fatamid dynasty** takes over the **Arab** kingdoms in **north Africa**. They conquer and rule **Egypt** from 969-1171.

997-1030 Reign of **Mahmud, Sultan of Ghazni (Turkestan)**, who conquers an empire in **eastern Afghanistan** and **northern India**. Ghazni becomes a centre of **Islamic*** culture.

The Far East

802 The **Angkor kingdom** is established in **Cambodia** under the **Khmer dynasty**.

842 The **Tibetan Empire** disintegrates.

c.852-1160 The **Fujiwara clan** controls the government in **Japan**.

868 The earliest printed book, the **Buddhist*** *Diamond Sutra*, is produced in **China**.

10th century **Indian kingdoms** break up into smaller states.

907-960 The **Epoch of the Five Dynasties** : **China** is divided by civil wars.

916 Founding of the **Khitan kingdom** in **Mongolia**.

947-1125 **Khitans** overrun **northern China** and set up the **Liao dynasty**.

960-1127 The **Northern Sung dynasty** reunites **central** and **southern China** and rules from **Kaifeng**.

Hindu statue from the **Chola dynasty**.

985-1014 Reign of **Rajara I**, of the **Chola kingdom, south India**.

990 **Yangtu (Peking)** becomes the capital of **northern China**.

997-1030 Reign of **Mahmud, Sultan of Ghazni (Turkestan)**, who conquers an empire in **northern India** and **eastern Afghanistan**.

c.1000 The **Chinese** perfect the invention of gunpowder.

1002-1050 **Angkor kingdom** grows in importance under **King Suryavarman**.

1044 A **Burmese state** is formed around **Pagan**.

1051-1062 **Nine Years' Civil War** in **Japan**: the beginning of the rise of the **samurai***.

Samurai warriors

1086-1088 **Three Years' Civil War** in **Japan**.

1126-1234 The **Chin dynasty** overrun **northern China**.

1127-1279 The **Southern Sung dynasty** is established at **Nanking, southern China**.

The Americas

c.750 **Teotihuacan*** is destroyed.

c.750 **Mayan civilization*** slowly declines.

900 The **Anasazi*** begin building **pueblos**, clusters of buildings nestling in cliffs, reached only by ladders. The Anasazi make cotton cloth and work in turquoise and other stones.

Anasazi pueblo

900-1200 **Post Classical Period** in **Central America**. The **Toltecs** destroy centres around **Teotihuacan*** and invade the coastal area and **Mayan*** territory. The Mayan city **Chichen**, is renamed **Chichen Itza**.

Pyramid at **Chichen Itza**.

c.900-1494 **Mixtec culture** in **Mexico**.

c.900 The centre of **Maya*** culture shifts to **Yucatan**.

947 **Mexico**: Birth of **Quetzalcoatl**, revered by the **Aztecs*** as a god.

980 The **Toltecs** establish their capital at **Tula**.

Statue of **Toltec** warrior from **Tula**.

982 **Eric the Red**, a **Viking***, begins to colonize **Greenland**.

999 **Quetzalcoatl** flees to the **Gulf coast** of **Mexico**.

1000 **Leif Ericsson**, son of **Eric the Red**, travels down the **American coast**.

Viking ship off the coast of **America**.

c.1000 The **Hopewellians*** discover how to etch designs with acid.

The Vikings

The **Vikings** (also called **Northmen** or **Norsemen**) were seafarers from **Scandinavia**, who raided much of **Europe** between the **8th** and **11th centuries**. They began by robbing and plundering, but later began to trade and settle. In **northern France** they became known as **Normans**, and in **Russia**, as **Varangians***. The first raids came from **Norway** from **790s-840s**, but from the **830s**, the **Danes** joined in on an even bigger scale.

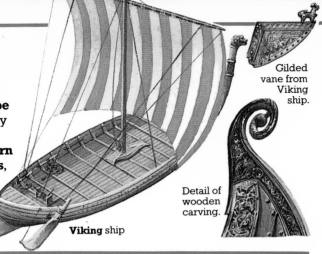

Gilded vane from Viking ship.

Detail of wooden carving.

Viking ship

Map of Viking voyages

Iona 795

793-795

Ireland 832-847

England 838

Normandy 896

Provence and Tuscany 859-862

Spain and Portugal 844

Greenland 982-984

The route to **America**.

Iceland 860

Vinland (Newfoundland) c.1000

Swedes Danes Norwegians

Viking routes

England under the Danelaw

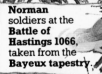

Viking raiders

Between **866-874** the **Danes** conquered all **England**, except **Wessex**. **Alfred the Great**, King of Wessex **(871-899)**, defeated them in **878** and set up the **Danelaw** – an area in which the Danes could live. Alfred and his successors, **Edward (899-924)**, **Ethelstan (924-939)** and **Edgar (959-975)**, gradually overran the Danish states and reestablished English rule.

The Vikings raided and looted all over **Europe**, reaching as far as **Constantinople** and the **Middle East**.

Viking treasure

However the English position grew weaker. **Ethelred the Unready (978-1016)** was forced to pay **Danegeld** – a tax to avoid being plundered by new Danish raiders. In **1016**, England was conquered by **Canute of Denmark (1016-1035)** and ruled by Danes until **1042**, when Ethelred's son, **Edward the Confessor (1042-1066)** came to the throne.

The Normans

Norman soldiers at the **Battle of Hastings 1066**, taken from the **Bayeux tapestry**.

In **895**, **Danes** attacked **Paris** and settled at the mouth of the **River Seine (896)**. The **Franks*** allowed them to keep the land, provided they defended it against other **Norsemen**. In **912** their leader, **Rollo**, was baptized and made **Duke of Normandy** (the Northmen's lands). In **1066**, **William of Normandy**, a descendant of Rollo's, defeated **Harold of Wessex** at the **Battle of Hastings** and conquered **England**, becoming **King William I**.

Franks, 22-23; Varangians, 29.

Russia

From the **8th century**, **Swedish** warrior merchants, or **Varangians**, settled around the **Baltic coast** to trade. They expanded down the **Russian** rivers, settling among the **Slavs** and developing trade between the Baltic and the **Islamic*** world. In **c. 862**, **Rurik**, head of the **Rus** tribe of Varangians, founded a state at **Novgorod**. It was called Rus (or **Russia**) and was ruled by his descendants until **1598**.

Varangians carrying their boat from one river to another.

Rurik's successor, **Oleg the Wise (879-912)**, won the allegiance of Slav tribes in the area and expanded south as far as **Kiev**, which he made the capital. Contacts with **Constantinople*** were encouraged under **Igor (912-945)** and **Christianity*** began to spread after **957**.

The **Virgin of Vladimir**, an icon painted **c.1125**.

Vladimir I "the Saint" **(978-1015)** brought together what had been a loose confederation of tribal areas into a single state. He married a **Byzantine*** princess and made Christianity the official religion. Kiev became a major European city and centre of culture, religion and the arts.

St Sophia, Novgorod c.1045- 1062

Kievan Russia reached its peak under Vladimir's son, **Yaroslav (1019-1054)**.

After **1054 Kievan Russia** went into an irreversible decline. A new wave of invasions by **Asiatic nomads*** drove many people north. The state dissolved into separate princedoms, which lasted until the invasion of the **Mongols*** (1237-1240).

The Slavs

The **Slavs** were tribes of **Indo-European*** origin who were originally settled in the **Pripet region**, west of the **River Dnieper**. In the **6th century** they were driven out by **Avars*** and spread across **eastern Europe**.

Slav expansion

Baltic Sea
Novgorod
Pomeranians
Boundary of **Kievan Russia**
Obodrites
Poles
Russians
Sorbs
Pripet marshes
Bohemians
Kiev
Moravians
Slovenes
Ukrainians
Croats
Bulgarian Slavs
Spread of **Christianity**

↳ Expansion of **Slavs**
↳ **Viking** trade routes
↳ Raids of **Asiatic** tribes

By the **9th century** the Slavs were settled in their new territories and were becoming politically organized. By **c.1000** most of the indigenous, non-Slav people had been assimilated. Independent Slav states were founded in **Moravia (830)**, **Poland (960)**, **Russia (c.862)**, **Croatia (815)** and **Bulgaria (716)**.

Moravian silver plaque

The Slavs were converted to **Christianity** by **Byzantine*** missionaries, led by two brothers, **St Cyril (826-869)** and **St Methodius (815-885)**. Cyril adapted the **Greek alphabet** for the Slav language and his version became known as the **Cyrillic alphabet**. In **990-992**, Poles and other western Slavs changed their allegiance to the **Western (Catholic) Church**, while the rest remained with the **Eastern Church**.

Reproduction of a scene from a **Greek** manuscript, showing the baptism of the **Bulgarians**.

Monasticism

Monasticism began in **Egypt** in the **3rd century**, when **Christians*** began withdrawing into the desert to live as **hermits**. Under **Basil of Caesarea (330-379)**, they were brought together into communities. Monasticism in the West was started by **Benedict of Nursia (480-543)**. He founded a monastery at **Monte Cassino (c.529)** and an order of **Benedictine monks**. They lived, worked and prayed together, following his **Rule** (a set of regulations).

Monastery of **St Catherine, Mount Sinai (mid-sixth century)**.

By the **8th century**, monasteries had been established all over **Christendom***. Until the spread of universities in the **13th century**, they were the most important centres of culture and learning. They also provided care of the poor and hospitality to travellers.

The monks copied the works of great **Christian** teachers, as well as **classical** texts.

The monasteries commissioned great works of sculpture and architecture. They were responsible for the development of the **Romanesque** style, which flourished in **Europe** between the **9th** and **11th centuries**. It was characterized by rounded arches, groined vaults and massive stone walls.

Features of **Romanesque** architecture.

Southern and Western Europe

1086 Domesday Book is compiled in **England**: a survey of all the property in the realm, according to the agricultural yield of the land.

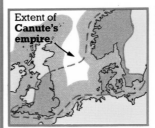

Domesday Book

1094 Portugal becomes independent and is recognized as a kingdom in **1179**.

1096 – 1099 First Crusade*.

1105 Roger II succeeds as **Count of Sicily**. He acquires **Calabria (1122)** and **Apulia (1127)** and is made **King of Sicily (1130 – 1154)**.

Under **Roger II** (right), **Sicily** becomes a great centre for **Christian** and **Arab** scholars.

1128 Mathilda, heir to **Henry I of England**, marries **Geoffrey of Anjou**, nicknamed "**Plantagenet**".

1135 Stephen of Boulogne seizes the **English** throne, on the death of his uncle, **Henry I**.

Roger II of Sicily

1137 – 1144 The building of **St Denis, Paris**, the first great **Gothic*** cathedral, by **Abbot Suger**.

1139 – 1148 Civil war in **England** between **Stephen** and **Mathilda**. Mathilda is defeated.

1147 – 1149 Second Crusade*.

c.1150 Paris University is founded.

Northern and Eastern Europe

990-992 Poland changes from the **Eastern (Greek Orthodox)** to the **Western (Roman Catholic) Church**.

993 Olaf Skutkonnung becomes the first **Christian** king of **Sweden**.

995-1000 Rule of **Olaf Tryggveson**, King of **Norway**. **Christianity*** is introduced in Norway.

998-1038 Reign of **Stephen I (St Stephen)*** – the first **Christian** king of **Hungary**.

1014-1035 Canute, King of **Denmark** rules an empire which covers Denmark, **England** and part of **Sweden**. **Norway** is subjugated 1028-1035.

Extent of **Canute's empire**

Norwegian stave church c.1150, made from strips of wood joined together.

1015-1028 Reign of **Olaf II** ("**the Saint**"), King of **Norway**. He flees to **Russia** in 1028.

1019-1054 Yaroslav the Wise rules **Kievan Russia***.

The monasteries became great landowners, but as they grew richer, discipline often relaxed. There were frequent attempts at reform and new orders were established. The first of these were the **Cluniacs**. They were founded at **Cluny, France** in **910** and expanded rapidly **c.950-1100**. The **Cistercians**, founded in **Cîteaux** in **1098**, aimed for a stricter, simpler way of life and became influential in the **12th century** under **St Bernard of Clairvaux (d.1153)**.

(left to right)
Cistercian
Dominican
Benedictine
Franciscan
Carmellite nun

The **12th century** was the great age of the monasteries, but by the end of the century their popularity was in decline. New orders were founded, such as the **Franciscans (1210)** and **Dominicans (1215)**, who were based in towns. They were called **mendicant friars**. They lived on **alms** (donations) and went about preaching.

Feudalism

The break-up of the **Roman Empire***, then that of **Charlemagne***, and the threat posed by the **Viking*** raids, created disruption in **western Europe**. People looked to powerful leaders to help defend them. In the **8th** and **9th centuries**, a system of rights and duties developed between **lords** and their **vassals** (those they protected), which we call **feudalism**. In return for protection, and often the granting of a **fief** (land), the vassal had to pay **homage*** to his lord, perform military duties and pay certain dues.

King

Nobles (great landowners)

Lesser nobility

Knights: mounted warriors who were granted a **fief** to support themselves and their entourage.

Free peasants or **freemen** lived on the **fief** and paid the lord rents and other dues.

Villeins and **serfs** had surrendered their freedom and were bound to the **fief**. They had to work for the lord so many days a year and pay rent and other dues.

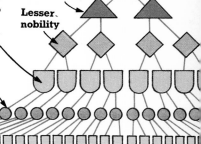

Middle East and Africa

1030 The **Seljuk Turks*** extend their influence in **Asia Minor**.

1052 The **Almoravids*** attack **Ghana**, inflicting great damage. Ghana is destroyed by **1076**.

1055 **Seljuks*** take **Baghdad**.

1056-1147 The **Almoravids*** conquer and rule a kingdom in **North Africa** and **Spain**.

1071 Battle of **Manzikert**. Seljuk **Turks*** take **Jerusalem** and destroy **Byzantine*** power in **Asia Minor**.

1076 The **Seljuk Turks*** conquer **Damascus**.

c.1090 The **Assassins** are founded in **Persia**; a branch of **Shi'ites*** who use murder to destroy their opponents.

1096-1099 **First Crusade***. **Crusaders** take **Jerusalem** and set up states in **Anatolia** and **Syria**.

c.1100s Growth of the kingdom of **Ife** in **Nigeria**.

Terracotta head from **Ife**.

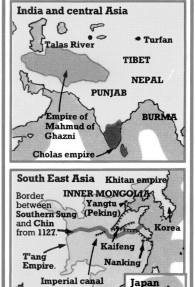

The Far East

India and central Asia

Talas River
Turfan
TIBET
NEPAL
PUNJAB
Empire of Mahmud of Ghazni
BURMA
Cholas empire

South East Asia Khitan empire
Border between Southern Sung and Chin from 1127.
INNER MONGOLIA
Yangtu (Peking)
Korea
T'ang Empire.
Kaifeng
Nanking
Imperial canal
Japan
NORTH VIETNAM
Kyoto
Angkor empire
Nara

The Americas

1000-1483 **Late Intermediate Period** in **South America**. Decline of the **Huari-Tiahuanaco*** centres. Local styles and cultures re-emerge. The **Chimu** peoples build large towns, including their capital, **Chanchan**, on the **north Peruvian** coast. Ancestors of the **Incas*** gather around **Cuzco**.

1168 Mexico: **Chichimec** people overrun **Tula**.

1190 Second era of **Mayan civilization***.

Pages from the *Dresden Codex*, a **Mayan** manuscript **c.900s-1100s**.

North America

Anasazi people
Hopewell people
Hohokam people
Mississippi mound builders
Mississippi River

Southern and Western Europe

1152 **Henry of Anjou**, son of **Mathilda***, marries **Eleanor of Aquitaine** and renews the struggle.

1153 **Stephen*** recognizes **Henry of Anjou** as his heir.

1154-1189 **Henry of Anjou** becomes **Henry II** and rules the **Angevin Empire** in **England** and **France**. The **Plantaganets*** rule England until **1399**.

1159 **Henry II of England** introduces **scutage**, a system which allows knights or barons to pay money instead of fighting in his wars.

1167-1168 **Oxford University** is founded.

The murder of **Thomas à Becket**.

1170 **Thomas à Becket**, Archbishop of Canterbury, is murdered on the orders of **Henry II**, with whom he has quarrelled over church rights. Becket is **canonized*** in **1173**.

1186 **Constance**, daughter of **Roger II*** of **Sicily**, marries **Henry VI, Holy Roman Emperor***.

1189-1192 **Third Crusade**.

1189-1199 Reign of **Richard I**, King of **England** (**1189-1199**). He recognizes the independence of **Scotland**.

1192 **Sicily** is united with the **Holy Roman Empire***.

Northern and Eastern Europe

1035 **Poland** becomes a **fief*** of the **Holy Roman Empire***.

1035 The **Norwegian kingdom** is restored by **Magnus the Good** (**1035-1047**), who returns from **Russia** after the death of **Canute***.

1054 The **Pope's** insistence on supremacy causes a **schism** (split) between the **Eastern (Orthodox)** and **Western (Roman Catholic) Churches**.

1071 **Battle of Manzikert**. The **Byzantines*** are defeated by the **Turks*** and lose **Asia Minor**.

1081-1085 **Comneni dynasty** rules the **Byzantine Empire***.

1081-1085 **Normans***, led by **Robert Guiscard**, invade the **Balkans**.

Norman horseman

1086 **Bohemia** is recognized as a kingdom by the **Holy Roman Emperor***.

1093 Sack of **Kiev** by the **Polovtsy***.

1095 **Byzantine*** emperor, **Alexius Comnenus** (**1081-1118**), calls on **Pope Urban II** for help against the **Turks***.

1096-1099 **First Crusade** (see below).

1105 **West Germans** begin colonizing **East Germany**.

1147-1149 **Second Crusade** (see below).

1189-1192 **Third Crusade** (see below).

The Crusades

In **1071**, the **Seljuk Turks*** defeated the **Byzantines*** at **Manzikert** and captured **Jerusalem**. This sparked off the **Crusades**, a series of military expeditions fought by **Christian* Europe** to recover the **Holy Land (Palestine)**. Militant **Muslims***, the Turks were less tolerant than their **Fatamid*** predecessors, and Christians were persecuted.

The **Crusaders** wore a cross on their tunics, to symbolize their role as "soldiers of Christ".

In **1095**, the Byzantine emperor, **Alexius Comnenus**, appealed to **Pope Urban II** for help against the Turks. The Pope preached a crusade, or holy war. The idea appealed to many, as it combined religious fervour with the chance to win riches and land.

The **First Crusade (1096-1099)** was composed of several different armies: **French, Flemish** and **Normans** from **Italy**. They captured **Nicaea (1097)**, **Antioch (1098)** and Jerusalem **(1099)**, killing many Muslims. The Holy Land was divided into four Christian kingdoms: Jerusalem, **Antioch, Edessa** and **Tripoli**, collectively known as **Outremer**.

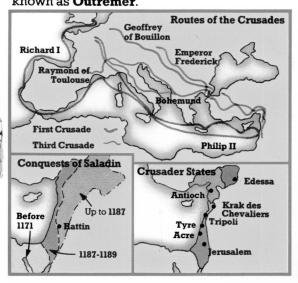

Routes of the Crusades

Richard I

Geoffrey of Bouillon

Emperor Frederick

Raymond of Toulouse

Bohemund

First Crusade

Third Crusade

Philip II

Conquests of Saladin

Before 1171

Up to 1187

Hattin

1187-1189

Crusader States

Edessa

Antioch

Krak des Chevaliers

Tripoli

Tyre

Acre

Jerusalem

Middle East and Africa

1135-1269 The **Almohads** rule a kingdom in **north Africa**.

1147-1149 Second Crusade.

1171 The **Fatamids*** are thrown out of **Egypt** by **Saladin (1171-1193)**, who founds the **Ayyubid dynasty**. He becomes ruler of **Syria (1174)** and **Aleppo (1183)**.

1187 **Saladin** defeats the **Christians*** at the **Battle of Hattin** and takes **Jerusalem**.

1189-1192 Third Crusade.

1190 Accession of **King Lalibela of Ethiopia**.

1191 **Crusaders** take **Acre**.

1192 Peace of Ramlah. **Saladin** keeps **Jerusalem**, but recognizes the **Christian*** kingdom of **Acre**.

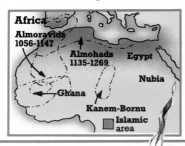

Africa
Almoravids 1056-1147
Almohads 1135-1269
Egypt
Nubia
Ghana
Kanem-Bornu
Islamic area

The Far East

c.1150 **Suryavarman II** of **Cambodia (1112-1152)** completes **Angkor Wat**.

Angkor Wat, a **Hindu** temple of the **Khmer dynasty** of **Cambodia**.

1156-1185 Civil wars in **Japan**: struggles between the **Taira**, **Fujiwara** and **Minamoto** clans.

1159 **Taira** clan control **Japan**.

1170 The height of the **Srivijaya** kingdom in **Java** under the **Indian Shailendra dynasty**.

c.1180 The **Angkor Empire*** is at its greatest extent.

1185 **Yoshitsume Minamoto** defeats the **Taira** clan. Start of the **Kamakura Period (1185-1333)** in **Japan** (named after the home district of the **Minamoto**).

1192 **Yoritomo Minamoto** is given effective power under the title **shogun** (hereditary military dictator*). His family rules **Japan** until **1219**.

The Americas

Mayan civilization
Zapotec culture
Chichen Itza
Teotihuacan civilization
Toltecs
Tula
Oaxaca
Yucatan
Mixtec states
Gulf coast culture
Central America

West coast of South America
Chimu people
Lake Titicaca
Huari culture
Tiahuanaco culture

Military orders of **monks** were set up in **Jerusalem** to protect pilgrims.

The **Knights Hospitallers** (founded **1110**).

The **Knights Templars** (founded **1118**).

The **Teutonic Knights** (founded **1190**).

Some **Crusaders** stayed to protect their new lands, while many returned to Europe, taking with them luxuries, such as silks and spices, and new ideas from **Islamic*** culture. Trade developed between the Muslims and some **northern Italian** cities. Meanwhile the Muslims were growing in strength.

Krak des Chevaliers, built by the **Knights Hospitallers**.

Edessa was recaptured **(1144)** and the **Second Crusade (1147-1149)** to win it back proved fruitless. The Muslims acquired a great leader, **Saladin**, who became **sultan*** of **Egypt** in **1171**, and in **1187**, recaptured Jerusalem.

Saladin and his soldiers

The **Third Crusade (1189-1192)** was led by **Emperor Frederick I**, **Richard I** of **England** and **Philip II** of **France**. It failed to retake Jerusalem, although a truce won the right for Christian pilgrims to enter the city. The **Fourth Crusade (1202-1204)** ended in the attack and plunder of **Constantinople** by Crusaders. Although there were further attempts, the great age of Crusades was over.

Angkor, 23; **Christian**, 19; **dictator**, 113; **Islam**, 24; **Fatamids**, 24; **sultan**, 114.

The medieval papacy

The **papacy** is the name given to the office of the **Pope**, or **Bishop of Rome**, at the head of the **Catholic Church**. In the **4th** and **5th centuries**, the Bishop of Rome grew in importance in relation to the other **bishops***, and filled the political vacuum left by the fall of the **Roman Empire***. The coronation of **Charlemagne*** by a pope symbolized the special position of the papacy at the head of **Christendom***.

Pope Innocent III (1198-1216). In 1202, he asserted the supremacy of the **papacy** over the **Holy Roman Emperor**.

In the **13th century**, the popes began claiming that they were superior to all **temporal*** rulers. This provoked clashes with **European** monarchs, especially the **Holy Roman Emperor***, over such matters as taxation, imperial elections and church appointments. Conflict came to a head during the reign of **Frederick II***.

The **Palace of the Popes, Avignon**, begun under **Pope Benedict XII (1334-1342)**.

The papal court was noted for its luxury and splendour, but also for its corruption and **nepotism***.

Papal bulls* *Clericos Laicos* **(1296)** and *Unam Sanctam* **(1302)** banned churchmen from paying taxes to temporal rulers and proclaimed the **sovereignty*** of the Church. There was strong opposition from **England** and **France**. **Philip IV** of France imprisoned the Pope in **1303** (he died soon after) and then ensured the election of a French pope, **Clement V (1305-1316)**. A series of Frenchmen were elected popes and, from **1309-1377**, the papal court was moved to **Avignon**. This period was known as the **Babylonian Captivity***, as the papacy came under the influence of the French kings. Pressure built up for reform and also for a return to Rome.

Areas following the **Pope** in **Rome**.

Areas following the **Pope** in **Avignon**.

Areas officially following **Rome**, but with local variations.

The Great Schism 1378-1417.

In **1378**, **Urban VI** was elected Pope and took up residence in Rome. A rival French pope, **Clement VII**, was elected in Avignon. Catholic Europe was divided in its support. This is known as the **Great Schism**. At the **Council of Pisa (1409)**, both popes were deposed and a new one elected, but the first two refused to stand down. At the **Council of Constance (1414-1418)**, all three were deposed. **Martin V** was elected and ruled from Rome.

The **Council of Constance**, a general council made up of representatives of the Church.

Criticism of the Church's corruption and wealth inspired a number of movements for reform. Complaints about abuses sometimes developed into attacks on authority and even on official doctrine. An opinion or belief which is contrary to the teaching of the Church is known as **heresy**.

Carcassonne, an **Albigensian** stronghold, which fell during the **Albigensian Crusade*** **(1209)**.

In **1184**, the **Inquisition** was founded by the papacy to discover and suppress heresy. **Heretics** (people accused of heresy) were often savagely punished and burnt to death. Despite this, heretical **sects** grew up, such as the **Cathars** (from the **11th century**). They gained a large following in **southern France** (where they were known as **Albigensians**), but were mostly wiped out after the fall of their stronghold at **Montsegur (1244)**.

Frederick II and the fall of the Hohenstaufen

In **1220**, **Frederick II of Hohenstaufen (1194-1250)**, **King of Sicily** and **Germany**, became **Holy Roman Emperor***. He lived in Sicily at the centre of a brilliant court. His reorganization of the Sicilian government (the **1231 Constitutions of Melfi**) made Sicily one of the most advanced states in **Europe**. Well-educated, with a rational, enquiring mind, Frederick's personality won him the nickname *Stupor Mundi* (Wonder of the World) and his attitudes offended many.

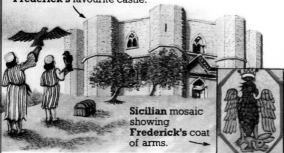

Falconers at **Castel del Monte** in **Apulia, Sicily**, **Frederick's** favourite castle.

Sicilian mosaic showing **Frederick's** coat of arms.

Frederick's ambitions in **Italy** brought him into conflict with the **papacy*** and he was **excommunicated*** (**1227** and **1239**) and deposed (**1245**). In **northern Italy** rivalry developed between two parties – the **Ghibellines** (Frederick's supporters) and the **Guelphs** (allies of the Pope).

Crown belonging to **Frederick's** wife, **Constance of Aragon**.

This continued after Frederick's death and led to the fall of the **Hohenstaufen dynasty**. There was political chaos in Germany and Italy, where independent city states grew up in place of imperial authority. The Pope gave Sicily to **Charles of Anjou**, who defeated Frederick's son, **Manfred**, and grandson, **Conradin**, at the battles of **Benevento (1266)** and **Tagliacozzo (1268)**. The Sicilians hated their new **French** rulers and massacred them in **1282** at the **Sicilian Vespers**. Sicily then passed to Frederick's granddaughter, **Constance of Aragon**.

The Wars of the Roses

The **Wars of the Roses** is the name given to the struggle between the descendants of **Edward III** for the **English** crown. They are named after the emblems of the rivals: the white rose of **York** and the red rose of **Lancaster**.

English Royal Family Tree

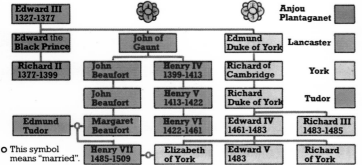

Anjou
Plantaganet

Lancaster

York

Tudor

o This symbol means "married".

Bitter rivalries developed during the long **minority*** rule of **Henry VI (1422-1461)**, of the house of Lancaster. When he came of age, he proved incompetent and subject to bouts of madness. Added to this was the humiliation of defeat in the **Hundred Years' War***. In **1454**, Parliament made **Richard, Duke of York, Protector***, but in **1455** he was excluded from the **Royal Council** and fighting broke out. The wars ended with the victory of **Henry Tudor**, as **Henry VII**, first king of the **Tudor dynasty (1485-1603)**.

Important dates

1455 Yorkists win at St Albans.

1460 Yorkists win at Northampton. Henry VI is taken prisoner. Lancastrians win at Wakefield. Richard of York is executed.

1461 Edward of York, supported by the Earl of Warwick, defeats Henry VI at Mortimer's Cross. Edward is crowned Edward IV.

1469 Warwick changes sides and defeats Edward IV at Edgecote, forcing him to flee to Flanders. Henry VI regains the throne.

1471 Edward IV defeats and kills Warwick at Barnet. Henry VI is murdered and Edward is restored to the throne.

1483 Edward IV dies, succeeded by his young son, **Edward V**. He is deposed by his uncle, **Richard of Gloucester**, who becomes Richard III. Edward and his brother, the Duke of York, are kept in the Tower of London and disappear, presumed murdered.

1485 Henry Tudor, the Lancastrian heir, invades and defeats Richard III at the Battle of Bosworth. He marries the Yorkist heiress, Elizabeth, and becomes Henry VII.

excommunicate, 113; **Holy Roman Emperor**, 26; **Hundred Years' War**, 39; **minority**, 114; **papacy**, 34; **Protector**, 114.

35

Southern and Western Europe

c.1200s Rise of **Gothic** architecture in **Europe**, characterized by the lancet arch, ribbed vault and flying buttress.

Notre Dame, Paris, an example of a **Gothic** cathedral built between **1163-1257**.

Stained glass rose window.

c.1200s Flourishing of the first universities, established in **Bologna (1119)**, **Paris (1150)** and **Oxford (1170)**.

1202 **Arabic numerals** are introduced in **Europe**.

1204 **England** loses **Normandy** to **France**.

1209-1229 Albigensian Crusade, led by **Simon de Montfort the elder** against the **Albigensians***.

1212 Battle of **Las Navas de Tolosa**: **Christian** kings of **Castile**, **Aragon** and **Navarre** defeat the **Arabs***. Starts the break up of the Arab kingdom in **Spain**.

1214-1294 Life of **Roger Bacon**, **English** monk, scholar and scientist.

1215 **Magna Carta***.

1225-1274 Life of **Thomas Aquinas**, **Italian** theologian and philospher.

1258-1265 Uprising of **English** barons against **Henry III**, led by **Simon de Montfort the younger**. Defeated by **Prince Edward** at **Evesham**.

1282 The death in battle of **Prince Llewelyn of Wales** marks the end of Welsh independence from **England**.

Harlech Castle, Wales.

Edward I (1272-1307) of **England** conquered **Wales** and built a series of castles.

1290 **Jews** are expelled from **England**.

1290 Death of **Margaret**, child **Queen of Scotland**. **Edward I** of **England** is asked to judge the claims of 13 rivals for the throne. He later claims it for himself.

1295 **Mateo Visconti** seizes control in **Milan**. His dynasty rules until **1447**.

1297 **French** occupy **Flanders**.

1297 Uprising against the **English** by **William Wallace** in **Scotland**.

1301 **Wales** becomes the principality of the heir to the **English** throne.

1302 **Flemish** craftsmen defeat the **French** army at the **Battle of Courtrai**.

1306 **Jews** are expelled from **France**.

1307-1314 The **Knights Templars*** are investigated for **heresy**.

1309-1378 The **Avignon Papacy***.

1314 **Robert Bruce**, King of Scotland (1306-1329) defeats the **English** at **Bannockburn**.

Northern and Eastern Europe

1204 The **Fourth Crusade***: Crusaders sack **Constantinople**. A **Latin Emperor** is crowned head of the **Byzantine Empire***.

1218 The ruling family in **Switzerland** dies out. Small independent states (**cantons**) are formed. War breaks out when the **Austrians** try to conquer them.

1220-1250 Reign of **Frederick II***, **Holy Roman Emperor*** and ruler of **Germany** and **Sicily**.

1220 **Frederick II*** grants special privileges to the **ecclesiastical princes*** of **Germany**.

1222 **Andreas II of Hungary** issues the **Golden Bull** (document), giving protection and power to the nobles and granting the **national assembly** the right to voice grievances.

1226-1283 The **Teutonic Knights*** are sent by **Frederick II*** to conquer and convert the **Prussians** to **Christianity**.

A **Teutonic Knight**.

Marienburg Castle, Poland, the headquarters of the **Teutonic Knights**.

1227 **Denmark** is defeated at **Bornhöved** by a group of **north German** princes and the city of **Lübeck**. German trade with the **Baltic** begins to expand.

1231 A statute grants the **secular*** princes of **Germany** the same rights of territorial **sovereignty*** as the **ecclesiastical princes***.

1237-1240 **Mongols*** invade **Russia**.

1241 **Mongols*** invade **Hungary** and **Poland**.

c.1242 The **Mongols*** establish the **Khanate of the Golden Horde**, at **Sarai, South Russia**.

1249 **Swedish** rule is extended to **Finland**.

1250-1266 **Birger Jarl**, conqueror of **South Finland**, gives trading privileges to the **Hanseatic League***.

This map shows **Hanseatic** towns and trade routes.

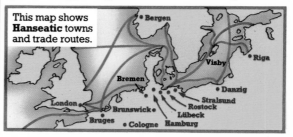

1250 The death of **Frederick II*** leads to the collapse of imperial power in **Germany** and **Italy**.

1253-1278 Rule of **Ottokar II of Bohemia**. **Bohemia** is at the height of its power and acquires **Austria** and parts of **Slovakia** and **Styria**.

1254-1273 **Great Interregnum** in the **Holy Roman Empire***: none of the elected emperors secures universal recognition.

1258-1282 **Michael Paleologus** restores **Byzantine** rule in the **Byzantine Empire***. The **Latin Empire** is dissolved in **1261**.

Africa and the Middle East

1200s Trans-Saharan trade continues. **Ghana*** is in decline.

1200s East Africa: trading cities, such as **Kilwa**, continue to flourish.

c.1200 Church of St George is built at Lalibela, Ethiopia.

The **Church of St George** was one of a series of cross-shaped churches, carved in rock, under the direction of **King Lalibela***.

1218 The **Ayyubid Empire*** breaks up, but the Ayyubids still rule in **Egypt**.

1228 Civil war between **Saladin's*** heirs.

1228-1229 Fifth Crusade*: **Frederick II*** reaches **Acre**. He makes a treaty with the **Sultan of Egypt** and is crowned **King of Jerusalem**.

c.1235 Sun Diata Keita establishes the kingdom of **Mali** which lasts until c.1500.

1240 Destruction of **Kumbi**, former capital of **Ghana***.

1244 Egyptians retake **Jerusalem**.

1248-1254 Sixth Crusade*, led by **Louis IX** of France against **Egypt**.

c.1250 North Africa: Berbers have established a number of states that flourish for over 200 years. Rivalries prevent their unification, but their power is such that **Europeans** call North Africa the **Barbary Coast**.

1250 The last **Ayyubid*** ruler of **Egypt** is murdered. **Mamelukes** seize power and found their own military state.

The **Mamelukes** (left) were slave soldiers from **central Asia**, employed by the **Ayyubids**.

1258 Baghdad is destroyed by **Mongols***.

1260-1277 Reign of **Sultan Baibars** of **Egypt**.

1261 Battle of Ain Jalut: the **Mongol*** advance is halted by the **Egyptians**, led by **Baibars**.

Asia

1206-1526 Rule of the **Islamic* Sultanate of Delhi**, known as the **slave dynasty**, because slaves assisted the first Sultan to power.

1206 **Genghis Khan*** unites the **Mongols*** and begins the conquest of **Asia**.

Pagan in **Burma** was raided by **Mongols** and fell into decline.

Ananda temple, Pagan*, built between **1084-1112**.

1218-1224 Mongols* attack the empire of **Khwarizm**.

1211 Mongols* invade **China**.

c.1220 Founding of the first **Thai** kingdom.

1221 Mongols* attack the Sultanate of Delhi.

1227 Death of **Genghis Khan***. His son, **Ogadei**, is elected **Great Khan** (1229-1241).

The gates of **Karakorum**, the **Mongol** capital founded by **Ogadei**.

1234 Mongols* overthrow the **Chin dynasty*** in **China**.

1239 Mongols* sack **Ani**, the capital of **Armenia**.

1251-1265 Hulagu, grandson of **Genghis Khan***, conquers **Persia** and establishes the **Il-Khan Empire**.

1252-1255 William Rubruque travels to **central Asia**, as the envoy of **Louis IX** of **France**.

1264 Kublai Khan* founds the **Yuan dynasty** in **China**.

1271-1295 Marco Polo of Venice travels across **Asia** to **China**. From 1275-1292, he works for **Kublai Khan***.

Marco Polo on his travels.

1274 Unsuccessful **Mongol*** invasion of **Japan**.

1279-1368 The **Yuan dynasty** rules all **China**.

The Americas

c.1200 North America: the **Mississippians** dominate a wide area. They develop a remarkable culture, influenced by **Mexico**, building large cities on flat-topped mounds.

A **Mississippi mound-builders'** town.

c.1200 North America: **Pueblo*** builders are at their peak in the south west.

c.1200 The **Aztecs***, whose culture is based on that of the **Toltecs*** and **Zapotecs***, begin to found small states in **Mexico**.

c.1200 The **Mayan*** capital, **Chichen Itza**, is abandoned and a new capital built at **Mayapán**, defended by five miles of wall.

c.1200-1300 Chimu kingdom* continues in **Peru**.

c.1200-1300 Beginning of the early **Inca*** period in **Peru**. **Manco Capac** founds **Cuzco** as his capital and makes small conquests in the area.

c.1300 North America: **Pueblo*** building ends abruptly, possibly as a result of drought and the arrival of **Athabascan Indians** migrating from the north west. By c.1500, they have completely taken over the south west.

c.1325 Rise of the **Aztecs*** in **Mexico**. The city of **Tenochtitlán** is built by a group led by **Chief Tenoch**, on islands in **Lake Texcoco**. It becomes the residence of the major tribe.

c.1335 Tenochtitlán is increased in size by the building of floating gardens in the lake.

c.1352 Acamapitzin is elected first King of the **Aztecs***.

Early 1400s Viracocha Inca* (8th Emperor) takes the title **Sapa Inca** (meaning supreme Inca).

c.1427 A causeway is built from **Tenochtitlán** to the mainland. **Emperor Itzcoatl** adopts an aggressive policy towards neighbours. He forces other tribes to pay **tribute*** and establishes a three city league with **Texcoco** and **Tlacopán**, to obtain political control.

Inside an **Aztec** city.

The unification of France

At the beginning of the **13th century** much of **France** was made up of semi-independent provinces in the hands of powerful nobles, including the king of **England**. The effective control of the French kings was limited to a small area, but by the end of the **15th century** they had succeeded in uniting most of France.

A reconstruction of the **Palace of the Louvre, Paris**, built by **Philip II** as a royal residence.

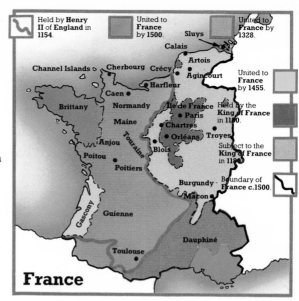

| Held by **Henry II of England** in 1154. | United to **France** by 1500. | United to **France** by 1328. |
| United to **France** by 1455. |
| Held by the **King of France** in 1180. |
| Subject to the **King of France** in 1180. |
| Boundary of **France** c.1500. |

France

In **1204**, **Philip II** of France conquered the English territory in northern France (**Normandy, Maine, Anjou** and **Touraine**). At the **Battle of Bouvines (1214)**, he retook the remaining English lands, except **Guienne** and **Gascony**. Despite early losses in the **Hundred Years' War***, the French succeeded in winning back nearly all their lands from the English.

Between **1234-1301**, **Chartres, Blois, Toulouse, Macon, Poitou** and **Bar** were acquired from French nobles. In **1349**, **Dauphiné** became the province of the heir to the throne, who became known as the **Dauphin**. **Louis XI** seized **Burgundy** and **Artois (1477)** and **Lorraine (1480)**. In **1491**, **Charles VIII** married **Anne of Brittany** and acquired **Brittany**.

The duchy of Burgundy

In **1363**, **John II** of **France** created his younger son, **Philip**, **Duke of Burgundy**. In the **14th** and **15th centuries**, the dukes of Burgundy increased their territory in France,

Burgundian costumes

Germany and the **Netherlands**, by purchase and inheritance. They became among the richest princes in **Europe** and influenced politics and culture for over a century. They were noted for their splendid courts and patronage of the arts.

The Burgundians caused a civil war in France **(1410-1411)** and sided with **England** in the **Hundred Years' War***. **Louis XI** of France planned the destruction of the duchy. **Duke Charles the Bold** was killed at **Nancy (1477)** and Louis seized Burgundy and **Picardy**. At the **Peace of Arras (1482)**, the rest of the inheritance passed to **Maximilian Habsburg** of **Austria**. This provided the **Habsburgs*** with a base from which, under **Charles V***, they rose to dominate Europe.

| French lands after 1482. | Habsburg lands after 1482. |

Holland 1328

Zeeland 1328

Artois 1384

Brabant 1430

Gelderland 1473

Flanders 1384

Limburg 1430

Arras

Picardy 1435

Hainault 1328

Luxembourg 1443

Paris

Nancy

This map shows the dates when territories were acquired by **Burgundy**.

Lorraine 1475

Alsace 1469

Dijon

Franche-Comté 1384

Burgundy

Charolais 1390

The Burgundian kingdom

The Hundred Years' War

The **Hundred Years' War** is the name given to the struggle between **England** and **France** which lasted from **1337-1453**. Since **1066**, there had been quarrels and wars over land held in France by the English kings, but added to this was a dispute over the crown itself. In **1328**, **Charles IV** of France died without a male heir. He was succeeded by his cousin, **Philip VI**, but in **1337**, Charles's nephew, **Edward III** of England, claimed the French throne.

The **Battle of Agincourt**.

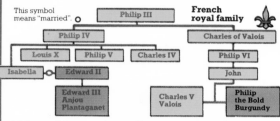

This symbol means "married". o

French royal family

- Philip III
  - Philip IV
    - Louis X
    - Philip V
    - Charles IV
    - Isabella ⚭ Edward II
      - Edward III Anjou Plantaganet
  - Charles of Valois
    - Philip VI
      - John
        - Charles V Valois
        - Philip the Bold Burgundy

Edward formed an alliance with **Flanders (1338)** and invaded France in **1339**. The English made early gains, winning victories at **Sluys (1340)**, **Crécy (1346)**, **Calais (1347)** and **Poitiers (1356)**, where they captured the French king. By the **Treaty of Brétigny (1360)** the English won large areas of France.

A reconstruction of a **15th century French** castle.

Civil war broke out in **Castile** in **1367**, and England and France backed rival candidates. By **1369** the war had spread to France. Truces were made in **1375** and **1389**, but hostilities began again in **1415**. the English king, **Henry V**, won victories at **Agincourt** and **Harfleur**, and in **1417** at **Caen**. By the terms of the **Treaty of Troyes (1420)**, he married a French princess and became heir to the French throne.

However, the real heir, the **Dauphin***, refused to accept this and fighting broke out again. In **1429**, the English besieged **Orléans**, which was saved by an army led by **Joan of Arc**, a young French peasant girl. The Dauphin was crowned **Charles VII**. Joan was burnt as a witch by the English in **1430**, but the French went on to take **Paris (1436)**, **Normandy (1449)**, **Cherbourg (1450)** and **Guienne (1451)**. The war ended in **1453**, with England keeping only Calais and the **Channel Islands**.

Joan of Arc at the **Siege of Orléans**.

The Birth of Parliament in England

In **1215**, a group of **English** barons forced **King John** to sign **Magna Carta**, a document establishing their right to a **Council** to discuss problems. This was the base from which **Parliament** later developed. Similar institutions grew up elsewhere in **Europe** – the **Estates-General** in **France**, the **Cortés** in **Spain** and the **Diet** in **Germany**.

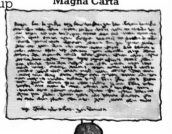
Magna Carta

Important dates

1265 **Simon de Montfort*** expands the **Council** by calling **burgesses** (freemen from towns) as representatives of certain boroughs.

1295 The Model Parliament: Edward I needs money for wars. He calls two **knights*** from each shire and two **burgesses** to vote taxes for him. This is the basis of the **House of Commons**.

1297 The rights of **Parliament** to approve taxes and customs dues are confirmed. Petitions from Parliament that get the King's approval are to become law. Parliament now has the right to initiate legislation.

1332 **Parliament** meets in two "houses" for the first time – the **Lords** and **Commoners**.

Dauphin, 38; **knights**, 31; **Simon de Montfort**, 36.

Southern and Western Europe

1317 The **Salic Law** in **France** bans women from inheriting the throne.

1323 The **Fraticelli**, a branch of **Franciscans***, are condemned as **heretics***, for their belief in the importance of the poverty of **Christ**.

1328 Start of the **Valois dynasty** in **France**.

1337-1453 The **Hundred Years' War***.

The **Black Death** killed one third of the population of **Europe**.

1347-1351 The **Black Death**, a bubonic plague carried by the fleas of black rats, reaches **Genoa** from the **East**, via the **Crimea**.

c.1350 **Firearms** are first in use in **Europe**.

1371 House of **Stewart** rules in **Scotland**.

1373 Treaty of **Anglo-Portuguese** friendship.

1378-1415 The **Great Schism***.

c.1380 **John Wycliffe**, an **English** scholar, begins preaching that the *Bible* alone is the authority for **Christian** belief. His teachings are condemned and his followers, the **Lollards**, are persecuted.

1381 The **Peasants' Revolt***.

1381 **Genoa** is defeated by **Venice** after a hundred years of war.

The **Doge** (ruler) of **Venice**.

1387 **Geoffrey Chaucer** (1340-1400), first great poet to write in **English**, writes the *Canterbury Tales*.

1400-1415 Rebellion of **Owen Glendower** in **Wales**.

1407 **Casi di San Georgio**, the first **European** public bank is established in **Genoa, Italy**.

1410-1411 Civil war in **France**. A struggle for power between the **Armagnacs** and the **Burgundians***, for influence over the monarchy.

1410-1435 **Burgundy*** sides with **England** in the **Hundred Years War***.

1415 **Henry V** wins the **Battle of Agincourt***.

1431 **Joan of Arc*** is burnt.

1434 **Cosimo de Medici** takes control of **Florence**. The start of the age of the **Medici** family.

The Dome of **Florence Cathedral**, built by **Brunelleschi** c.1420-1436.

1442 **Alfonso of Aragon** conquers **Naples**.

1447 The **French** house of **Orléans** claims **Milan** by inheritance.

1450 **Francesco Sforza** becomes **Duke of Milan**.

Lorenzo de Medici on horseback.

1455-1480 The **Wars of the Roses***.

1462-1492 Rule of **Lorenzo de Medici (the Magnificent)** in **Florence**. Artists at his court include **Botticelli** and **Michelangelo**.

Northern and Eastern Europe

1261 **Greenland** is conquered by **Norway**.

1262-1264 **Iceland** comes under **Norwegian** rule.

1263 **Norway** is defeated by **Scotland** and cedes* the **Hebrides** to **Scotland**.

1266 **Norway** cedes* the **Isle of Man** to **Scotland**.

1273-1291 **Rudolf of Habsburg** becomes **Holy Roman Emperor***, despite the efforts of his enemy, **Ottokar II**.

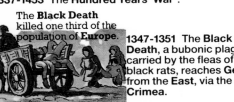

Stained glass showing **Rudolf of Habsburg**.

1278 **Ottokar II** of **Bohemia** is killed at **Marchfeld**. **Bohemia** and **Moravia** become **estates** of the **Holy Roman Empire***.

1282 **Rudolf of Habsburg** makes his son, **Albert, Duke of Austria**.

1291 Three **Swiss cantons** sign the **Pact of Rutli**, establishing Swiss independence.

1293 **Sweden** conquers **Karelia**.

1298-1308 Rule of **Albert I Habsburg** as **Holy Roman Emperor***.

1301 The end of the **Arpad dynasty*** in **Hungary**.

1308-1313 **Henry VII of Luxembourg** becomes **Holy Roman Emperor***. In **1310**, **John of Luxembourg** inherits **Bohemia**.

1320 The unity of **Poland** is restored by the coronation of **Vladislav Lokiekek** as king.

1328-1340 The expansion of **Moscow*** under **Duke Ivan I**.

1333-1370 **Casimir III the Great** strengthens the kingdom of **Poland**.

1343 **Teutonic Knights*** acquire **Estonia** from **Denmark**.

Map showing territory held by the **Teutonic Knights**.

1346 The **Black Death** (see first column) reaches the **Crimea** from the **East**.

1354 The **Ottoman Turks*** acquire **Gallipoli**, their first **European** possession.

1355 **Charles IV of Luxembourg** (1316-1378) becomes **Holy Roman Emperor***. The kingdom of **Bohemia** and the city of **Prague** flourish during his reign.

1361 **Denmark** is defeated by the **Hanseatic League***.

1370 The **Lithuanians** are defeated at **Rudan** by the **Teutonic Knights***.

1370 **Peace of Stralsund** between **Denmark** and the **Hanseatic League***. The League's power is at its height.

1386 Union of **Poland** and **Lithuania**.

1389 **Battle of Kosovo**: the **Ottoman Turks*** gain control of the **Balkans**.

1397 The **Union of Kalmar** brings **Scandinavia** under one ruler: **Margaret, Queen of Denmark** and **Norway** (1387-1412).

Africa and the Middle East

1262-1263 **Baibars*** takes the **Ayyubid*** lands in **Syria**.

1265-1271 **Baibars*** takes most of **Outremer***.

1268 **Baibars*** captures **Antioch**.

1270 **Seventh Crusade***, led by **Louis IX** of **France**, who dies of sickness in **Tunis**.

1281-1326 Reign of **Osman I***, emir (chief) of a small **Turkish** princedom. In **1290** he declares himself **Sultan of the Turks** and becomes founder of the **Ottoman Empire***.

1291 **Mamelukes*** take **Acre**, the last stronghold of **Outremer***.

c.1300 Emergence of the empire of **Benin** in **Nigeria**.

Works of art in ivory from **Benin**.

1324 **Mansa Musa**, King of **Mali**,* goes on pilgrimage to **Mecca***. He visits **Cairo** and impresses everyone with his wealth.

Mansa Musa, as shown on a **14th century** map.

1350 Founding of the kingdom of **Songhai**.

1352 **Ibn Battuta**, a **Berber** scholar, visits **Mali*** and writes an account of all he sees. He reaches **Timbuctoo** in **1353**. From the writings of other **Arab** scholars, and archaeology, other states are known: **Kanem-Bornu**, **Congo** and **Benin**.

1375 **Mamelukes*** take **Sis**: the end of **Armenian** independence.

1397 **Portuguese*** explorers reach the **Canary Islands**.

c.1400s **Chinese** traders join the **Arab** and **Indian** merchants trading in **East Africa**.

East African port.

1401 **Tamerlane*** conquers **Damascus** and **Baghdad**.

1415 **Portuguese** conquer **Ceuta**.

Asia

1281 Second attempted invasion of **Japan** by **Mongols***. The Mongol fleet is scatttered by **kamikaze** (divine winds).

The **Mongol** fleet being destroyed by a typhoon.

1293 The first **Christian** missionaries reach **China**.

c.1300 **Persia** is converted to **Islam***.

1307 The first Archbishop is established in **Peking**.

c.1325 The development of **No plays** in **Japan**: classic Japanese drama, using music and dancing.

1325-1351 The reign of **Mohammed Ibn Tughluk, Sultan of Delhi**. He expands his territories and briefly conquers **South India (Deccan)**.

India — PUNJAB, Delhi, Sultanate of Delhi, BENGAL, DECCAN, CEYLON, Vijayanagar Empire. **Tughluk's** tomb.

1333 **China** suffers drought, famine and floods, followed by plague. 5 million die.

1333 End of the **Kamakura shogunate*** in **Japan**. Emperor **Go-daigo** rules without a **shogun*** (1333-1336).

1336 The **Il-Khan Empire*** is dissolved and replaced by a local **Turcoman** dynasty.

c.1340 The **Hindu*** empire of **Vijayanagar** in **India** becomes a centre of resistance to **Islam***. It becomes dominant in southern India c.1370.

1349 The earliest **Chinese** settlement in **Singapore**.

c.1350 Cultural peak of the **Majapahit Empire** in **Java**.

Majahapit temple, **Java**.

The Americas

c.1436-1464 Rule of **Emperor Montezuma I** of the **Aztecs***.

1438 **Peru**: Late **Inca*** or Empire Period begins with the reign of **Pachacuti Inca** (1438-1471), who starts conquering an empire.

c.1440 An aqueduct is built from **Chapultec** spring to give **Tenochtitlán*** a new water supply.

1460 **Mayapan*** is destroyed by a peasant uprising. The **Mayan*** civilization comes to an end.

c.1470 **Incas*** conquer the **Chimu kingdom***.

Chimu gold carving.

1471-1493 Reign of **Emperor Topa Inca**, who extends the empire south.

1493-1525 Reign of **Huayna Capac**, the greatest **Inca*** conqueror. He founds a second capital at **Quito**.

Inca nobles and warriors.

1492 **Christopher Columbus*** (1451-1506) reaches the **West Indies**.

1494 Treaty of Tordesillas: **Pope Alexander VI** fixes a line to partition the **New World*** into **Spanish** and **Portuguese** empires.

1497 **John Cabot**, an **Italian** explorer employed by **Henry VII** of **England**, reaches **Newfoundland**.

1498 **Christopher Columbus*** reaches the **South American** mainland.

Columbus landing in the **West Indies**.

1499-1502 **Amerigo Vespucci** explores the **South American** coast. The continent is later named **America**, after him.

ATHABASCANS, Newfoundland, MISSISSIPPIANS, PUEBLO. **North America**

The Mongol Empire

The **Mongols** were **nomadic*** tribes of mixed origin, from the part of the **Steppes** now called **Mongolia**. In **1206** they were united by **Temujin (c.1162-1227)**, who overpowered the other Mongol tribes and became **Genghis Khan** (supreme ruler). He and his sons and grandsons conquered one of the largest empires in history, and threatened the civilizations of **Europe** and **Asia**. After subduing his neighbours,

Genghis Khan attacked the **Chin Empire*** in **northern China (1211-1215)**, and in **1221** invaded **India**. When he died in **1227**, his son, **Ogadei**, became **Great Khan** and the empire was divided between him and his three brothers. Between **1237-1241** they invaded **Russia***, **Hungary** and **Poland**. In **c.1242**, they established the **Khanate of the Golden Horde** in South Russia.

The Mongol Empire

Labels on map: • Moscow; KHANATE OF THE GOLDEN HORDE; • Kiev; • New Sarai; Old Sarai; Constantinople; CHAGATAI KHANATE; Karakorum; Peking; Samarkand; Baghdad; IL-KHAN EMPIRE; EASTERN KHANATE; Empire of Tamerlane; Empire of Genghis Khan; • Delhi

The Mongols invaded **Persia (1251-1265)** and set up the **Il-Khan Empire**, which survived until **1336**. They sacked **Baghdad (1258)**, bringing an end to the **Abbasid caliphate***. Their advance in the **Middle East** was halted in **1260**, by the victory of the **Mamelukes*** at the **Ain Jalut**.

Mongols attacking a **Muslim** city. The Mongols were cruel and merciless, but had well-organized and disciplined armies.

The unity of the empire came to an end in **1259** with the election of Genghis's grandson, **Kublai Khan** as Great Khan. His power was limited to the **Eastern Khanate**. Between **1268-1279** Kublai conquered the **Sung Empire*** in **southern China**, and set up the **Yuan dynasty (1280-1368)**. He was an efficient ruler, but after his death the empire was weakened by internal divisions.

The Court of **Kublai Khan** at **Peking**.

The only **Westerner** to reach **China** during this period was **Marco Polo**, a **Venetian**, who wrote a book about his experiences.

There was a resurgence of power under **Timur the Lame**, or **Tamerlane (1336-1405)**, who conquered a second Mongol empire from **Samarkand**. Tamerlane's empire broke up after his death and Mongols became increasingly under attack. The territories of the Golden Horde were gradually absorbed by Russia and in **1696**, Mongolia itself came under Chinese rule.

The burial place of **Tamerlane** in **Samarkand**.

Abbasid caliphate, 24; Chin, 27; Mamelukes, 37; nomadic, 114; Russia, 43; Sung, 27.

Russia and the emergence of Moscow

Russia was conquered by **Mongols***, also known as **Tartars**, between **1237-1240**. In **1240**, they took **Kiev***, destroying the cultural centre of **medieval*** Russia. In **c.1242**, they withdrew to South Russia, and established the **Khanate of the Golden Horde**, while exacting **tribute*** from the rest of the country. Contacts between Russia and **Western Europe** came to an end.

The **Battle of the River Neva**.

Meanwhile in the north, **Alexander of Novgorod** fought off attacks by the **Swedes** at **Battle of the Riva Neva (1240)** and the **Catholic Teutonic Knights*** at **Lake Peipus (1242)**. Alexander, nicknamed **"Nevsky"**, became regarded as a hero of national resistance and a saint of the **Orthodox Church**, although he too was forced to pay tribute to the Mongols.

Alexander Nevsky's youngest son, **Daniel**, became **Prince of Moscow (1280-1303)**. Under his dynasty, **Moscow** slowly expanded in size and importance to become the state of **Muscovy**. In **1328** Moscow became the residence of the **Metropolitan**, the head of the Orthodox Church in Russia. Mongol power began to decline. In **1380** the Mongols were defeated by Muscovites at **Kulikova**, and were weakened further by the attacks of **Tamerlane*** in **1390-1395**.

Moscow at the end of the 13th century.

Expansion to 1462.

Expansion under **Ivan III** (1462-1505).

The expansion of Moscow

Ivan III (the Great) (1462-1505) married **Zoë Palaeologa**, a **Byzantine*** princess and adopted many Byzantine customs. In **1478** he took **Novgorod** and in **1480** declared himself **Tsar** (sole ruler) of all the **Rus***. He refused to pay tribute to the Mongols and so ended their overlordship of Moscow.

The rise of the Ottomans

The **Ottomans** were **Turkish Muslims***, driven west from **Turkestan** by the **Mongols***. By **c.1250**, they had settled in **Asia Minor**, taking service with the **Seljuks***. In **1288**, their **emir** (chief), **Osman I (1281-1326)**, proclaimed himself **Sultan of all the Turks** and became founder of the **Ottoman Empire**.

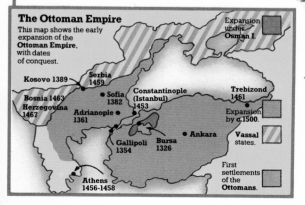

Istanbul, during the reign of **Mehmed II the Conqueror (1432-1481)**.

The Ottoman Empire
This map shows the early expansion of the **Ottoman Empire**, with dates of conquest.

Kosovo 1389
Serbia 1459
Bosnia 1463
Herzegovina 1467
Sofia 1382
Constantinople (Istanbul) 1453
Adrianople 1361
Trebizond 1461
Ankara
Gallipoli 1354
Bursa 1326
Athens 1456-1458

Expansion under **Osman I**.

Expansion by c.1500.

Vassal states.

First settlements of the Ottomans.

Osman built up a huge well-organized army, which included the **janissaries**, **Christian** children taken as slaves and raised as Muslims. In **1453** the Ottomans conquered **Constantinople**, and overthrew the **Byzantine Empire***. The city was renamed **Istanbul** and became the Ottoman capital. By the end of the **15th century**, the Ottomans had destroyed many Christian states in **Eastern Europe** and the **Balkans** and established themselves as the leaders of **Islamic*** world.

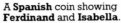
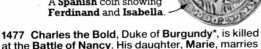

Southern and Western Europe

1469 **Ferdinand** of **Aragon** marries **Isabella** of **Castile**.

A **Spanish** coin showing **Ferdinand** and **Isabella**.

1477 **Charles the Bold**, Duke of **Burgundy***, is killed at the **Battle of Nancy**. His daughter, **Marie**, marries **Maximilian Habsburg** of **Austria**.

1477-1493 War between **France** and **Austria** over the **Burgundian*** inheritance. At the **Peace of Senlis**, Austria keeps Burgundy and the **Netherlands**.

1479 **Ferdinand of Aragon** succeeds his father as King of **Aragon** and unites the kingdom with **Castile**.

1483 **Charles VIII** of **France** claims **Naples** as part of the **Anjou*** inheritance.

1485 The **Battle of Bosworth***; **Henry Tudor** becomes first king of the **Tudor dynasty** in **England**.

1487 Rebellion in **England** by **Lambert Simnel**, claiming to be the **Duke of York***.

1492 The conquest of the **Arab** kingdom of **Granada** by **Ferdinand** and **Isabella** completes the **Reconquista*** in **Spain**. **Jews** are expelled and many go to **eastern Europe**.

Despite the **Christian** advance, **Granada** had been the centre of a brilliant culture in the **14th century**.

The **Alhambra**, a magnificent **Moorish (Spanish Arab)** palace in **Granada**.

1494-1495 **France** invades **Italy** and is driven back after early successes. The start of a struggle for power between **France** and the **Habsburgs**.

1497 Rebellion in **England** by **Perkin Warbeck**, claiming to be the **Duke of York***.

1498 **Louis XII** of **France** invades **Italy** and takes **Milan**.

Northern and Eastern Europe

1410 **Poles** defeat the **Teutonic Knights*** at **Tannenberg**.

1415 **John Huss**, a **Bohemian** religious reformer influenced by **Wycliffe***, is burnt as a **heretic***. His death leads to **Hussite wars (1419-1436)** between **Bohemia** and **Moravia** and the **Holy Roman Empire***.

The arrest of **John Huss**.

1415 **Frederick VI** of **Hohenzollern** is made **Elector*** of **Brandenburg**.

1422 First siege of **Constantinople** by the **Ottoman Turks***.

1437 **Albert II** of **Habsburg** becomes King of **Hungary** and **Bohemia** and is elected King of **Germany** in 1438-1439.

1439 **Russian** and **Greek Orthodox Churches** are formally separated.

1445 **Johann Gutenberg** (1397-1468), a **German**, publishes the *Gutenberg Bible*, the first printed book in **Europe**.

A page from the *Gutenberg Bible*.

1453 **Ottomans*** capture **Constantinople**. The end of the **Byzantine Empire***.

1456-1467 **Ottomans*** take over **Balkan** states.

1462-1505 Rule of **Ivan III*** of **Moscow**.

1468-1469 **Denmark** pawns **Orkney** and **Shetland** to **Scotland**.

1471-1480 **Turkish** raids in **Styria**.

1480 **Ivan III*** liberates **Moscow** from **Mongol*** rule and declares himself first **Tsar*** of **Russia**.

1488 **Swabian League** is founded in **South Germany**, to preserve peace.

Moscow, rebuilt by **Ivan III**.

1499 **Peace of Basle** establishes **Swiss** independence.

Italian city states in the 15th century

Milan, Mantua, Genoa, Ferrara, Venice, Bologna, Pisa, Florence, Siena, Papal states, Rome, Naples

Britain

SCOTLAND, IRELAND, ENGLAND, Lancaster, York, Wakefield, WALES, Tewkesbury, Northampton, Gloucester, St Albans, Barnet, London, Canterbury

The Holy Roman Empire

Bornhöved, Area belonging to the Hohenstaufen Empire, BOHEMIA, MORAVIA, AUSTRIA, STYRIA, Venice, MILAN, Florence, Bologna, Rome, Papal states, NAPLES

The Balkans

Byzantine Empire in the 15th century.

BOSNIA, HERZEGOVINA, Kosovo, SERBIA, Salonica, Adrianople, Gallipoli, Athens

Africa and the Middle East

1416 **Venetians** defeat the **Turks*** off **Gallipoli**.

1419 **Portuguese** reach **Madeira**.

1431 **Portuguese** reach the **Azores**.

A cross left by **Portuguese** navigators.

1445 **Portuguese** reach the mouth of the **River Congo**.

1451-1481 Reign of **Sultan Mehmed II** (the **Conqueror**) of the **Ottoman Empire***.

1463-1479 **Ottoman Turks*** are at war with **Venice**.

1464-1492 Reign of **Sunni Ali**, ruler of **Songhai***, who expands his empire at the expense of **Mali***.

Timbuctoo

1471 **Portuguese** conquer **Tangier**.

1482 **Portuguese** settle on the **Gold Coast**.

1487 **Bartholomeu Diaz*** rounds the **Cape of Good Hope**.

Portuguese ships, called **caravels**.

1490 **King Nzinga Nkuwu** of the **Kongo** becomes a **Christian**.

1493 The **Songhai Empire*** reaches its peak.

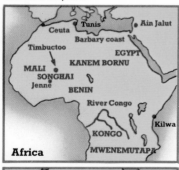

Africa

The Middle East

Asia

1368 The **Yuan dynasty*** in **China** is overthrown and replaced by the native Chinese **Ming dynasty***.

1369 **Thais** invade **Cambodia**.

1369-1405 **Tamerlane*** rules the **Mongols***. He conquers **Herat** (1381), destroys **Delhi** (1398-1399) and annexes* the **Punjab**.

Chinese trading ships.

1405-1433 **China** opens new trade routes.

1421 **Peking** becomes the capital of **China**.

1428 **Chinese** are expelled from **Vietnam**.

1447 The empire of **Tamerlane*** breaks up. **Indian**, **Persian** and **Afghan** provinces win independence.

1451-1489 Rule of **Bahlol Lodi**, the first **Pathan** king of **Delhi**.

1467-1477 First **Onin War*** in **Japan**.

1471 **Vietnamese** expand south.

1477-1568 **Provincial wars*** in **Japan**.

1494 **Babar**, a descendent of **Genghis Khan*** and **Tamerlane***, becomes **Prince of Ferghana**, central **Asia**.

Babar, Prince of Ferghana.

1498 **Vasco da Gama***, a **Portuguese** navigator, makes the first **European** sea voyage to **India** via **Africa** and back.

The Far East

The Americas

Central America

The Inca empire in Peru

Spain and Portugal: the Reconquista

The *Reconquista*, or reconquest of **Arab*** territory by the **Christian** kingdoms of **Spain** and **Portugal**, began in the early **11th century**, though their progress was hampered by civil wars. The marriage of **Ferdinand of Aragon** and **Isabella of Castile** led to the unification of the two main kingdoms in **1479**. In **1492**, they captured **Granada**, the last Arab stronghold, and the kingdoms of Spain and Portugal were formed.

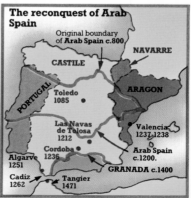

The reconquest of Arab Spain

Towns and trade

In the **12th** and **13th centuries**, most of **Europe** generally enjoyed growing prosperity. The population increased and new land was brought into cultivation. Some landlords began allowing peasants to pay rent instead of labour dues, which meant they were no longer tied to the manor. Towns grew and trade flourished.

Italian cities, such as **Venice** (above), grew rich partly as a result of the **Crusades**.

A **European** town in the **Middle Ages**.

Guilds, associations of merchants and craftsmen, began forming in the **11th century**. By the **12th century**, each trade had its own guild. The guilds were in charge of regulating prices and wages, caring for members in trouble, and establishing standards of work and trading practice. By the **13th century**, they were beginning to divide into **aristocratic guilds** (richer merchants), who came to dominate city governments, and **plebeian guilds** (ordinary craftsmen), who declined in influence.

The **guilds** performed in **Mystery Plays**, plays based on the life of **Christ**.

Prosperous towns grew up in main trading areas. The **Baltic** and **North Sea** trade became dominated by the **Hanseatic League** – a group of **German** and Baltic cities, including **Hamburg**, **Lübeck** and **Cologne**, which set up trading associations, or *hanse*, for mutual protection.

The first *hanse* was established at **Visby (Gotland)** in **1160**, but activity soon shifted to **Lübeck** (above). The **Hanseatic League** was formed between **1259-1358**.

The **northern Italian** cities controlled the luxury trade in silks and spices from the **East**. In **1381**, **Venice** defeated her rival, **Genoa**, and became the foremost naval and trading power.

Usury (lending money and charging interest) was against the law of the **Catholic Church**, and so became a service often provided by **Jews***. However, by the **13th century**, demand for money and credit had grown. A banking system was introduced by the **Lombards**, North Italian merchants. Other bankers followed, the most famous being the **Medici*** family of **Florence**. They began as cloth traders, rose to public office in the **14th century** and in **1434** became rulers of the city.

Gold coins from **Florence**.

In the early **14th century**, bad weather brought poor harvests and famine (**1315-1317**). This, with the **Black Death***, led to a fall in population. Wages rose at first, but then fell again, causing hardship. Struggles took place between poorer craftsmen and the richer guilds and there were a number of uprisings against taxes and conditions.

14th century uprisings

1302 Craftsmen in **Ghent** and **Bruges** seize power from the wealthy, **pro-French** merchant guilds. They defeat the **French** at **Courtrai**, but are beaten at **Cassel**.

1355 Parisians, led by a cloth merchant, **Etienne Marcel**, rise against taxes.

1358 The Jacquerie: uprisings of **French** peasants against harsh conditions. They try to ally with the **Parisian** rebels, but are crushed by nobles and merchants.

1378 An uprising of the **Ciompi** (clothworkers) in **Florence** is put down by the guilds.

1381 Peasants Revolt: an uprising of **English** peasants, led by Jack Straw and Wat Tyler. They disperse when the king agrees to some of their demands.

1382 Uprising in **Paris** against taxes.

The Renaissance

The **Renaissance** means literally "rebirth". It is the name given to the renewed interest in the art and learning of **Greece*** and **Rome***, that stimulated **Europe** into changes which mark the end of **medieval*** and the beginning of modern times. A gradual process, it began in **Italy** and reached its height in the **15th** and **16th centuries**.

Illustration from a **Renaissance** painting showing a contemporary battle scene.

The city of **Florence** led the **Renaissance** in the arts.

It was not just a revival of the past, for it was also a time of **exploration*** and new ideas. But classical examples inspired the new thought, particularly the stress on human possibilities, rather than human shortcomings which had preoccupied medieval man. This new attitude became known as **humanism**. Learning was no longer solely in the hands of the Church. New schools and universities were founded and scientific and medical experiments were carried out.

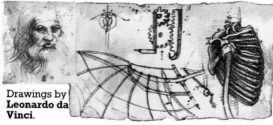

Drawings by **Leonardo da Vinci**.

Painters and sculptors aimed at showing the human body, and its surroundings, in a more natural, realistic style. Classical statues were studied, as well as human anatomy. Perspective was used to make paintings look less flat. Subjects now included portraits, contemporary and classical events, as well as religious themes. Certain artists achieved greater prestige and independence than was enjoyed by the medieval craftsman.

Many Renaissance rulers believed in the ideal of the "universal man", with wide-ranging talents and interests. Thus **Lorenzo de Medici**, ruler of **Florence**, was a soldier, politician, banker and poet. These men were the patrons of great artists and lived in palaces built by great architects, such as **Alberti (1404-1472)**.

Renaissance architects used classical forms, such as round arches, central domes and barrel vaults.

The **Palazzo Pitti, Florence**.

Italy developed the **capitalist*** skills which financed the Renaissance, and the political links between city states which developed into **diplomacy**. Scientific and technical discoveries, such as the invention of **printing***, helped the new ideas to spread. Eventually all Europe was influenced by the new spirit.

Italian Renaissance people

Dante (1265-1321), writer.

Giotto (1266-1337), painter.

Petrarch (1304-1374), poet and scholar.

Boccaccio (1313-1375), writer.

Brunelleschi (1377-1446), architect.

Donatello (1386-1466), sculptor.

Botticelli (1444-1510), painter.

Leonardo da Vinci (1452-1519), painter, inventor, musician, architect and sculptor.

Machiavelli (1469-1527), author of *The Prince*.

Michelangelo (1475-1564), painter and sculptor.

Raphael (1483-1520), painter and architect.

Cellini (1500-1571), sculptor, goldsmith and autobiographer.

capitalist, 113; exploration, 48-49; Greece, 12-13; medieval, 114; printing, 40; Rome, 18.

The Age of Discovery

In the **15th** and **16th centuries**, **European** seafarers began to explore the world. Up until then, Europeans had had only a vague knowledge of the rest of the world. The areas they knew were limited to the north and west coasts of **Africa** and the overland routes to the **East**.

In the early **15th century**, **Prince Henry (the Navigator)** of **Portugal (1394-1460)** set up a school of navigation. Portuguese sailors began searching for a sea route to **India**, in order to gain direct access to the valuable spice trade of the East. In 1488, **Bartholomeu Diaz** reached the **Cape of Good Hope**, and in 1497, **Vasco da Gama** sailed into the **Indian Ocean**, reaching **India** in 1498.

Portuguese ships, called **caravels**, off the coast of **Africa**.

In 1492, **Christopher Columbus**, a **Genoese** navigator employed by **Spain**, tried sailing west instead, and accidentally discovered the **West Indies**. Further Spanish expeditions followed, reaching the **South American** mainland. The new discoveries became known as the **New World**, though at first people believed it was **Asia**, not realizing that a new continent had been discovered.

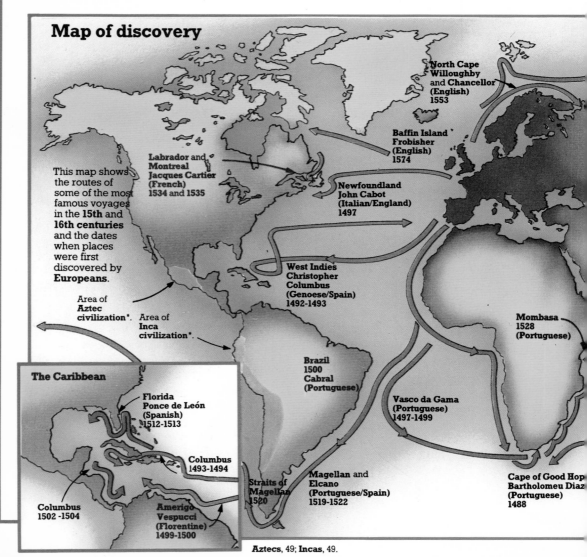

Map of discovery

This map shows the routes of some of the most famous voyages in the **15th** and **16th centuries** and the dates when places were first discovered by **Europeans**.

North Cape
Willoughby and **Chancellor** (**English**) 1553

Baffin Island Frobisher (**English**) 1574

Labrador and Montreal Jacques Cartier (**French**) 1534 and 1535

Newfoundland John Cabot (**Italian/England**) 1497

West Indies Christopher Columbus (**Genoese/Spain**) 1492-1493

Mombasa 1528 (**Portuguese**)

Area of **Aztec** civilization*.

Area of **Inca** civilization*.

Brazil 1500 Cabral (**Portuguese**)

Vasco da Gama (**Portuguese**) 1497-1499

The Caribbean

Florida Ponce de León (**Spanish**) 1512-1513

Columbus 1493-1494

Columbus 1502-1504

Amerigo Vespucci (**Florentine**) 1499-1500

Straits of Magellan 1520

Magellan and Elcano (**Portuguese/Spain**) 1519-1522

Cape of Good Hope Bartholomeu Diaz (**Portuguese**) 1488

16th century navigational instruments.

By the **Treaty of Tordesillas (1494)**, Spain and Portugal agreed to divide up the world between them. The **French** and **English** challenged this view and **privateers***, such as **Hawkins*** and **Drake***, attacked Spanish shipping in the New World. Others sought alternative routes to the East, by sailing north west, which led to the discovery of **North America**.

Europeans confronting Eskimos in North America.

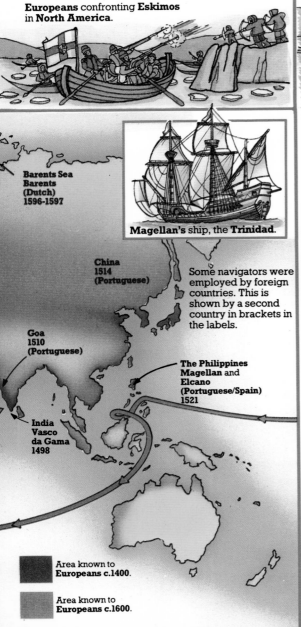

Barents Sea
Barents
(Dutch)
1596-1597

Magellan's ship, the **Trinidad**.

China
1514
(Portuguese)

Some navigators were employed by foreign countries. This is shown by a second country in brackets in the labels.

Goa
1510
(Portuguese)

The Philippines
Magellan and
Elcano
(Portuguese/Spain)
1521

India
Vasco
da Gama
1498

Area known to Europeans c.1400.

Area known to Europeans c.1600.

The conquest of Mexico and Peru

The early explorers of the **New World*** had returned to **Europe** with legends of great wealth to be found. They were followed by **Spanish** *conquistadors* (conquerors), in search of land and gold. The most famous of these were **Hernándo Cortés**, conqueror of **Mexico (1519-1521)**, and **Francisco Pizarro**, conqueror of **Peru (1532-1534)**.

The **Aztec** city of **Tenochtitlan**, built in the centre of the **Lake of Mexico**.

Aqueducts

Temples

Cortés and Pizarro encountered two great warrior civilizations – the **Aztecs** of Mexico and the **Incas** of Peru. Both had large, well-organized empires, beautiful cities, strict laws and complex religious beliefs.

The **Aztecs** worshipped many different gods and human sacrifice was widely practised.

The god, **Quetzacoatl**, the plumed serpent.

The god, **Huitzilopochtli**, the humming bird of the south.

The empires were soon conquered and destroyed. The Spaniards had the advantage of horses and cannons. Many of the natives (called **Indians**, because the Spaniards thought it was the **East Indies**) caught European diseases and died. Silver was discovered in Peru **(1545)** and in Mexico **(1548)** and shipped back to Europe, boosting the wealth and prestige of Spain. Indians were forced to work in the silver mines, and on the estates of the conquerors, but they were physically unsuited to the work and many died.

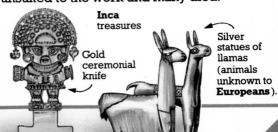

Inca treasures

Gold ceremonial knife

Silver statues of llamas (animals unknown to **Europeans**).

Drake, 55; **Hawkins**, 55; **New World**, 48; **privateers**, 114.

Western and Southern Europe

1501 **Louis XII** of **France** conquers **Naples**.

1509-1547 Reign of **Henry VIII*** of **England**.

1510 **Ferdinand of Aragon** takes the **Spanish Navarre**.

1510 The **French** invade **Milan**, but are defeated and expelled from **Italy**.

1513 **Battle of Flodden** between **England** and **Scotland**. **James IV of Scotland** is killed.

1513 **Machiavelli (1469-1527)**, a **Florentine** statesman, writes *The Prince,* advocating ruthlessness and cunning in order to achieve political success.

1515-1547 Reign of **Francis I of France**.

The **Chateau of Chambord**, built by **Francis I** of **France**.

1515 **Francis I** defeats the **Swiss** at the **Battle of Marignano** and conquers **Milan**.

1516 **Charles of Habsburg** becomes **Charles V*** of **Spain**.

1516 **Coffee** is first imported into **Europe**.

1520 The **Field of the Cloth of Gold**: a meeting between **Henry VIII*** and **Francis I**, to conclude peace between **England** and **France**.

The **Field of the Cloth of Gold, Flanders**.

1520 **Chocolate** is first imported into **Europe**.

1521 **Silk** manufacture begins in **France**.

1521 **France** and **Spain** go to war over **Italy**.

1525 **Battle of Pavia**: **Spain** defeats **France** and **Francis I** is taken prisoner.

1527 **Charles V's*** troops **sack*** **Rome**.

1527-1530 **Medici*** are expelled from **Florence**.

1529 **Peace of Cambrai**: the **French** renounce their claims to **Italy** and **Charles V*** renounces his claim to lost **Burgundian*** lands.

1530 The **Knights Hospitallers*** establish a base in **Malta**.

1531 The **Inquisition*** is established in **Portugal**.

1532 **Calvin*** begins work in **Paris**.

1536 The **English** and **Welsh** systems of government are unified.

1541 The **Reformation*** begins in **Scotland**.

Central and Northern Europe

1517 **Luther*** issues his **95 theses**.

1519 **Zwingli*** begins preaching reform in **Zurich**.

German soldiers, called *Landsknechts,* **c.1520**.

1519 **Charles V*** is elected **Holy Roman Emperor***.

1521 The **Diet of Worms***.

1521 **Charles V*** gives the **Austrian Habsburg** lands to his brother, **Ferdinand**.

1521 **Belgrade** falls to the **Ottoman Turks***.

1522-1523 The **imperial knights*** rebel against their overlord, the **Archbishop of Trier**, in protest against their declining economic and social position.

1523 **Sweden** gains independence from **Denmark** and **Gustavus Vasa** is proclaimed king.

1523 The **imperial knights*** are defeated by an alliance of princes at **Landstuhl**.

1524-1525 An uprising of peasants against their landlords in **south** and **central Germany**.

1525 **Albert of Hohenzollern, Grand Master of the Teutonic Knights*** and ruler of **Prussia**, becomes a **Lutheran*** and **secularizes*** the state.

1526 **Battle of Mohacs**: **Lewis II of Hungary** is defeated and killed by the **Turks***. **Charles V's*** brother, **Ferdinand**, and **John Zapolya** are both elected kings of **Hungary**.

1529 The **Turks*** besiege **Vienna**.

1529 **Second Diet of Speyer** (an assembly of the **Holy Roman Empire***). Protests by **Lutheran*** princes lead to the use of the name **Protestant**.

Speyer cathedral.

1529 War between **Catholics** and **Protestants** in **Switzerland**.

1530 **Charles V*** is crowned **Holy Roman Emperor*** by the **Pope**: the last imperial coronation by a pope.

1531 The **League of Schmalkalden** is formed by **Protestant German** princes against **Charles V***.

1531 **Copernicus (1473-1543)**, a **Polish** astronomer, circulates his revolutionary theory demonstrating that planets move around the Sun, not around the Earth (which was the Church's teaching).

An engraving from a **17th century** atlas, showing **Copernicus's** idea of the **Solar system**.

The Middle East and Africa

1500 Mohammed Turre (1494-1528) of **Songhai*** captures **Zaherma, Bagana** and **Dandi.**

1502 **Safavid dynasty** is established in **Persia** by **Ismail I.**

1504 **Nubians** destroy the **Christian** kingdom of **Meroë*.**

1504-1546 Reign of the **Christian*** king, **Afonso** of the **Kongo.**

1505 The **Songhai*** invade the **Mali Empire*.**

1505-1507 **Portuguese** establish forts on the **East African coast.**

1508 **Portuguese** set up a factory in **Mozambique.**

1509 **Spanish** capture **Oran, North Africa.**

1513 **Portuguese** go up the **Zambesi River** and establish posts at **Sena** and **Tete.**

1514 **Sultan Selim** of **Turkey** begins fighting the **Persians** and settles **Kurds** in **Armenia.** (Sporadic warfare continues for **200 years.**)

1516-1518 **Selim** conquers **North Iraq, Syria** and **Palestine.**

1517 **Turks** conquer **Egypt:** the end of **Mameluke*** rule.

1518 The first full cargo of **slaves*** is shipped from **Guinea** to the **New World*.**

1520-1566 Reign of **Suleiman the Magnificent:** the golden age of the **Ottoman Empire*.**

Suleiman's mosque, Damascus.

1521 **Turks*** take **Cyrenaica** and **Belgrade.**

1522 **Turks*** take **Rhodes.**

1535 **Charles V*** takes **Tunis.**

1538 **Turks*** capture **Aden.**

1543 **Ethiopian Christians,** helped by **Portugal,** repel the **Muslim*** advance into **Ethiopia.**

1545 **Turks*** occupy **Massawa** and complete their occupation of **Ethiopia.**

The Far East

1504 **Babar*** becomes **Master of Kabul, Afghanistan.**

1510 **Portuguese** annex* **Goa.**

1511 **Portugese** take **Malacca.**

1514 **Portuguese** reach **China.** By **1516,** they start trading from a base in **Canton.**

1521 **Portuguese** reach the **Molucca Islands.**

16th century Chinese junk (ship).

1521 **Magellan** is killed in the **Philippines,** during the first circumnavigation (see also next column) of the **World** (1519-1522).

1523 **Europeans** are expelled from **China.**

Chinese porcelain from the **Ming** period.

1525 **Babar*** conquers the **Punjab.**

1526 **Babar*** wins a victory over the **Sultan of Delhi** at **Panipat.** The **Moguls*** are established in **India.**

1527 **Babar*** defeats **Hindus*** at **Kanwaha.**

1529 **Babar*** wins a victory at **Gogra.**

1533 **North Vietnam** splits into **Tongking** and **Annam.**

1539 **Burmese** kingdom of **Toungoo** conquers the **Mons** kingdom of **Pegu.**

1540 **Babar's*** son, **Humayun,** is driven out of **India** by the **Afghan, Sher Shah.**

Goa Cathedral, begun in 1562.

1542 **Francis Xavier,** a **Portuguese Jesuit*** missionary, arrives in **Goa.**

1545 **Humayun** captures **Kandahar.**

1547 **Humayun** captures **Kabul.**

1549-1551 **Francis Xavier** and his missionaries spread **Christianity*** in **Japan.** The **Jesuits*** participate in trade.

The Americas

1500 **Aztec Empire*** reaches its greatest extent under **Ahuizotl.**

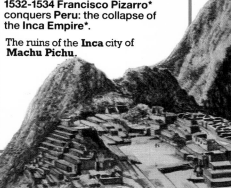

Aztec shield, adorned with feathers.

1501 **Anglo-Portuguese** expedition to **Newfoundland.**

1504 **Amerigo Vespucci,** a **Florentine** navigator, publishes an account of his voyages to **South America.** The new discoveries are called the **New World*.**

1507 The **New World*** is named **America,** after **Amerigo Vespucci.**

1510 The first **African slaves*** are brought to **America.**

1513 **Ponce de León,** a **Spaniard,** discovers **Florida.**

1513 **Nuñez de Balboa** (Spanish) crosses the **Isthmus of Panama** and discovers the **Pacific Ocean.**

Aztec feather crown, presented to **Cortés** by **Montezuma II,** the last **Aztec** ruler.

1519-1521 **Hernando Cortés*** conquers **Mexico:** the end of the **Aztec Empire*.**

1520 **Ferdinand Magellan,** a **Portuguese** navigator, finds the **Magellan Straits.**

1521-1549 The **Spanish** colonize **Venezuela.**

1526 **John Cabot*** sails to the **River Plate.**

1528 **Germans** attempt to colonize **Venezuela.**

1530 **Portuguese** begin to colonize **Brazil.**

1531 **Rio de Janeiro** is discovered.

1532-1534 **Francisco Pizarro*** conquers **Peru:** the collapse of the **Inca Empire*.**

The ruins of the **Inca** city of **Machu Pichu.**

The empire of Charles V

In the first half of the **16th century**, **Europe** was dominated by the vast empire of **Charles V (1500-1558)**, a member of the **Austrian Habsburg** family. As **King of Spain** and **Holy Roman Emperor***, he became the most powerful monarch in Europe. He defeated his great rivals, the **French Valois** kings, in **Italy** and stopped the advance of the **Ottoman Turks*** in Europe. Under him, Spain acquired wealth and prestige, as a result of the discovery of the **New World***.

Charles V's family tree

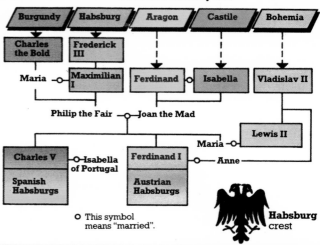

○ This symbol means "married".

Habsburg crest

Map of Charles V's empire 1519-1556

In **1506**, Charles inherited the **Burgundian lands** (**Franche-Comté**, **Luxembourg** and the **Netherlands**) from his father, **Philip of Burgundy**.

In **1516**, on the death of his grandfather, **Ferdinand of Spain***, Charles became King of **Aragon**, **Sicily** and **Naples**. He also became **regent*** of **Castile** on behalf of his mother, **Joan**, who was mad.

Lands claimed by Ferdinand.

London • NETHERLANDS

• Paris LUXEMBOURG

Rhineland • Vienna AUSTRIA

TYROL STYRIA

FRANCHE-COMTÉ

CASTILE

• Lisbon ARAGON

Rome • NAPLES

SICILY

In **1519**, on the death of his other grandfather (the **Emperor Maximilian**) he inherited **Austria**, **Tyrol**, **Styria**, **Carinthia**, **Carniola** and the **Habsburg** lands on the **Rhine**, together with the claim to the **Imperial throne**.

Charles himself acquired territory in the Netherlands: **Tournai (1521)**, **Friesland (1523)**, **Overijssel** and **Utrecht (1528)**, **Groningen (1536)** and **Guelders (1543)**.

In **1521**, **Charles** handed over the **Habsburg** lands in **Austria** to his brother, **Ferdinand**. In **1526**, Ferdinand claimed **Bohemia** and **Hungary**, through his wife, **Anne**, on the death of her brother, **King Lewis** of Hungary. Ferdinand was elected king by the Bohemian nobles and some of the Hungarians, but the others chose **John Zapolya, Duke of Transylvania**. (This part of Hungary became a **Turkish** province in **1541**.) Charles V abdicated in **1556** and his kingdom was divided. He left the imperial title to Ferdinand and the **Spanish** possessions to his son, **Philip II**.

The Holy Roman Empire

In the early **16th century** the **Holy Roman Emperor*** was still the **temporal*** head of **Christendom***. The Empire itself consisted of hundreds of separate units, with varying relationships to the Emperor.

Princely states, such as **Brandenburg** and **Saxony**, were ruled by princes who were **vassals*** of the Emperor. Seven of these princes were **Electors**, which meant that they elected the Emperor.

Independent imperial cities, such as **Augsburg**.

Austrian lands, ruled by the **Habsburg** family. (The Austrian Emperor was always the Holy Roman Emperor in this period.)

Bishoprics, such as **Trier**, ruled by bishops and archbishops (**ecclesiastical*** princes).

Lands ruled by **imperial knights** (**secular*** princes), directly subject to the Emperor.

Other lands, such as **Bohemia** and **Silesia**, which were technically outside the Empire, but subject to the Habsburgs.

Christendom, 113; ecclesiastical, 113; **Ferdinand of Spain**, 45; **Holy Roman Emperor**, 26; **New World**, 48; **Ottoman Turks**, 43; regent, 114; secular, 114; temporal 114; vassals, 31.

The provincial wars in Japan

From the end of the **14th century** onwards, **Japan** was divided by civil wars. The emperors, who were worshipped as gods, had become honorary rulers, delegating authority to the **shoguns** (hereditary military **dictators***). Real power lay in the hands of the **daimyos**, local barons who waged continual war against each other, and rebelled against the shoguns.

16th century Japanese castle town.

The daimyos lived in fortified castle towns and employed huge armies. They inspired loyalty from their **vassals***, the **samurai**, a caste of professional warriors. Military specialists, called **gunpaisha**, were employed to study the art of warfare and improve weapons.

Japanese armour consisted of leather, iron plates and cord. It was lighter and more flexible than **European** armour.

Samurai warriors

The **Onin War (1467-1477)** was followed by the **Provincial Wars (1477-1568)**. These ended in the victory of **Oda Nobunaga (1534-1582)**, who began to unify the country. By **1573** Nobunaga controlled half the country. He was killed in a rebellion in **1582** and was succeeded by **Toyotomi Hideyoshi (1535-1598)**, who continued his work for national unity.

The Ming dynasty

The **Ming dynasty** was established in **1368** and ruled **China** until **1644**. It was a period of order and stability. Agriculture improved and the population began to grow. Industry, trade and the arts prospered, with the manufacture of porcelain, jade, silk and lacquer.

Peking under the **Ming dynasty**.

The **15th century** was a time of expansion for the Ming. They invaded **Mongolia** and **Vietnam**, sent diplomatic missions across the world and made sea voyages as far as **Africa**.

Avenue leading to the tombs of the **Ming** emperors.

By the **16th century** the Ming were under attack from **Mongols*** and from **Japanese** pirates. They reverted to a defensive policy, deploying huge armies along the **Great Wall***. This, coinciding with a period of weak government and corruption, provoked a series of rebellions in the early **17th century** and the dynasty was overthrown.

South East Asia

KOREA
Great Wall
Peking
Boundary of
Ming China
CHINA
BURMA
Ava
Hanoi
Toungoo
Pegu
SIAM
Canton
Macao
ANNAM
Manila
Taiwan
JAPAN
Kyoto
Nagasaki
PHILIPPINES
SUMATRA
BORNEO
Molucca
Islands
JAVA

dictator, 113; **Great Wall**, 11; **Mongols**, 42; **vassals**, 31.

53

Western and Southern Europe

1542 **Mary Stuart (1542-1587)** becomes **Queen of Scotland** at the age of one week.

1543 Alliance of **Henry VIII*** and **Charles V*** against **France** and **Scotland**.

1545 **Council of Trent***: the start of the **Counter-Reformation***.

1547 **England** invades **Scotland** and defeats the **Scots** at the **Battle of Pinkie. Mary, Queen of Scots** is sent to **France** to marry the **Dauphin***.

1547-1559 Reign of **Henry II** of **France**.

1547-1553 Reign of **Edward VI** of **England**.

1552-1556 War between **Henry II** and **Charles V***.

1553 **Tobacco** is first introduced into **Europe** (from **America** to **Spain**).

Tobacco plant

1553-1558 Reign of **Mary I** of **England**, who marries **Philip II** of **Spain** (see below). **England** returns to **Catholicism** and 300 **Protestants** are burnt.

1555 **English Muscovy Company** is given a **charter*** to explore and trade with **Russia**.

1556 Abdication of **Charles V***. His son becomes **Philip II** of **Spain**, and inherits **Habsburg*** land in **Italy**, **Burgundy**, the **Netherlands** and the **New World***.

1558 **England** loses **Calais** to **France**.

1558-1603 Reign of **Elizabeth I** of **England**. She reintroduces the **Protestant Church of England***.

Hatfield Palace, the childhood home of **Eizabeth I**.

1559 **Mary, Queen of Scots** is widowed and returns to **Scotland** from **France**.

1559 **Jean Nicot** imports **tobacco** into **France** (from **America**. (The word **nicotine** is named after him.)

1559 **Treaty of Cateau-Cambresis**: peace between **France** and **Spain**.

1560-1574 Reign of **Charles IX** of **France**.

1562 Start of the **French Wars of Religion***.

1563 **English Poor Law**: **Justices of the Peace** are given the power to raise a **poor rate** to look after the poor in each parish.

1564-1616 Life of **William Shakespeare, English** playwright and poet.

The **Globe Theatre, London**, where **Shakespeare's** plays were performed.

1567-1625 Reign of **James VI** of **Scotland**.

1571 **Battle of Lepanto: Turks** are defeated by **Spanish** and **Venetians**. The end of Turkish sea power in **Europe**.

1572 **St Bartholomew's Day Massacre** of 20,000 **Huguenots** (French Protestants) in **France**.

Central and Northern Europe and Russia

1532 **Peace of Nuremburg: Protestants** in the **Holy Roman Empire*** are allowed to practise their religion.

1532-1533 War between **Turkey** and **Austria** over **Hungary**.

1533-1584 Reign of **Ivan IV (the Terrible)** in **Russia**.

Ivan IV

1534-1535 The city of **Münster** in **northern Germany** is taken over by **Anabaptists**, a group who deny the need for any form of government.

1536 **Calvin*** goes to **Geneva**.

1541-1688 **Hungary** becomes a **Turkish** province.

1547 **Charles V*** defeats the **Protestant League of Schmalkalden** at **Muhlberg**.

1547 **Ivan IV** takes the title **Tsar of all the Russias**.

St Basil's Cathedral, begun by **Ivan IV** in **1555**.

1548-1572 Reign of **Sigismund II** of **Poland**.

1553-1555 Expeditions of **Chancellor**, an **English** navigator, to **Russia**.

1555 **Peace of Augsburg: Charles V*** allows the **Protestant** princes freedom of worship.

1556 **Charles V*** abdicates. His brother, **Ferdinand***, becomes **Holy Roman Emperor***.

1557-1582 **Russia, Poland, Sweden** and **Denmark** fight over the **Baltic** territories.

1564-1576 Reign of **Maximilian II, Holy Roman Emperor***.

Illustration of the **Holy Roman Emperor** from a **16th century** drinking glass.

1566 Rebellions break out in the **Netherlands** against **Spanish** rule.

1572 **Poland** introduces a system of electing kings.

1572 Beginning of the **Dutch Revolt***.

The **Sea Beggars** (**Dutch** rebels) capture the port of **Brill**.

The Middle East and Africa

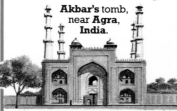

The King of **Mali**.

1546 The destruction of the **Mali Empire*** by the **Songhai***.

1549-1582 Reign of **Askia David**, King of **Songhai***.

c.1550s **England** starts trading with **West Africa**.

1551 **Turks** take **Tripoli**. War between **Turkey** and **Hungary**.

1562 **England** joins the **slave trade***, shipping slaves from **West Africa** to the **Caribbean**. **John Hawkins**, a naval commander, allies with two kings in **Sierra Leone** and attacks their neighbours, taking captives as slaves.

Slaves taken captive.

1566 The **Ottoman Empire*** is now at its greatest extent.

1566-1574 Reign of **Sultan Selim II** of **Turkey**.

1571 **Battle of Lepanto**: Turkish naval power is broken after defeat by **Don John** of **Austria**.

1573 **Don John** of **Austria** captures **Tunis** and **Turkey** goes to war with Austria.

1574 **Portuguese** colonize **Angola**.

1574-1575 The **Turks** retake **Tunis** and conquer the rest of **Tunisia**.

1578 **King Sebastian** of **Portugal** invades **Morocco**, but is defeated at the **Battle of al-Ksar al-Kabir**. **Ahmed al Mansur** of **Fez** establishes the **Sharifian dynasty** and **Morocco** expands in power.

Moroccan warriors on horseback.

1580-1617 Reign of **Idris Alooma**, greatest of the kings of the **Kanem-Bornu***.

The Far East

1550 The **Mongol*** leader, **Altan-Khan**, invades **northern China**. **Japanese** pirates raid **China**.

1555 **Humayun*** regains his **Indian** empire from **Sher Shah***.

1555 The King of **Toungoo** captures the **northern Burmese** kingdom of **Ava**. This results in a unified **Burmese state**, which grows at the expense of the **Thai kingdom**.

1556-1605 Reign of **Akbar the Great***, greatest of **Mogul*** rulers. A new phase of conquest begins.

Akbar's tomb, near **Agra**, **India**.

1556 **Astrakhan** is **annexed*** by **Russia**.

1557 **Portuguese** establish a settlement at **Macao**. (Trade with **China** is restricted to **Macao**.)

1560 **Oda Nobunaga*** becomes leading **daimyo*** in **Japan**.

1564 **Spaniards** occupy the **Philippines** and build **Manila**.

1565 **Akbar*** extends the **Mogul Empire*** to the **Deccan**.

1567 **Oda Nobunaga*** becomes military dictator of **Japan**.

1570 **Nagasaki, Japan** is opened to foreign traders. Trade comes via **Macao**, bringing silk.

Portuguese settlement at **Nagasaki**.

1573 **Oda Nobunaga*** now rules half **Japan**.

1573-1577 **Akbar*** conquers **Gujerat** and **Bengal** and unifies **northern India**.

1579 A **Portuguese** trading station is established in **Bengal**.

1581 **Akbar*** subdues **Afghanistan**, formally **annexing*** it in **1585**.

1581 **Russians** take **Siberia**.

1582 **Hideyoshi*** succeeds as leader in **Japan**.

1584 **Phra Narai** creates an independent kingdom of **Siam**.

The Americas

1534 A **French** expedition, led by **Jacques Cartier**, reaches **Labrador, Canada**.

1535 **Buenos Aires** and **Lima** are founded.

1535 **Jacques Cartier** discovers the **St Lawrence River**, and sails to **Montreal**.

1535-1538 **Quesada**, a **Spanish** *conquistador**, conquers **Colombia**.

1536 **Jesuits*** found **Asunción**, **Paraguay**.

1536 **Inca*** rebellion in **Peru**, led by **Manco Inca**. He rules from **Villcabamba** until **1545**.

Manco Inca

1540-1544 **Valdivia**, a **Spanish** *conquistador**, explores **Chile**.

1541 **Indian*** revolt in **Mexico**.

1542 **Charles V's*** New Laws abolish **Indian*** slavery in **Spanish** colonies and limit the control of the Spanish colonists.

1545 **Silver mines** are discovered in **Peru** and **Mexico** (1548).

1554 The founding of **São Paulo** in **Brazil**.

1560 **Titi Cusi Inca*** rules at **Villcabamba, Peru**.

1562-1565 **French** colony in **Florida** destroyed by **Spanish**.

1562 **John Hawkins** (see **Africa** column) makes his first **slave trade*** voyage to **Hispaniola** (**Haiti**). Second and third voyages follow: **1564-1565** and **1567-1568**.

1572 **Topa Amaru**, the last **Inca*** ruler, is captured and executed.

1572 **Francis Drake**, an **English** navigator and **privateer***, begins attacking **Spanish American** harbours.

Francis Drake is knighted by **Elizabeth I**.

1576-1577 **Martin Frobisher** (**English**) explores **North Atlantic** and discovers **Baffin Island**.

Frobisher's ship off **Baffin Island**.

The Reformation

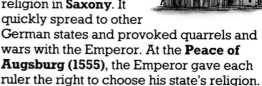

Worms Cathedral

The **Reformation** began as an attempt to reform the **Catholic Church**, but it provoked a religious and political upheaval that led to the creation of the **Protestant Churches** and a permanent split in **Christendom***. It also became associated with social and political protest and helped inspire movements such as the **Dutch Revolt***. The Reformation was led by **Martin Luther (1483-1546)**, a monk and professor of theology at **Wittenburg** in **Germany**. In **1517**, he nailed **95 theses** (propositions) to the church door.

Luther nailing his **95 theses** to the church door (a standard way of starting a debate). The theses contained criticisms of the sale of **indulgences** (pardons for sins) and other practices.

For many years people had been criticizing the Church for abuses such as **absenteeism** (the absence of a priest from his parish), **nepotism** (the practice of giving clerical **benefices**, or positions, to relations) and **simony** (the selling of benefices, relics or indulgences). The clergy were criticized for their ignorance and Church leaders for their wealth and involvement with politics.

16th century printing press and **Reformation** pamphlet.

The invention of **printing** in the **15th century** and the growth of literacy meant that these criticisms could now reach a wider public.

Luther's theses were printed and attracted wide public interest. He was accused of **heresy*** and **excommunicated*** in **1520**. In **1521** he was called to account for himself at the **Diet of Worms** (a council held by the Emperor at Worms). There he denied the **infallibility*** of the Pope and asserted the need to base religious beliefs on the *Bible*, rather than the Church's teachings.

Anti-Catholic medallion, showing a bishop one way up, and a jester, the other.

Bishop
Jester

Luther was condemned as a **heretic*** and went into hiding in **Wartburg Castle**. There he began developing his ideas for the organization of a **Lutheran Church**. In **1525**, Lutheranism became the official religion in **Saxony**. It quickly spread to other German states and provoked quarrels and wars with the Emperor. At the **Peace of Augsburg (1555)**, the Emperor gave each ruler the right to choose his state's religion.

Zwingli

In **1523, Zwingli (1484-1531)**, a priest at **Zurich Cathedral**, inspired by Luther, wrote **67 theses** providing for even greater changes in belief, services and church organization. They were accepted by the city council and his influence spread in **Switzerland** and **South Germany**.

Calvin

Another great leader of the Reformation was **John Calvin (1509-1564)**, a Frenchman based in **Geneva**. In **1536** he published *Institutes*, containing his ideas for reform. **Calvinism** was stricter and more severe than Lutheranism, but better organized, and it quickly made converts.

Inside a **Calvinist** church.

Many **Protestant** churches were plain and simple, in reaction against the decoration and sculptures of **Catholic** churches.

In **1541** Calvin began organizing the Genevan Church. The Church was to govern itself, electing **pastors** (to preach), **doctors** (to decide doctrine), **elders** (to enforce discipline) and **deacons** (to care for the poor) – with a **synod** (committee) to arrange elections.

The Counter-Reformation

St Peters, Rome, built in the 16th and 17th centuries.

The successes of the **Reformation*** forced the **Catholic Church** to speed up reform and counter-attack. This movement is known as the **Counter-Reformation**. By the early **17th century**, **Protestant** successes in **Poland**, **France**, **Bavaria**, **Austria** and the **southern Netherlands** had been reversed and the Protestant share of **Europe** had fallen considerably.

Ignatius Loyola, founder of the **Jesuits**.

Colleges were set up to educate the clergy of non-Catholic countries. New religious orders were founded: **Capuchins (1525), Paulines (1530), Jesuits (1534)** and **Ursulines (1535)**. The most important of these were the Jesuits, who worked as teachers and as missionaries abroad.

The **Council of Trent** (a council of the Church) met in **1545-1547, 1551-1552,** and **1562-1563** and launched a campaign to reconvert Protestants. The **Inquisition*** was re-established and Protestants were convicted of **heresy*** and burned. The **Baroque** movement in the arts also helped win people back to Catholicism, with flamboyant religious painting, church music and elaborate architecture.

Inside a **Baroque** Church.

Map of Europe 1560

This map shows the different **Christian** groups in **Europe** in the 16th century.

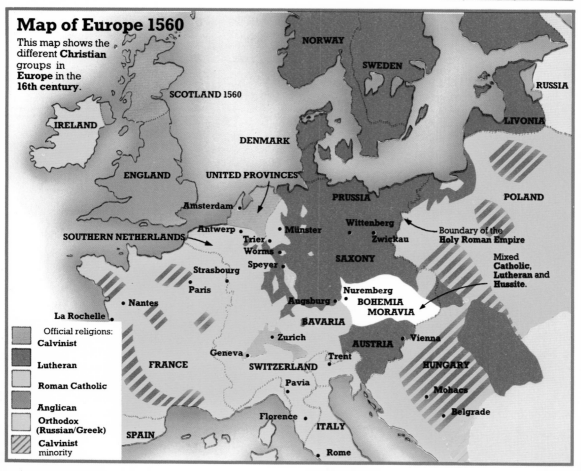

NORWAY
SWEDEN
RUSSIA
SCOTLAND 1560
LIVONIA
IRELAND
DENMARK
ENGLAND
UNITED PROVINCES
PRUSSIA
POLAND
Amsterdam
Antwerp
Wittenberg
Boundary of the Holy Roman Empire
SOUTHERN NETHERLANDS
Münster
Trier
Zwickau
Worms
SAXONY
Mixed Catholic, Lutheran and Hussite.
Speyer
Strasbourg
Nuremberg
Paris
Augsburg
BOHEMIA
Nantes
MORAVIA
La Rochelle
BAVARIA
Zurich
AUSTRIA
Vienna
Geneva
Trent
FRANCE
SWITZERLAND
HUNGARY
Pavia
Mohacs
Belgrade
Florence
SPAIN
ITALY
Rome

Official religions:
Calvinist
Lutheran
Roman Catholic
Anglican
Orthodox (Russian/Greek)
Calvinist minority

The Reformation in England

The **English Reformation** was prompted by political rather than religious motives. **Henry VIII (1509-1547)** was desperate for a son to secure his dynasty, but all his children by his wife, **Catherine of Aragon**, had died, except **Mary**. The **Pope** was unlikely to give his consent to a divorce, as he was in the power of Catherine's nephew, **Charles V***. So Henry chose to break with the Church in **Rome**. This led to the formation of the **Anglican (English Protestant) Church**.

Important dates

1531 The English clergy recognize **Henry** as **Supreme Head of the English Church**.

1533 Henry's marriage is declared void. He marries **Anne Boleyn** and is **excommunicated***.

1534 **Act of Supremacy** is passed in **Parliament**, cutting off all ties with **Rome**.

1534-1539 The **Dissolution of the monasteries**: monasteries are closed and sold on the pretext of the discovery of fraud, immorality and other abuses.

A monastery in ruins after evacuation.

1536-1537 **Pilgrimage of Grace**: a **Catholic** uprising against the **Reformation** in the north.

1539 **Six Articles** are issued, setting out points of **Catholic** doctrine still to be followed.

1547-1553 Reign of **Edward VI**.

1549 The **Act of Uniformity** and a new **Prayer Book** are issued to establish the new faith.

1552 A **Second Act of Uniformity** and **Prayer Book** bring the **Anglican Church** closer to **Swiss Protestants***.

1553-1558 Reign of **Henry VIII's** daughter, **Mary Tudor**. The **Catholic Church** is reinstated.

1558-1603 Reign of **Henry VIII's** daughter, **Elizabeth I**, who reinstates the **Anglican Church**.

Elizabeth I

1559 New **Act of Supremacy** and **Prayer Book**, closer to the moderate 1549 version. These are unacceptable to radical **Protestants** who want to move closer to **Calvinism***.

1563 **39 Articles** sets out the beliefs of the **Anglican Church**.

1570 **Elizabeth I** is **excommunicated***. Catholics are now under suspicion as possible traitors.

1593 **Act against sectaries** (members of **Protestant sects** who find the **Anglican Church** too moderate; also called **non-conformists** or **Puritans**).

Africa

Timbuctoo in the **16th century**.

By the **16th century** larger political units were developing in **Africa**, particularly in **West Africa**, with increases in territory, population and trade. Kingdoms such as **Kanem-Bornu***, **Kongo*** and **Songhai*** (based around the trading cities of **Timbuctoo**, **Jenne** and **Gao**) were reaching their peaks.

In **Nigeria**, the kingdom of **Benin** and the **Yoruba kingdom** of **Oyo** flourished, producing highly-skilled works of art in bronze.

Benin bronze

In **East Africa**, the **Luo** (**nomadic*** cattle herders from the **Sudan**) moved into **Uganda**. Some **Bantu*** farmers stayed and were assimilated. In **Southern Africa** the **Mwenemutapa kingdom*** of **Zimbabwe** was revived under the **Rozwi** kings.

Ruins of the **Palace of Zimbabwe**. It was probably first built **c.1350s** and enlarged in the **16th century** by the **Rozwi**.

Along the East African coast trading cities such as **Kilwa**, **Mombasa**, **Zanzibar** and **Malindi** had been established for several centuries. They handled trade in gold, ivory and tropical products.

Bantu, 113; **Calvin**, 56; **Charles V**, 52; **excommunicate**, 113; **Kongo**, 41.

Kanem-Bornu, 27; **Mwenemutapa**, 37; **nomads**, 113; **Songhai**, 41; **Swiss Protestants** (see **Calvin** and **Zwingli**, 56).

The Mogul Empire

The **Muslim*** **Mogul Empire** was established in **1526** when **Babar**, a descendant of the **Mongol***, **Tamerlane***, entered **India** from **Afghanistan** and defeated the **Sultan of Delhi**. Under Babar's successors, **Akbar (1556-1605)**, **Jahan (1627-1656)** and **Aurangzeb (1656-1707)**, the Moguls gradually extended control by conquest over most of India. Akbar attempted to unite India culturally, by allowing **Hindus*** to practise their religion – the predominant faith in India.

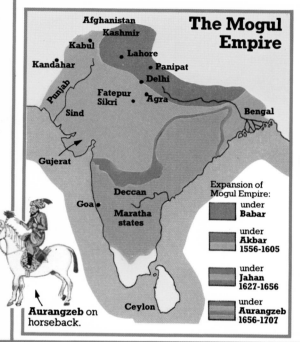

The Mogul Empire

Afghanistan
Kashmir
Kabul
Lahore
Kandahar
Panipat
Delhi
Punjab
Fatepur Sikri
Agra
Sind
Bengal
Gujerat
Deccan
Goa
Maratha states
Ceylon

Expansion of Mogul Empire:
under **Babar**
under **Akbar** 1556-1605
under **Jahan** 1627-1656
under **Aurangzeb** 1656-1707

Aurangzeb on horseback.

The **Taj Mahal**, built by **Jahan** in 1632-1653, as a tomb for his favourite wife, **Mumtaz Mahal**.

The **Mogul** period was a golden age for the arts, particularly architecture.

The Empire reached its greatest extent in the mid **17th century**, but decay set in too. Persecution of Hindus undermined their loyalty and there was resistance to heavy taxes. Relations worsened with the Hindu **Maratha** princes, who were growing in power. By the **18th century**, although the Moguls still nominally held power, India consisted of a collection of more or less independent states.

In the **16th century**, the **Portuguese** began establishing forts along the east coast to protect their sea route to **India**. They took over the trade for themselves and the prosperity of the area declined.

Portuguese fort

In **North Africa**, the **Arabs** had been making converts to **Islam*** for centuries. In the **16th century** the **Ottomans*** took control of **Egypt, Tripoli, Tunisia** and, indirectly, **Algeria. Muslim Morocco** remained independent and expanded south, taking over Songhai.

The **mosque** at Jenne.

The **slave trade*** from West Africa began during this period. Slave raids brought about a fall in population and widespread disorder. By the end of the century, most African kingdoms were in decline.

Africa in the 16th century

al-Ksar al-Kabir
Oran
Tripoli
Cyprus
Algeria
Tunisia
Morocco
Egypt
Songhai
Massawa
Timbuctoo
River Niger
Gao
Kanem-Bornu
Yoruba
Jenne
Oyo
Ethiopia
Benin
Kongo
Mombasa
Malindi
Kilwa
Zanzibar
River Zambesi
Tete
Mwenemutapa
Sena
Rozwi
Zimbabwe

Western and Southern Europe

1580-1640 Union of **Spain** and **Portugal**.

1582 The **Gregorian Calendar** (used today) is introduced in **Catholic** countries only.

1584 **Potatoes** are imported from **America**.

1587 **Mary, Queen of Scots*** is executed by **Elizabeth I***, for plotting against her.

1588 The **Spanish Armada** (a fleet of ships sent by **Philip II*** to conquer **England**) is defeated.

Spanish Armada, 1588.

1589 **Henry of Navarre** becomes **Henry IV*** of **France**. The start of the **Bourbon dynasty**.

1592 **Presbyterianism** (a form of **Calvinism***) is adopted in **Scotland**.

1596 The **English** attack **Cadiz (Spain)** and hinder the preparation of a second **Armada**.

1597 **Irish** rebellion against the **English**, led by **Hugh O'Neill, Earl of Tyrone**.

1598 **Henry IV*** of **France** issues the **Edict of Nantes**, allowing religious toleration to **Huguenots (French Protestants)**. This ends the **French Wars of Religion***.

Central and Northern Europe

1575 **Pacification of Ghent** (see below).

1576 **Russians** begin expanding across the **Ural mountains**.

1578 **Peace of Arras** (see below).

1579 **Union of Utrecht** (see below).

1581 **Russians** begin the conquest of **Siberia**.

1581 The seven northern provinces of the **Netherlands** proclaim independence as the **United Provinces** and elect **William of Orange** as their ruler.

1582 Peace between **Russia** and **Poland**. Russia is cut off from the **Baltic**.

1584 **William of Orange**, ruler of the **United Provinces**, is assassinated.

1596 **France**, **England** and the **United Provinces** unite against **Spain**.

1596 **Galileo Galilei** (1564-1642), an **Italian** astronomer, mathematician and physicist, invents the **thermometer**.

1598 Death of **Tsar Theodor**, last of the **Rurik dynasty***: the start of a period known as the **time of troubles** in **Russia**.

Russian aristocrats, called *boyars*, c.1570s.

The Dutch Revolt 1568-1648

In the early **16th century**, **Calvinism*** made many converts in the provinces of the **Netherlands**. In **1555**, they were inherited by **Philip II*** of **Spain**, an unpopular foreigner who ruled through a series of governors. When Philip tried to impose religious uniformity (**Catholicism**), many people opposed it, including the nobles **Egmont**, **Hoorne** and **William of Orange** (1533-1584).

In **1566**, **Protestants** began to worship openly and there were attacks on Catholic churches. The governor, the **Duke of Alva**, imposed widespread persecution, and in **1568** Egmont and Hoorne were executed. Many of the opposition, who became known as **Sea Beggars**, escaped in ships and began attacking Spanish ships. This began the struggle for independence, known as the **Dutch Revolt (1568-1648)**.

The Netherlands

Northern provinces

The Hague

Utrecht

Brill
Flushing

Sea Beggars' ship.

Ghent

Southern provinces

Arras

Important dates

1572 **Sea Beggars** capture **Brill** and **Flushing**.

1576 The **Spanish Fury**: Spanish soldiers sack **Antwerp**. This leads to the **Pacification of Ghent**: all 17 provinces unite against **Spain**.

1578 **Peace of Arras**: the ten southern (**Catholic**) provinces unite with **Spain**.

1579 **Union of Utrecht**: the seven northern (**Calvinist**) provinces unite against **Spain**.

1581 Northern provinces proclaim independence as the **United Provinces**. They elect **William of Orange** as hereditary **Stadtholder** (governor).

1648 **Peace of the Hague**: **Spain** recognizes the **United Provinces**. The southern provinces remain under Spanish rule as the **Spanish Netherlands** (later **Belgium**).

The Middle East and Africa

1581 Moroccans begin penetrating the **Sahara**.

1581 Peace between **Turkey** and **Spain**.

1585 The **Ottoman Empire*** begins to decline.

1586-1622 Reign of **Shah Abbas the Great** in **Persia**.

Persian warriors at the time of **Abbas the Great**.

1590 Moroccans reach the **River Niger** and take **Timbuctoo**.

1590 Shah Abbas of Persia makes peace with **Turkey**.

1591 Battle of Tondibi: **Moroccans** invade and defeat **Songhai*** and cause the collapse of the kingdom.

1592 The **Portuguese** take **Mombasa**.

1598 The **Dutch** take **Mauritius**.

1598 Shah Abbas makes **Isfahan** the capital of **Persia**.

The Far East

1587 Akbar* takes **Kashmir**.

1591 First **English** voyage to the **East Indies**.

Hindu statue from Java.

1592 Japanese invade **Korea**.

1592 Annamese take **Hanoi** and unite **North Vietnam**.

1592 Akbar* conquers **Sind**.

1593 The **Japanese** leave **Korea**, under pressure from the **Chinese**.

1594 English begin trading in **India**.

1594 Akbar* takes **Kandahar**. The **Mogul Empire*** reaches its peak.

1595 Dutch colonies are established in the **East Indies**.

1597 The **Japanese** invade **Korea** again, but the **Chinese** help the **Koreans** to expel them.

1598 Death of **Toyotomi Hideyoshi***, ruler of **Japan**. He is succeeded by a child and five **regents*** compete for power.

1599 Akbar* begins to subdue the **Deccan**.

The Americas

1577 Humphrey Gilbert (English) is granted a **patent*** to found colonies in **North America**.

1579 Francis Drake* claims **New Albion (California)** during his voyage round the world (1577-1580).

1583 Humphrey Gilbert (see above) establishes his first **English** colony in **Newfoundland**.

1584 Walter Raleigh, (English) discovers and **annexes*** Virginia. He founds a colony in **1585**, but it is abandoned by settlers in **1586**. A second colony is set up in **1587-1591**.

Arms of the **Virginia Company**, formed to establish a colony in **Virginia**.

1585-1587 John Davis (English) searches for a north west passage to **Asia** and explores the **Davis Strait**.

Wars of Religion in France 1562-1598

Rival **Catholic** and **Protestant** factions developed at the **French** Court, as some noblemen converted to **Calvinism***. In **1560** a child, **Charles IX**, became king, with his mother, **Catherine de Medici**, as **regent***. Struggles between the factions led to a civil war, the **French Wars of Religion**, which lasted from **1562-1598**.

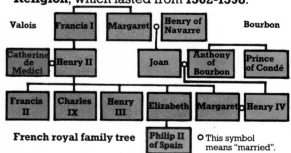

French royal family tree

Valois — Bourbon

Francis I — Margaret — Henry of Navarre

Catherine de Medici ○ Henry II — Joan — Anthony of Bourbon — Prince of Condé

Francis II — Charles IX — Henry III — Elizabeth ○ Philip II of Spain — Margaret ○ Henry IV

○ This symbol means "married".

The Catholics were led by the **Guise** family, supported by Catherine de Medici. The Protestants (or **Huguenots**) were led by the **Coligny** brothers and the **Bourbon Prince of Condé** and **King of Navarre**.

A ball at the **French Court**.

Important dates

1562 Massacre of **Huguenots** at **Vassy** by the **Duke de Guise** and his retainers leads to civil war.

1563 Murder of the **Duke de Guise**.

1567-1570 Second civil war ends with a general **amnesty*** at the **Peace of Saint Germain**.

1572 The **St Bartholomew's Day Massacre** of **Huguenots** leads to another civil war.

1584 The **Guise** family and **Philip II*** form the **League of Joinville** against the **Huguenots**.

1586 War of the Three Henries: **Henry III** of **France**, **Henry of Navarre** and **Henry de Guise**.

1589 Henry III is murdered and the crown is claimed by **Henry of Navarre**, as **Henry IV**, first king of the **Bourbon** dynasty.

1590 Henry IV defeats **Catholics** at **Ivry**.

1593 Henry IV becomes a **Catholic**.

1594 Henry IV enters **Paris** and begins his reign.

1598 Edict of Nantes gives religious toleration to **Huguenots**.

Colonial expansion in the 17th century

In the **17th century** most colonies were founded, not by nations, but by groups of settlers or traders. Great trading companies, such as the **East India Companies**, were given trade **monopolies*** by their governments, granting them sole rights to trade in an area. Sometimes the companies started colonies too.

The **Pilgrim Fathers (English Puritans)** arriving in **Massachussetts** in **1620**.

Hugly (est.**1640**), headquarters of the **Dutch East India Company** in **Bengal, India**.

As **Spanish*** and **Portuguese*** power declined, the **English, Dutch** and **French** became major colonial powers. They competed for trade with **India** and the **Far East**, setting up colonies and bases there. The Dutch established a monopoly of trade with the **"spice islands"** (the **East Indies**).

However, in terms of colonies, the biggest advances were made in the **West Indies** and **North America**. Many North American colonies attracted settlers in search of land, or freedom from religious persecution.

African slaves on a sugar plantation.

Other colonies were developed for growing products such as sugar or tobacco. From **1660** until the **19th century**, increasing numbers of **slaves** (people with no freedom) were captured and sent from **West Africa** to work on the plantations.

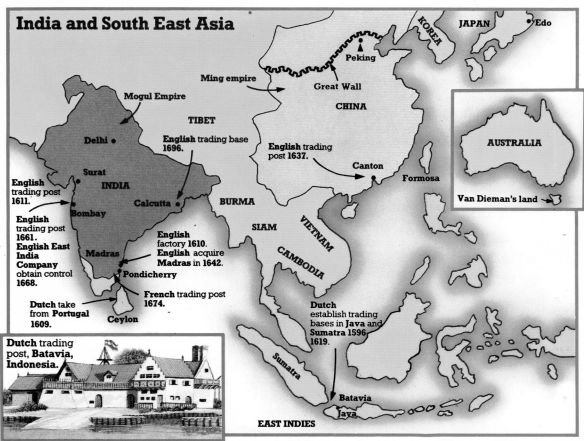

India and South East Asia

JAPAN
Edo
KOREA
Peking
Ming empire
Great Wall
CHINA
Mogul Empire
TIBET
Delhi
English trading base **1696**.
English trading post **1637**.
Canton
Formosa
Surat
INDIA
English trading post **1611**.
Calcutta
BURMA
Bombay
English trading post **1661**.
English East India Company obtain control **1668**.
Madras
English factory **1610**. **English** acquire **Madras** in **1642**.
SIAM
VIETNAM
CAMBODIA
Pondicherry
French trading post **1674**.
Dutch take from **Portugal 1609**.
Ceylon
Dutch establish trading bases in **Java** and **Sumatra 1596, 1619**.
Sumatra
Batavia
Java
EAST INDIES

AUSTRALIA
Van Dieman's land

Dutch trading post, **Batavia, Indonesia**.

monopoly, 114; **Portuguese, Spanish** (see **Age of Discovery**, 48-49).

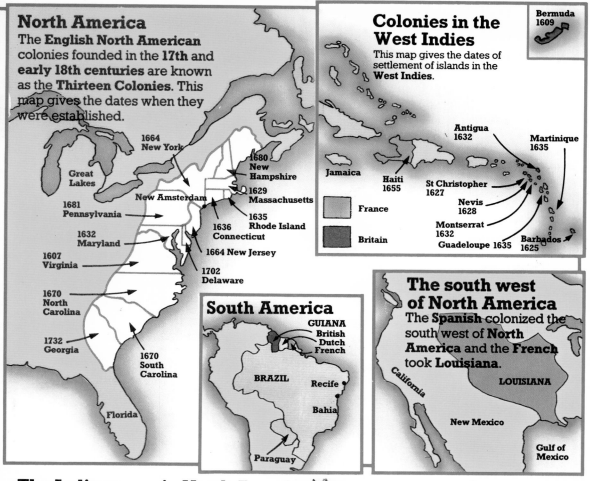

North America

The **English North American** colonies founded in the **17th** and **early 18th centuries** are known as the **Thirteen Colonies**. This map gives the dates when they were established.

Great Lakes

1664 New York

1680 New Hampshire

New Amsterdam

1629 Massachusetts

1681 Pennsylvania

1635 Rhode Island

1636 Connecticut

1632 Maryland

1664 New Jersey

1607 Virginia

1702 Delaware

1670 North Carolina

1732 Georgia

1670 South Carolina

Florida

Colonies in the West Indies

This map gives the dates of settlement of islands in the **West Indies**.

Bermuda 1609

Jamaica

Haiti 1655

Antigua 1632

Martinique 1635

St Christopher 1627

Nevis 1628

Montserrat 1632

Guadeloupe 1635

Barbados 1625

France

Britain

South America

GUIANA
British
Dutch
French

BRAZIL

Recife

Bahia

Paraguay

The south west of North America

The **Spanish** colonized the south west of **North America** and the **French** took **Louisiana**.

California

LOUISIANA

New Mexico

Gulf of Mexico

The Indian wars in North America

The huge growth of the **British** colonies in **North America** threatened the land and livelihood of the native **Red Indian** tribes. Sometimes the Indians tried to play off one **European** colonizing power against another, but in the end they were defeated and their land taken away.

Iroquois   **Sioux**   **Florida Indians**

A variety of **Indians**, described by early settlers.

Pequot village in **Connecticut**.

There were major wars in the **17th** and **early 18th centuries** – the **Pequot War (1636-1637)**, **King Philip's War (1675-1676)** and Indian uprisings in the **Carolines (1712-1716)**. **English** settlers won a series of victories and destroyed many important Indian towns and settlements.

Despite frequent wars and massacres, the advance of the white settlers continued and the Indians were gradually pushed westwards. In the **18th century**, the advance of **French** and English settlers led to frequent conflict there too. By **1810**, most former Indian land in the **northern states** (south of the **Great Lakes** and east of the **Mississippi River**) was under **American** control. Between **1820** and **1840**, Indians were driven from their territories in the **southern states** too.

63

Southern and Western Europe

1603 Death of **Queen Elizabeth I*** of **England**. **James VI** of **Scotland** becomes **James I** of England and Scotland.

1604 Peace between **England** and **Spain** after fighting since **1587**.

1605 **Guy Fawkes' gunpowder plot**: an unsuccessful attempt by a group of **Catholics** to blow up the **English Houses of Parliament**. It leads to a wave of anti-Catholic laws.

1608 The first **telescope** is invented by **Hans Lippershey**, a **Dutch** lens maker.

The **Italian** scientist, **Galileo**, made his own telescope in **1609**. Here are two of his later telescopes.

1624-1642 **French** policy is controlled by **Cardinal Richelieu**, advisor to **Louis XIII**.

1628 **William Harvey**, an **English** doctor, publishes his discovery of the **circulation of the blood**.

1628 **Richelieu** captures the **Huguenot*** stronghold of **La Rochelle**, ending the Huguenot threat to **French** unity.

1629-1640 The **Eleven Years Tyranny***: **Charles I*** dissolves **Parliament** and rules on his own.

The **Huguenot** fortress at **La Rochelle**.

Northern and Eastern Europe

1598-1613 The period known as the **time of troubles** in **Russia**, with power struggles over the succession. **Boris Gudonov** becomes **Tsar** from **1598-1605**. **Polish** troops occupy **Moscow** in **1605**.

Moscow c.1600.

1607 War between **Sweden** and **Poland**. Sweden retakes **Estonia**.

1608 Formation of a **German Protestant Union**.

1609 **Maximilian of Bavaria** forms a **Catholic league**.

1609 **Johan Kepler** (1571-1630) a **German** astronomer, announces his **laws of planetary motion**, explaining how planets orbit the sun.

Kepler's diagram explaining the structure of the planetary system.

Stockholm Palace at the time of **Gustavus Adolphus**.

1611 **Poles** take Smolensk and occupy Moscow. **Swedes** take Novgorod.

1611-1632 Reign of **Gustavus Adolphus II** of **Sweden**, a great soldier and statesman.

The decline of the Ottoman Empire

The **Ottoman Empire*** expanded greatly in the **16th century**. The **Turks** took control of **Egypt** and parts of **North Africa** and occupied most of the territories known today as **Syria**, **Lebanon**, **Israel**, **Iraq** and the **Yemen**, as well as large parts of the **Caucasus**. They also had territories in **Europe**, including **Greece**, **Bulgaria**, **Serbia**, **Romania**, **Hungary** and the **Crimea**. However, from the end of the **16th century**, their power began to decline.

The Ottoman Empire to 1683

RUSSIA
Vienna • AUSTRIA POLAND Azov •
Venice • HUNGARY TRANSYLVANIA Crimea Caucasus Caspian
Mohacs SERBIA Belgrade Mountains Sea
 BULGARIA Constantinople GEORGIA
Algiers TURKEY
 MOREA
Tunis • Baghdad •
Tripoli Mediterranean Sea PERSIA

Ottoman Empire 1520

Acquired by 1566.

Acquired by 1683.

EGYPT

The striped areas show states that were subject to the **Ottoman Empire**. Red Sea

There were a number of causes for the decline. To some extent the Empire had simply become too big to control and there was a succession of weak rulers. Enemies on the borders, such as **Russia** and **Austria**, were growing in strength. As **Muslims***, the Ottomans came into conflict with **Christian Europe**. There were clashes too with their Muslim neighbours, the **Persian Safavids***.

The Americas

1602 **Spanish** explore **Californian** coast.

1603 Start of **French** colonization in **North America** – **Newfoundland**, **Nova Scotia** and **New France**.

1605 **Spanish** found **Santa Fé, New Mexico**.

1607 First permanent **English** settlement in **North America**, at **Jamestown, Virginia**.

1608 The state of **Paraguay** is founded by **Jesuits***.

1608 **French** found **Quebec**.

The house belonging to **de Champlain**, founder of **Quebec**.

1609 First **English** settlement on **Bermuda**.

1609 **Dutch** found **Manhattan**.

1610-1611 **Henry Hudson** (**English**) explores **Hudson Bay**.

1610 **Etienne Brulé** (**French**) discovers **Lake Huron**.

The Far East and Oceania

1596-1619 **Dutch** establish trading bases in **Java** and **Sumatra**.

1600 Civil War in **Burma**; the **Burmese Empire** breaks up.

1600 **English East India Company*** is founded.

1600 **Ieyasu Tokugawa*** defeats his rivals at the **Battle of Sekigahara** and establishes supremacy throughout **Japan**.

17th century trading ship.

1602 Founding of **Dutch East India Company***. The first **Dutch** traders arrive in **Cambodia** and **Siam**.

1604 **Russians** expand across **Siberia** and found **Tomsk**.

1604 **Ieyasu Tokugawa*** assumes the title of **shogun*** and founds the **Tokugawa dynasty**.

1604 **French East India Company*** is founded.

Africa, India and the Middle East

1600 **Oyo kingdom*** is at its height.

1602-1627 Wars between the **Persian Safavids*** and the **Ottomans** (see below).

Oyo carvings

1605 Death of the **Mogul*** Emperor, **Akbar the Great***.

1609 **Dutch** take **Ceylon** from **Portugal**.

1610 **English East India Company*** establishes a factory at **Madras**.

Cloth made at an **English** factory in **India**.

1611 **English East India Company*** establishes its first trading post in **India**, at **Surat**.

1612 **Persians** take Baghdad from the **Turks** (see below).

By **1683**, when the Turks unsuccessfully besieged **Vienna** for the last time, the Empire was already in decline. They had been forced to make concessions to Persia, **Poland** and Russia. They lost Hungary in **1699** and the Crimea by **1784**.

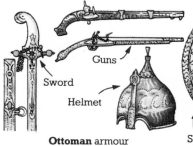

Guns

Sword

Helmet

Shield

Ottoman armour

Important dates

1603 **Ottomans** lose **Baghdad** to **Persia**.

1618 **Ottomans** lose **Georgia** to **Persia**.

1638 **Ottomans** recapture **Baghdad**.

1669 **Ottomans** acquire **Crete** from **Venice**.

1672-1676 War with **Poland**. **Ottomans** acquire the **Polish Ukraine**.

1677-1681 War with **Russia**. **Ottomans** lose most of the **Ukraine**.

1683 Unsuccessful siege of **Vienna**.

1686 **Austrians** take **Budapest, Hungary**.

1687 Battle of **Mohacs**: **Ottomans** are defeated and **Hungary** becomes a hereditary **Habsburg*** possession.

1689 **Austrians** take **Belgrade**.

1690 **Ottomans** drive **Austria** from **Bulgaria**, **Serbia** and **Transylvania** and recapture **Belgrade**.

1696 **Russia** seizes **Azov** from the **Ottomans**.

1699 Treaty of **Karlowitz**: **Turks** lose **Hungary**, **Croatia**, **Transylvania** and **Slavonia** to **Austria**. The **Morea** and most of **Dalmatia** are acquired by **Venice**, and **Podolia** goes to **Poland**.

1717 Treaty of **Belgrade**: **Austria** gives up **northern Serbia** and **Belgrade** to **Turkey**.

1743-1746 War between **Turkey** and **Persia** marks the end of a long period of warfare. Borders are fixed between the two states.

1768-1774 War between **Turkey** and **Russia**.

1783 The **Crimea** is **annexed*** by **Russia**.

Southern and Western Europe

1635 France declares war on **Spain**.

1640 **Charles I*** is forced to summon **Parliament**, as he needs money to fight a **Scottish** invasion. The **Short Parliament** is followed by the **Long Parliament**, which tries to control the power of the crown.

1642-1648 **English Civil War***.

1643-1661 **French** policy is controlled by **Cardinal Mazarin**, while **King Louis XIV*** is still a child.

1643 The **French** beat the **Spanish** at **Rocroi**. The start of French military superiority in **Europe**.

1648 **Peace of Münster** ends the **Dutch Revolt***. **Spanish** recognize independence of the **United Provinces**. War continues between **French** and **Spanish**.

1648 Riots in **Paris**. The start of a period of civil disorder known as **the Fronde**.

1649 Execution of **Charles I***. **Oliver Cromwell*** suppresses rebellions in **Ireland** and **Scotland**.

1649-1660 **England** is ruled by the **Commonwealth** (1649-1653), followed by the **Protectorate** (1653-1660), under **Oliver Cromwell***.

1652-1654 **First Anglo-Dutch Trade War**.

1659 **Peace of the Pyrenees** between **France** and **Spain**. Beginning of the rise of France and the decline of Spain.

1660 Restoration of the **Stuart*** monarchy in **England**, under **Charles II** (1660-1685).

1661 **Louis XIV***, King of France since 1643, takes control of government, aged 22.

1661 **Robert Boyle** (1627-1691), an **Irish** scientist, defines **chemical elements**.

Louis XIV entering **Paris** to begin his reign.

1665 **Second Anglo-Dutch Trade War**. England gains **New York** and islands in the **Caribbean**.

1665 **English** and **Portuguese** defeat **Spain**, securing Portugal's independence.

1665 The **Great Plague** in **London**.

1665 **Isaac Newton** (1643-1727), an **English** scientist, discovers **gravity**. Watching a falling apple made Newton aware of the force of gravity.

Falling apple demonstrating gravity.

1666 The **Great Fire of London**.

The **Great Fire of London**.

Northern and Eastern Europe

1613 The founding of the **Romanov** dynasty (1613-1917) in **Russia** by **Tsar Michael**.

Tsar **Michael Romanov**.

1617 **Treaty of Stolbovo**: **Russia** gives up **Ingria** and **Karelia** to **Sweden**.

1618-1648 **Thirty Years War***.

1621 **Gustavus Adolphus*** gains **Livonia** from **Poland**.

1632 **Gustavus Adolphus*** is killed at the **Battle of Lützen**.

1632 **Galileo Galilei** (1564-1642), an **Italian** astronomer and mathematician, publishes his *Dialogues*, which revolutionize scientific thinking.

The front page from **Galileo's** *Dialogues*.

1632-1654 Reign of **Queen Christina** of **Sweden**, guided by the great statesman, **Oxenstierna**.

1640-1688 Under **Frederick William I (the Great Elector)**, the state of **Brandenburg-Prussia** grows in importance.

1643 **Torricelli** (1608-1647), a **Florentine** mathematician and physicist, invents the **barometer**.

1643-1645 War between **Sweden** and **Denmark**. The **Danes** cede* **Gotland** and lease **Halland** to the **Swedes**, leaving Sweden the major power in the **Baltic**.

1646 **Swedes** take **Prague** and invade **Bavaria**.

1648 **Peace of Westphalia** ends the **Thirty Years War***.

1649 The **Code of Laws** marks the final establishment of **serfdom*** in **Russia**.

1654-1657 War between **Russia** and **Poland**. Russia acquires **Smolensk** and the **eastern Ukraine** (including **Kiev**).

1654-1660 War between **Sweden** and **Poland**.

Map showing territories of **Brandenburg-Prussia** under **Elector Frederick William I**.

1657 The **Elector of Brandenburg** obtains the sovereignty* of **Prussia**, which was previously under **Polish** overlordship.

1658 **Peace of Roskilde**: the **Danes** give up all claims to **southern Sweden**.

The Americas

1612 Beginnings of tobacco cultivation in **Virginia**.

1613 **Samuel de Champlain*** explores the **Ottawa River**.

1613 **English** destroy **French** settlement at **Port Royal, Jamaica**.

1619 First **slaves*** imported into **Virginia** from **West Africa**.

1620 The **Mayflower** sails from **Plymouth** to **Massachusetts**, carrying the **Pilgrim Fathers (English Puritans*)**.

American settlers building houses.

1621 **Dutch West India Company** founded.

Headquarters of the **Dutch West India Company**.

1625 **French** establish a port at **Cayenne, Guiana**.

1626 **Dutch** found **New Amsterdam** (now **New York**).

1627 **Cardinal Richelieu*** of **France** organizes the **Company of the Hundred Associates** to colonize all the lands between **Florida** and the **Arctic Circle**.

1629 **English** capture **Quebec** from **France** and settle the **Bahamas**.

1630-1642 Great migration to the **Massachusetts Bay Colony**. 16,000 settlers arrive from **England**.

1631 **Luke Foxe (English)** sails around **Hudson Bay**.

1631 First settlers in **Maryland**.

1632 **England** restores **Quebec** to **France**.

1634 **Dutch** establish a base at **Curaçao, West Indies**.

1634 **Jean Nicolet (French)** explores **Lake Michigan** and reaches the **St Lawrence** and **Mississippi Rivers**.

1636 Founding of **Dutch Guiana** (becomes **British Guiana** in **1814**).

The Far East and Oceania

1605 **Hidetada Tokugawa*** becomes ruler in **Japan**.

1613-1646 Reign of **Sultan Agung of Mataram**, who attempts to rule all **Java**.

1614-1636 **Europeans** begin to discover **Australia**.

1619 **Dutch** found a base at **Batavia** in the **East Indies**.

Dutch base at **Batavia, East Indies**.

1623 The **Amboyna Massacre**: **Dutch** destroy the **English** base in the **East Indies**, at **Amboyna**.

1623-1651 Rule of the powerful **shogun*, Iemitsu Tokugawa***, in **Japan**.

1626-1662 **Dutch** trade with **China** from **Taiwan**.

1627 **Manchus*** overrun **Korea**, which becomes a **vassal*** in **1637**.

1627 Rebellions against the **Ming dynasty*** in **China**.

Crown belonging to a **Ming Empress**.

1637 **English** establish a trading post in **Canton, China**.

1637 **Japan** adopts isolationist policies. Japanese are forbidden to travel abroad and foreigners are forbidden to enter Japan.

1641 **Dutch** seize **Malacca** from **Portugal** and dominate trade in the **East Indies**.

1642 **Abel Tasman (Dutch)** discovers **Van Diemen's Land (Tasmania)** and **New Zealand**.

Natives of **Tasmania**, encountered by **Tasman**.

Africa, India and the Middle East

1616 **Dutch** and **French** explore **West Africa** and establish trading posts in **Senegal** and the **Gold Coast**.

1627-1650 Rule of **Mogul*** Emperor, **Shah Jahan***, who adds further territories to the Empire.

Shah Jahan

Helmet belonging to **Shah Abbas**.

1629 Death of **Shah Abbas the Great*** of **Persia**.

1631 First permanent **English** settlement is established in **Africa**, at **Kormatin**.

1631-1642 **Dutch West India Company** ousts the **Portuguese** from the **Gold Coast**.

1632-1653 **Shah Jahan*** builds the **Taj Mahal***, as a tomb for his wife.

1637 **Dutch** take **El Mina, West Africa**, from the **Portuguese**.

The **Blue Mosque, Isfahan**, completed in **1638**.

1637 The **French** establish trading posts in **Senegal**.

1638 **Ottomans*** recapture **Baghdad** from the **Persians**.

1639 **Ottomans*** capture **Iraq** from the **Persians**.

1642 The **English** acquire **Madras, India**.

1643 The **French** establish **Fort Dauphin, Madagascar**.

1644 **Dutch** settle in **Mauritius**.

1648 **Arabs** recapture **Muscat** from **Portugal**.

1651 **English** occupy **St Helena**.

The Thirty Years War

The **Thirty Years War** began in **1618** as a revolt by **Protestants** in the **Bohemian provinces** of the **Holy Roman Empire***. It soon broadened into a number of separate conflicts involving most **European** powers, but fought mainly on **German** and **Bohemian** soil.

Many **German** cities suffered great damage and population losses during the war.

The **Defenestration of Prague (1618)**, an event which helped set off the war. Angry **Bohemian** noblemen threw two imperial governors out of the window (which is what "defenestration" means).

At first, it was largely a religious affair, with the **north German** and **Danish Protestants** allied against the **Catholic Habsburgs***, **Bavarians** and other Catholic German states. Neither group won clear-cut victories, although the imperial armies, under the command of **General Wallenstein (1583-1634)**, won several major and destructive battles.

In **1630**, **Sweden** entered the war, under the brilliant military commander, **King Gustavus Adolphus (1594-1632)**. His aim was partly to support the Protestants, but also to expand his own power in the **Baltic**. **France** was already at war with **Spain**, and indirectly supported Sweden. In **1635**, France joined the war directly.

Armour from the **Thirty Years War**.

Sword
Cannon
Musket
Arquebus

Europe in 1648

NORWAY
SWEDEN
Baltic Sea
LIVONIA
RUSSIA
SCOTLAND
Lund
LITHUANIA
IRELAND
DENMARK
Lübeck
BRANDENBURG-PRUSSIA
Dunkirk
Limerick
ENGLAND
POLAND
London
Beachy Head
La Hogue
Courtrai
Palatinate
Namur
Boundary of the
Holy Roman Empire.
Rocroi
BOHEMIA
MOLDAVIA
Paris
Strasbourg
AUSTRIA
Orléans
Lorraine
TRANSYLVANIA
La Rochelle
HUNGARY
CROATIA
WALLACHIA
Limit of **Ottoman**
sphere of influence.
Savoy
SERBIA
Black Sea
FRANCE
Turin
Venice
DALMATIA
BULGARIA
PORTUGAL
SPAIN
ITALY
TURKEY
Crete
Cyprus
Mediterranean Sea

 Habsburgs, 52; Holy Roman Empire, 52.

Peace came at the **Treaty of Westphalia** in **1648**. The **Dutch** and **Swiss** were granted independence and the survival of the Protestant German states was assured. As a result, the threat of the Habsburg domination of Europe was finally ended. The status of **Spain** declined, while that of France increased. Sweden emerged as the major power in the north and **Brandenburg-Prussia** also began to rise in importance. The **Austrian Empire** emerged as the leading Catholic power.

Important dates in the Thirty Years War

1620 Battle of the **White Mountain**: a victory for the imperial forces.

1625 Denmark enters the war.

1629 Peace of Lübeck.

1630 Sweden enters the war.

1631 Battle of Breitenfeld: an imperial defeat.

1632 Battle of Lützen: the **Swedes** win, but **Gustavus Adolphus** is killed.

1634 Battle of Nördlingen. **Sweden** loses **South Germany**.

1635 France enters the war.

1648 Peace of Westphalia.

Germany

The United Provinces

The rise of the Dutch

The **17th century** was a golden age for the **Dutch Republic** (also known as the **United Provinces**). Having gained independence from **Spain**, the Dutch became a successful trading nation. **Amsterdam** grew to be one of the largest and most prosperous **European** cities. Dutch engineers became experts at land drainage and reclamation and their farms were the most productive in Europe.

The port of **Amsterdam** in the **17th century**.

The Dutch also founded a major colonial empire in **Asia**, **South Africa** and the **New World***. The **English** were their greatest rivals and after **1650** there were three **Anglo-Dutch Trade Wars**. However, by the **1680s**, the growing strength of **France** brought the two countries into alliance once more. The Dutch ruler, **William III of Orange**, married the English **Princess Mary**. In **1688** he became **King of England** after the fall of **James II***.

17th century **Dutch** china, influenced by porcelain imported from the **Far East**.

Under the patronage of wealthy merchants, the Dutch made important contributions to the arts and to science and technology. Dutch painters of the period include **Rembrandt (1606-1669)**, **Rubens (1577-1640)**, **Van Dyck (1599-1641)**, **Vermeer (1632-1675)**, **Frans Hals (1580-1666)**, **Jan Steen (1626-1679)** and **Jacob van Ruysdael (1628-1682)**. Scientists and philosophers include **Grotius (1583-1645)**, **Spinoza (1632-1677)** and **Leeuwenhoek (1632-1723)**.

An early microscope, made by **Anton van Leeuwenhoek**.

James II, 72; New World, 48.

Southern and Western Europe

1666 **Isaac Newton*** develops his theories on colour.

One of **Newton's** experiments, showing light breaking up into a spectrum, through a glass prism.

1666-1667 **Anglo-Dutch War*** continues, ending in the **Peace of Breda**. **France** declares war on **England**, in support of the **Dutch**.

1668 **Treaty of Lisbon**: **Spain** recognizes the independence of **Portugal**.

1668 **Treaty of Aix-la-Chapelle** ends the war between **France** and **Spain**.

1668 **Isaac Newton*** invents the **reflecting telescope**.

1670 **Treaty of Dover**: a secret treaty between **Charles II** of **England** and **Louis XIV***, supplying Charles with funds to fight the **Dutch** and restore **Catholicism** in England.

1672-1674 **Third Anglo-Dutch Trade War**.

1672-1678 War between **France** and **Netherlands**, ending in **Treaty of Nijmegen**.

1672 **William III of Orange** becomes hereditary **Stadtholder** (ruler) of the **Netherlands**.

Newton's reflecting telescope.

Northern and Eastern Europe

1661 The first **European bank-note** is issued by the **Bank of Stockholm, Sweden**.

1663-1699 **Ottoman Turks*** attack **Central Europe**.

1664 **Ottomans*** invade and occupy **Hungary**.

1667 End of a 13 year truce between **Russia** and **Poland**. **Kiev** is **ceded*** to Russia.

1669 **Crete** is **ceded*** by **Venice** to the **Ottoman Empire***, marking the end of Venice's colonial empire.

1670 A rebellion of **Ukrainian Cossacks** and peasants subject to **Poland** is crushed by the Polish leader, **Jan Sobiewski**.

1671 **Ottomans*** declare war on **Poland**, in support of the **Cossacks**.

1672 **Turks** and **Cossacks** invade **Poland**. The Poles surrender **Podolia** and the **Ukraine**.

1673 **Poles** defeat the **Turks** at the **Battle of Khorzim**.

1674 **Jan Sobiewski** is elected **King of Poland**.

1675 The **Elector of Brandenburg** defeats the **Swedes** at the **Battle of Fehrbellin**.

1676 **Peace of Zuravno** ends the war between **Poland** and **Turkey**. Turkey receives the **Polish Ukraine**.

Cossack soldiers

The English Civil War and Commonwealth

Cavaliers or **Royalists**, supporters of the **King**.

Roundheads, supporters of **Parliament**.

The **English Civil War** broke out in **1642** as a result of a growing rift between **Parliament** and the early **Stuart** kings. Both sides wanted more power, but the limits of power of either party were not clearly defined. There were religious differences too. Many **Members of Parliament** became **Puritans***, while the Stuarts were suspected of having **Catholic** sympathies. Both **James I** and **Charles I** showed an increasing tendency to rule without Parliament, culminating in the **Eleven Years Tyranny (1629-1640)**.

By **1646**, Parliament had won the Civil War, with the help of the **New Model Army**, established by **Oliver Cromwell**. Fighting broke out again in **1648-1649**, ending in the King's defeat and execution. England was then ruled by the **House of Commons**, under the **Commonwealth (1649-1653)**.

Britain during the Civil War

Parliamentary gains 1642-1644.

Area controlled by **Parliament** in 1642.

- Tippermuir
- Dunbar
- Marston Moor
- Preston
- Nantwich
- Controlled by the **King** in 1645.
- Naseby
- Edgehill
- Lostwithiel

Area controlled by the **King** in 1644.

Area controlled by the **King** in 1645.

The Americas

1637 Dutch take **Recife, Brazil,** from the **Portuguese.**

1642 French found **Montreal.**

1648 French establish settlements on **St Martin, St Bartholomew, St Croix, The Saints, Maria Galante, St Lucia** and **Grenada.**

1654 First sugar plantations in the **West Indies.**

1655 England acquires **Jamaica** from **Spain.**

1664 England obtains **New Netherlands** (**New York** and **New Jersey**) from the **Dutch.**

New Amsterdam in the **17th century.**

1670 Hudson's Bay Company is founded in **England** to explore and acquire territory in the **Hudson Bay** areas of **Canada.**

1673 Marquette and Joliet (**French**) reach the headwaters of the **Mississippi River.**

1674 Plantations in **Quebec** become **French** royal colonies.

The Far East and Oceania

1643 **Abel Tasman*** discovers the **Fiji islands.**

Tasman arriving in **Fiji.**

1644 The **Ming dynasty*** is overthrown by rebels. The **Manchu dynasty*** is founded in northern China.

1644 Abel Tasman* explores the north and west coasts of Australia.

1647 The **Manchus*** take **Canton, China.**

1648 The **Bering Strait** is discovered by the **Cossack** explorer, **Dezhnev.**

1649 The **Russians** reach the **Pacific Ocean** and found **Okhotsk** in **Eastern Siberia.**

1652 Most of **China** is united under **Manchu*** control.

Africa, India and the Middle East

1652 The **Dutch** found the **Cape of Good Hope, South Africa.**

A **Cape Dutch** farmhouse.

1656 The **Dutch** displace the **Portuguese** in **Ceylon.**

1658-1707 Rule of **Aurangzeb***, the last great **Mogul*** Emperor. He defeats and deposes his father, **Akbar**, and conquers **Kandahar, Kabul** and the **Deccan.** The Empire reaches its greatest extent, but decay sets in.

Elephants dressed for a **Mogul** celebration.

c.1660-1670 The rise of the **Bambara kingdoms** of the **Upper Niger, West Africa.**

Important dates

1640 Charles I is forced to call **Parliament,** to raise money to put down an uprising of **Covenanters** (Scottish **Puritans***, called **Presbyterians**).

1641 **Irish Catholic** uprising leads to arguments as to who should lead an army to suppress it. Both **King** and **Parliament** recruit soldiers.

1642 Battle of **Edgehill:** the first battle between **King** and **Parliament.**

1643 Alliance of **Parliament** and **Scots Covenanters** against the **King.**

1644 Battle of **Marston Moor: Parliament** defeats **Charles I** and occupies **northern England.**

1644 Battle of **Lostwithiel: Parliament** loses control of **south west England** to the **King.**

1644 Battle of **Tippermuir: Scottish royalists** defeat the **Covenanters.**

1645 Battle of **Naseby: Parliament** defeats **Charles I** and wins control of the country.

During the Commonwealth there was an increase in religious sects and radical political groups, such as the **Levellers.** In **1653,** Cromwell took power as **Lord Protector.** His death in **1658** left a political vacuum, and in **1660** the Stuart monarchy was restored under **Charles II.**

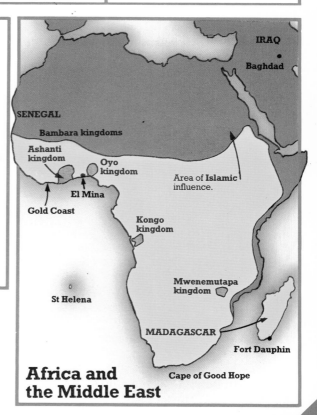

Africa and the Middle East

France under Louis XIV

Under **Louis XIV (1643-1715), France** became the dominant power in **Europe**. Louis won a series of brilliant military victories, which extended France's boundaries in the north and east. Many European powers feared his ambitions and various leagues were formed against him. Despite some major defeats towards the end of his reign, France's power and prestige was maintained for over a century.

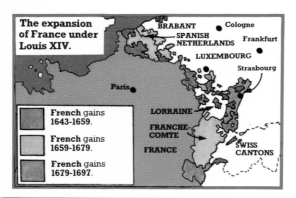

Louis XIV was nicknamed the **"Sun King"**. This is a decoration from a gate at **Versailles**.

Under **Colbert (1619-1683)**, Louis's finance minister, the economy was modernized. France made gains overseas, extending her colonial empire in **North America**.

Louis was able to control his nobles, and to exercise complete power himself. He is famous for his claim *"L'état, c'est moi"* (I am the state). His **autocratic*** rule set an example for other European rulers. Louis has been called the perfect **absolute monarch. Absolutism** is the belief that the power of the state is embodied in one person (the king), who is not accountable to anyone. This doctrine was developed by theorists such as **Hobbes (1588-1679)** and **Bodin (1530-1596)**.

The expansion of France under Louis XIV.

BRABANT — Cologne
SPANISH NETHERLANDS — Frankfurt
LUXEMBOURG
Strasbourg
Paris
LORRAINE
FRANCHE-COMTE
FRANCE
SWISS CANTONS

French gains 1643-1659.
French gains 1659-1679.
French gains 1679-1697.

Southern and Western Europe

1679 The **Exclusion Crisis**. A parliamentary bill prevents the **Catholic Duke of York** from succeeding his brother as **King of England**. **Charles II** dismisses **Parliament**.

1685 The revocation of the **Edict of Nantes*** forces half a million **Huguenots*** to flee **France**.

1685 Death of **Charles II** of **England**. Revolts break out as the **Catholic James II** becomes King.

The Coronation procession of **James II**.

1686 The **League of Augsburg** is formed between the **Holy Roman Empire***, Spain, Sweden, Saxony, **Bavaria** and the **Palatinate** against **France**.

1688 The **Glorious Revolution. William of Orange*** is invited by the **House of Lords** to save England from **Catholicism**. Start of the reign of **William and Mary (1688-1702)**. The end of the **Stuart dynasty*** and a decade of conflict between King and Parliament.

Plate showing **William** and **Mary**.

Northern and Eastern Europe

1676 **Swedes** defeat the **Danes** at the **Battle of Lund**.

1677 **Swedes** defeat the **Danes** at **Rostock** and **Landström**.

1677 War between **Russia** and **Turkey**.

1678 War between **Russia** and **Sweden**.

1679 Peace between **Sweden** and **Brandenburg**.

1679 **Russia** gains most of the **Ukraine** from the **Ottoman Empire*** by the **Treaty of Radzin**.

1683 **Ottoman Turks*** besiege **Vienna** and fail. The Turkish threat in **Europe** declines and **Austrian** power grows.

The **Siege of Vienna** by **Turks** in 1683.

1684 The **Holy League** (Holy Roman Empire*, **Poland** and **Venice**) is formed by **Pope Innocent XI** to fight the **Ottoman Turks***.

1687 Battle of Mohacs: **Ottoman Turks*** are defeated and **Hungary** becomes the hereditary possession of the **Habsburgs***.

French influence on European culture was at its height. Louis's court at **Versailles** was noted for its magnificence. There was a flowering of French literature, music and drama, producing writers such as **Corneille (1606-1684)**, **Racine (1639-1699)**, **Molière (1622-1673)** and **La Fontaine (1621-1695)**. French became spoken in courts and diplomatic circles throughout Europe.

Important dates

1667-1678 War of Devolution against **Spain**. Louis makes claims to **Brabant**.

1670 France occupies **Lorraine**.

1671 Spain and **United Provinces** ally against **France**.

1672-1678 War with the United Provinces.

1673 Holy Roman Emperor*, **Lorraine**, **Spain** and the **United Provinces** ally against **France**.

1678 Peace of Nijmegen ends the war with **Spain** and the **United Provinces**. **France** acquires **Franche-Comté**.

1681 Strasbourg is **annexed*** by **France**.

1682 Holy Roman Empire* and **Spain** form a defensive league against **France**.

1684 France invades the **Spanish Netherlands** and occupies **Luxembourg**.

1686 The League of Augsburg (Holy Roman Empire*, **Sweden, Spain, Saxony, Bavaria** and the **Palatinate**) against **France**.

1688-1697 War of the League of Augsburg: Louis takes **Heidelberg**. At the **Peace of Rijswijk** he is forced to make concessions, but keeps **Strasbourg**.

1701-1714 War of the Spanish Succession*: England, Netherlands, Austria and German states form a **Grand Alliance** against **France**.

The Americas

1676 Defeat of the Indians* in **New England** gives the **European** settlers control of the **North American** seaboard.

1679 De la Salle (French) explores the **Great Lakes**.

The **Niagara Falls**, discovered by **de la Salle**.

1680 The Portuguese establish the colony of **Sacramento, California**.

1681 William Penn (English) is granted a **charter*** to found **Pennsylvania**.

De la Salle exploring the **River Mississippi**.

1682 De la Salle claims **Louisiana** for **France** and takes the **Mississippi Valley**.

The Far East and Oceania

Lhasa, capital of **Tibet**.

1661 Two Jesuits* become the first **Europeans** to visit **Lhasa**.

1661-1688 Rule of King Narai of Siam. He tries to resist **Dutch** attempts to monopolize trade by enlisting **French** help. This proves unpopular and his dynasty is overthrown, along with the **French** garrisons.

17th century Siamese Buddha.

1662-1722 Rule of the powerful Manchu* Emperor, K'ang Hsi.

1663 French missionaries enter **Vietnam**.

1677 The Dutch extend their possessions in **Java**.

Africa, India and the Middle East

1662 Battle of Ambuila: the destruction of the **Kongo kingdom*** by the **Portuguese**.

Carving from the **Kongo kingdom**.

1662 Tangier, North Africa is **ceded*** to **England** by **Portugal**.

1664 The French East India Company* is founded.

1666-1668 Civil wars in India.

1668 English East India Company obtains control of **Bombay**.

1669 Aurangzeb* bans the **Hindu*** religion in **India** and persecutes Hindus.

1672 English Royal Africa Company is founded. Interest in **West African** trade increases, including the **slave trade***.

1674 The French establish a trading station at **Pondicherry**.

1674 Sivaji Bhonsla, leader of the **Marathas***, makes himself independent of the **Mogul Empire*** and founds a **Maratha state** in **India**.

Southern and Western Europe

1689 The **English Parliament** confirms the abdication of **James II* (Catholic)**. The **Bill of Rights** safeguards Parliamentary government and bars Catholics from the throne.

1690 The **Battle of the Boyne**: Irish Catholic supporters of the exiled **James II*** are defeated by the **English** forces.

1697 The **Treaty of Rijswik** ends the war between **France, Spain, England** and the **Netherlands**. France recognizes **William III** as the King of England, and also the **Protestant** succession of **Queen Anne (1702-1714)**.

St Paul's Cathedral, London.

St Paul's was built by **Sir Christopher Wren** between **1675-1710**.

1698 **England, France**, the **United Provinces** and the **Holy Roman Empire*** agree on the **Spanish Succession*** and the partition of the **Spanish Empire**. **Charles II** of Spain makes his first will, leaving his territories to the **Infant Elector Prince of Bavaria**.

1699 The death of the **Infant Elector of Bavaria** opens up the question of the **Spanish Succession***.

Northern and Eastern Europe

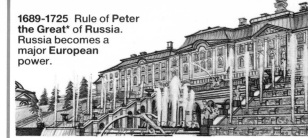

1689-1725 Rule of Peter the Great of Russia. Russia becomes a major European power.

The **Summer Palace, St Petersburg**, built by **Peter the Great**.

1690 **Ottoman Turks*** take **Belgrade** in a major counter-attack against the **Austrian Empire**.

1691 War continues between **Austria** and the **Ottoman Empire***. The Turks are defeated at **Zelankemen**. The **Habsburgs*** conquer **Transylvania**, which is brought under their control.

1695 **Russo-Turkish War**: **Peter the Great** fails to take **Azov**, an important fortress on the **Black Sea**, and returns to **Moscow**.

1696 **Russia** captures **Azov** from **Turkey** and conquers **Kamchatka**.

1697 **Battle of Zenta**: **Prince Eugene of Savoy** defeats the **Ottoman Turks***.

1699 **Treaty of Karlowitz**: the **Austrians** recover **Hungary, Croatia** and **Transylvania** from the **Ottoman Empire***. **Poland** takes the **Turkish Ukraine** and **Venice** gains the **Peloponnese** and **Podolia**.

The rise of the Manchu dynasty

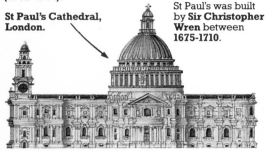

The **Manchu Summer Palace**, outside **Peking**. It was first built in the **18th century** by **Emperor Quiantong**.

Between **1600-1615** a **Manchu** nation emerged in **Manchuria, northern China**. The Manchus then expanded into other parts of China and invaded **Korea (1627)** and **Inner Mongolia (1629-1635)**. In **1644**, the **Ming dynasty*** was overthrown by rebels. The Manchus moved in, establishing a new dynasty – the **Ch'ing**, which ruled from **Peking** until **1911**. Despite Ming resistance in the south, by **1652** most of the country was under Manchu control.

There were unsuccessful rebellions by the governors of the southern and western provinces (the **Rebellion of the Three Feudatories 1674-1681**). These were followed by a long period of peace and population growth.

In the **17th** and **18th centuries, China** had a flourishing export trade in tea, porcelain, silk and crafts.

Ch'ing porcelain

Tea

Silk

Under **Emperor K'ang Hsi (1662-1722)**, the Manchus built up a powerful empire. It reached its greatest extent at the end of the **18th century** after wars with **Burma** and **Tibet**. Under **Emperor Ch'ien Lung (1736-1796)**, the Manchus became increasingly hostile to **Europeans** and to the imports of opium, which began in the late **18th century**.

The Americas

1683 **William Penn*** founds **Philadelphia** and the **Quaker** colony of **Pennsylvania**. Arrival of the first **German** immigrants. Penn makes a treaty with the **Indians***, which keeps Pennsylvania at peace.

Penn signing a treaty with the **Delaware Indians**.

1684 **Bermuda** becomes an **English Crown Colony***.

1691 **Massachusetts** absorbs the **Plymouth Colony*** and receives a new **charter***.

1691 The **English** found **Kingston, Jamaica**.

1699 The **French** found the colony of **Louisiana**.

The Far East and Oceania

1679 War between **Vietnam** and **Cambodia**. Cambodia loses the **Mekong Delta**.

1680 The **Dutch** join together their territories in the **East Indies**.

1683 **Manchus*** conquer **Formosa**.

1683 **Dutch** traders are admitted to **Canton, China**.

The port at **Canton**.

1684 The **Dutch** establish control in **Java**.

1885 **Chinese** ports are opened to foreign trade.

1688 Death of **King Narai*** of **Siam**. Siamese policies become isolationist until the **1850s**.

1688 **William Dampier (English)** explores **Australia**.

1697 The **Chinese** conquer **Western Mongolia**.

1699 The voyages of **Dampier** increase **European** knowledge of the **South Seas**.

Africa, India and the Middle East

The **Golden Temple, Amritsar**, the centre of the **Sikh** religion.

1676 Uprising of **Sikhs**, a reformed **Hindu*** sect, in **India**.

1680-1708 The **French** increase their trading interests in **Madagascar** and **Nigeria**.

1681 **Prince Akbar** leads an unsuccessful revolt in **India** against his father, **Aurangzeb***. Akbar flees to the **Deccan**, which Aurangzeb then conquers.

1686 **Madagascar** is annexed* by the **French East India Company***.

1687 The **English East India Company*** transfers its headquarters from **Surat** to **Bombay**.

1691 The **Mogul Empire*** reaches its greatest extent.

1696 The **English** establish a trading base at **Calcutta**.

Japan under the Tokugawas

In the **16th century**, there were almost continuous civil wars in **Japan***. However in **1600**, **Ieyasu Tokugawa** won power at the **Battle of Sekigahara** and in **1603** became **shogun** (military **dictator*** on behalf of the Emperor). The Tokugawa family ruled Japan from their capital **Edo (Tokyo)** until **1867**. Under the Tokugawas, Japan was strictly organized into social classes. There was a new system of **daimyo** (feudal lords) and **han** (fiefs*), closely regulated by the shogun himself.

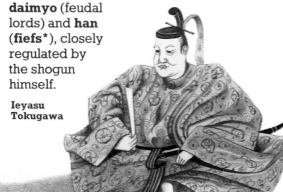

Ieyasu Tokugawa

The city of **Edo** had about a million inhabitants in the **18th century**. It may have been the largest city in the world.

After **1639**, Japan became virtually isolated from European contact until the **1850s**. This was a deliberate policy of the Tokugawas. The powerful ruler, **Iemitsu (1623-1651)**, expelled missionaries and forbade the Japanese to go abroad. During this period of peace and isolation, towns grew and trade flourished. By the **19th century** Japan was one of the most prosperous, well-governed and literate societies in the world.

The War of the Spanish Succession 1701-1713

The War of the Spanish Succession was fought by the major **European** powers to decide who would inherit the kingdom of the childless **Charles II** of **Spain**. With possessions in **Italy** and the **Spanish Netherlands** and rich colonies in the **Americas**, it was an important prize. There were strong claims both by the **French Bourbons*** and the **Austrian Habsburgs***.

Battle of Blenheim

The war was fought mainly in **Italy**, the **Netherlands** and **Germany**.

Major battles

1704 Battle of Blenheim. Prince Eugene and the Duke of Marlborough defeat the French and Bavarians.

1706 Battle of Ramillies. Marlborough wins control of the Southern Netherlands.

1708 Battle of Oudenarde. The French are forced to withdraw from the Southern Netherlands and Italy.

1709 Battle of Malplaquet. Prince Eugene and Marlborough defeat the French.

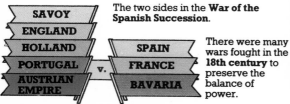

SAVOY
ENGLAND
HOLLAND
PORTUGAL
AUSTRIAN EMPIRE

v.

SPAIN
FRANCE
BAVARIA

The two sides in the **War of the Spanish Succession**.

There were many wars fought in the **18th century** to preserve the balance of power.

In **1700, Louis XIV*** proclaimed his grandson **Philip V** of Spain. Unwilling to see **France** united with Spain, **England** and **Holland** formed an alliance in support of the Austrian Emperor's son, **Charles**. They were joined in **1703** by **Portugal** and **Savoy** and won a series of brilliant victories, led by **John Churchill, Duke of Marlborough** and **Prince Eugene of Savoy**.

In **1711** Charles became **Emperor Charles VI** and ruler of the Austrian lands. This altered the balance of power, so the English and Dutch switched their support to Philip – on the condition that France and Spain would never unite. Peace was made at **Utrecht (1713-1714)**. Philip won Spain, and Austria acquired the Spanish Netherlands, **Naples, Sardinia** and **Milan**.

Maria Theresa

When **Emperor Charles VI** died in **1740**, his possessions fell to his 23 year old daughter, **Maria Theresa, Archduchess of Austria** and **Queen of Hungary** and **Bohemia (1740-1780)**. Although she

Maria Theresa

inherited a bankrupt and decaying empire, whose throne and lands were coveted by various claimants, she was to emerge as one of the great rulers of modern history.

Frederick II* of **Prussia** quickly took the opportunity of Charles's death to seize the rich Austrian province of **Silesia**. This, and the refusal by **Bavaria** (a rival claimant to the Austrian throne) and **France** to recognize a woman as Empress of Austria, led to the outbreak of the **War of the Austrian Succession (1740-1748)**.

FRANCE   PRUSSIA

BRITAIN   AUSTRIA

RUSSIA

The two sides in the **War of the Austrian Succession**.

Maria Theresa fought this war and the **Seven Years War* (1756-1763)**, to preserve the **Austrian Empire** for the **Habsburgs***. This she achieved brilliantly. In **1748** her husband was crowned **Holy Roman Emperor*** as **Francis I**. When he died in **1765**, she ruled alongside her son, **Joseph II (1765-1790)**. Maria Theresa is remembered not only for Austria's revival as a great power, but for her magnificent court and palaces.

Under **Maria Theresa**, **Vienna** became one of the cultural centres of **Europe**, where painting, architecture and, especially, music flourished.

Palace of Schönbrunn, Vienna.

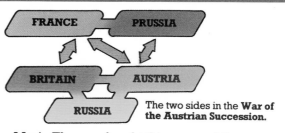

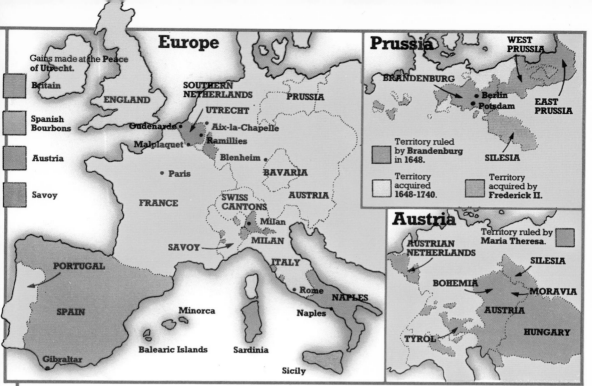

Europe

Gains made at the **Peace of Utrecht**.

- Britain
- Spanish Bourbons
- Austria
- Savoy

ENGLAND
SOUTHERN NETHERLANDS
PRUSSIA
UTRECHT
Oudenarde •
• Aix-la-Chapelle
Malplaquet •
• Ramillies
• Blenheim
BAVARIA
• Paris
AUSTRIA
FRANCE
SWISS CANTONS
• Milan
MILAN
SAVOY →
PORTUGAL
ITALY
SPAIN
• Rome
NAPLES
• Minorca
Naples
Gibraltar •
Balearic Islands
Sardinia
Sicily

Prussia

WEST PRUSSIA
BRANDENBURG
• Berlin
EAST PRUSSIA
• Potsdam
SILESIA

- Territory ruled by Brandenburg in 1648.
- Territory acquired 1648-1740.
- Territory acquired by Frederick II.

Austria

Territory ruled by **Maria Theresa**.

AUSTRIAN NETHERLANDS
SILESIA
BOHEMIA
MORAVIA
AUSTRIA
HUNGARY
TYROL

Frederick the Great and the rise of Prussia

Prussian soldiers

By the time of **Frederick William I**, the **Prussian** army was regarded as one of the best in **Europe**, with a reputation for perfect discipline and obedience. Their military uniforms were much admired and imitated.

At the beginning of the **17th century**, **Prussia** was a weak duchy under **Polish** overlordship, ruled by the **Elector of Brandenburg**, who held other, scattered territories within the **Holy Roman Empire***. Yet in just over 200 years, Prussia rose to become the nucleus of a **German Empire***. The rise began under the **Great Elector* (1640-1688)**, who built up a strong army, increased his territory and began a process of centralization. His successor, **Elector Frederick III**, was granted the title "**King in Prussia**" by the Emperor, and crowned himself **Frederick I** in **1701**. All his territories, including **Brandenburg**, came to be known as Prussia.

Prussia developed into a strong military state under **Frederick William I (1713-1740)**. His son, **Frederick II the Great (1740-1786)**, was interested in the ideas of the **Enlightenment*** and had published a book condemning the ideas of **Machiavelli***. However, within a year of becoming king, he invaded **Silesia** and provoked a war with **Austria**. By 1772 he had created a continuous Prussian state, making Prussia the second strongest German power, after Austria.

Frederick the Great's palace at **Sanssouci**, near **Potsdam**.

Frederick was an **enlightened despot***. He aimed to modernize the country and provide strong, efficient government, while keeping power in his own hands. He promoted education, agriculture and industry. He introduced a fairer legal system, abolished torture and censorship and declared religious freedom.

Northern and Eastern Europe

1700-1721 Great Northern War: a struggle for supremacy in the **Baltic** between **Russia** and **Sweden**.

1700 Sweden defeats **Russia** at **Narva**.

1701 Sweden invades **Poland**.

1701 Elector Frederick III of Brandenburg crowns himself **Frederick I***, "**King in Prussia***" (1701-1713).

Frederick I and his coronation procession in **Berlin**.

1703 Peter the Great* founds the city of **St Petersburg** in **Russia**.

1703-1711 Hungarians revolt against **Austria**.

1706 Treaty of Altranstadt: Augustus II (Elector of Saxony and **King of Poland**) renounces the Polish throne in favour of **Stanislaus Leszczynski**.

1708 Charles XII of Sweden invades **Russia**.

1709 Battle of Poltava. Major victory for **Russia** over **Sweden. Denmark** and **Saxony** ally with Russia against Sweden.

1710-1711 War between **Russia** and **Turkey**.

1710 Russia conquers **Swedish Baltic** provinces.

1711 Peter the Great* is forced to return **Azov** to the **Turks** and to withdraw from **Poland**.

1713 Peace of Utrecht: Elector of Brandenburg is recognized as **King of Prussia***.

1715 Turks expel the **Venetians** from the **Greek Morea**.

1716-1718 War between **Turkey** and **Austria**.

1718 Peace of Passarowitz: Turkey cedes **Belgrade** to **Austria** and **Hungary** is liberated from **Austria**.

1719 Russia invades **Sweden**. A coalition of **Denmark, Sweden, Prussia*** and **Britain** is formed to oppose Russia.

Russia under Peter the Great

Baltic Sea
Karelia
Narva
St Petersburg
Estonia
Livonia
Moscow
Hamburg
Orenburg
Black Sea Steppes
RUSSIA
Land acquired by Peter the Great
Moldavia
Poltava
Azov
Crimea
Caspian Sea

1721 Peace of Nystadt between **Russia** and **Sweden** ends the **Great Northern War**. Russia makes great gains (**Estonia, Livonia** and part of **Karelia**) and ends Swedish domination of the **Baltic**.

Southern and Western Europe

Venice, home of the **Italian** composer, **Vivaldi (1675-1741)**.

c.1700 Great age of **Baroque** music.

1701-1714 War of the Spanish Succession*.

1704 England seizes **Gibraltar** from **Spain**.

1707 Union of England and **Scotland** renamed **Great Britain**.

The **Union Jack**, combining the crosses of St George and St Andrew, is adopted as the national flag.

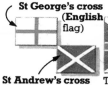

St George's cross (**English** flag)

St Andrew's cross (**Scottish** flag)   The first **Union Jack**

1713-1714 Peace of Utrecht ends the **War of the Spanish Succession***.

1714-1727 Reign of **George I of England**, the first king from the house of **Hanover**.

1715 Uprising in **Scotland** by **Jacobites**, supporters of **James Edward**, son of **James II*** and **pretender*** to the throne of **England** and **Scotland**.

1721-1742 Robert Walpole becomes the first **Prime Minister of Britain**.

1727-1729 War between **Spain** and **England** over **Gibraltar**.

1733 John Kay (British) invents the **flying shuttle loom**, which improves woollen weaving.

1734 Spain takes the kingdom of **Naples**.

1739 War of Jenkins' Ear between **England** and **Spain**. (Named after a **Captain Jenkins** who claimed that Spaniards had boarded his ship and cut off his ear.)

1740 The death of **Charles VI** of **Austria** and the succession of his daughter, **Maria Theresa*** (1740-1780), leads to the **War of the Austrian Succession*** (1740-1748).

1744 War breaks out between **France** and **Britain** in **Europe, India, North America** and the **West Indies** and lasts intermittently until **1815**.

1745 Second **Jacobite** uprising in **Scotland** attempts to put **Charles Edward Stuart (Bonnie Prince Charlie)** on the throne of **England** and **Scotland**. They are defeated by English troops at **Culloden (1746)**.

The **Battle of Culloden**

1746 France seizes the **Austrian Netherlands (Belgium)**. They are restored to **Austria** in **1748**.

1748 Peace of Aix-la-Chapelle ends the **War of the Austrian Succession***.

1750-1777 Reign of **King Joseph I** of **Portugal**. The chief minister, **Marquis de Pombal**, becomes virtual military **dictator*** from **1755**.

Africa and India

1697-1712 Expansion of the **Ashanti kingdom** in **West Africa**.

Ashanti gold weights.

c.1700 Decline of the **Yoruba kingdoms*** in **West Africa**.

c.1700 East Africa: rise of the **Bantu*** kingdom of **Buganda**.

c.1700 Oman controls **Zanzibar** and extends its influence along the **East African** coast at the expense of **Portugal**.

1705 Turkish rule is overthrown in **Tunis** and **Hussain Ibn Ali** establishes the **Hussainid dynasty**.

1707 Mogul Empire* disintegrates after the death of **Aurangzeb***.

1708 English East India Company possessions are divided into three presidencies: **Bengal**, **Madras** and **Bombay**.

1708 Revolution in **Ethiopia**: a difficult period after a time of expansion.

Illustration from a **17th century Ethiopian** manuscript of the *Gospels*.

1710 The **Dutch** leave **Mauritius** and the **French** take control.

1711 Tripoli becomes independent of **Turkey**.

1712-1755 Growth of **Bambara kingdoms** of the **Upper Niger**.

1714 Ahmed Bey establishes the **Karamanli dynasty** in **Tripoli**.

1714-1720 The **Marathas*** increase their territory in **northern India**.

1721 The French annex* **Mauritius**.

1723 British Africa Company acquires land in **Gambia**.

1726 France establishes a settlement on the **Seychelles**.

1731-1743 War between **Kano** and **Bornu**.

Bornu horsemen

Asia

1700 English East India Company* establishes a base in **Borneo**.

1709 Afghans rise against their **Persian** overlords and set up an independent **Afghan state**.

1714-1733 Reign of **King Taninganway Min** of **Burma**. Flourishing period of Burmese culture and power.

Shrine of **Schwe Dagon**, near **Rangoon, Burma**.

1715 China conquers **Mongolia** and **East Turkestan**.

1717 The **Bugis** from **Selangor, Malaya**, extend their influence in **Johore**. They control Johore from 1721-1777.

1720 China conquers **Tibet**.

1722-1730 Persia comes under Afghan rule.

1724-1727 War between **Persia** and **Turkey**.

1728 The **Bugis** invade **Perak**.

1729 War between the **Persians** and **Afghans**. The Afghans are expelled from **Persia** in **1730**.

1736-1747 Persia is ruled by **Nadir Khan**, who extends Persian influence in **India**.

Nadir Khan

1736-1796 China is ruled by the powerful emperor, **Ch'ien Lung**, who reorganizes the Manchu Empire* and reduces **Jesuit*** and **European** influence. A period of prosperity and increase in population.

1737-1747 Persians occupy **Afghanistan**.

Emperor Ch'ien Lung

1743 Mataram, **Java** becomes a Dutch vassal*.

America and Australasia

1701 Peace treaty between the **French** and **Indians** in **New France**.

1713 At the **Peace of Utrecht**, **Britain** acquires **Nova Scotia**, **Hudson Bay** and **Newfoundland** from **France**.

1714-1716 War between the **French** and **Indians** in **New France**.

1718 New Orleans is founded by the **French**.

1721-1722 Jacob Roggeveen (Holland) discovers **Samoa**, the **Solomons** and **Easter Island**.

Statues discovered by explorers on **Easter Island** in the **Pacific Ocean**.

1728 Bering, a Danish explorer sent by **Peter the Great***, discovers the **Bering Straits**.

1733 Foundation of **Georgia**, the last of the **Thirteen Colonies***.

Harbour at **Savannah, Georgia**.

1742 Russians explore **Alaska**.

1744-1748 King George's War, between **Britain** and **France** in **North America**.

1745 Bering discovers the **Aleutian Islands**.

1759 British, led by **General Wolfe**, capture **Quebec** from **France**.

1760 British take **Montreal** from the **French** and establish control of the **St Lawrence River**.

1762 Britain captures **Grenada** and **St Vincent**.

1763 The **Peace of Paris** ends **Anglo-French** rivalry in **North America**, establishing **British** supremacy. Britain gains **Canada** and most territory west of the **Mississippi River**. France cedes **Louisiana** to Spain. Britain acquires **Florida** from Spain, in exchange for **Cuba**.

1763 The capital of **Brazil** is moved to **Rio de Janeiro**.

1763 Britain draws the **Proclamation line** in **North America**, to define the limits of settler expansion. All land to the west of it is reserved for the **North American Indians**.

Northern and Eastern Europe

1722-1723 War between **Russia** and **Turkey**. Russia makes gains on the **Caspian Sea**.

1733-1735 War of the Polish Succession. France and **Sweden** support **Stanislaus Leszczynski***, but **Austria** and **Russia** support **Augustus II's*** son, who succeeds as **Augustus III**.

1735-1739 War between **Russia** and **Turkey**. Russia obtains **Azov** and extends to reach the **Black Sea**.

1740 Frederick II* (1740-1786) invades **Silesia**.

1741 Ivan VI of Russia is deposed by a military revolt and replaced by **Tsarina (Empress) Elizabeth (1741-1762)**. During her reign, **German** influence and the power of the nobility both expand.

Winter Palace, St Petersburg, built during **Elizabeth's** reign by an **Italian** architect, **Rastrelli (1754-1762)**.

1741 Prague is occupied by **French, Bavarian** and **Saxon** troops. **Charles Albert of Bavaria** is recognized as King of **Bohemia**.

1744 Frederick II* of **Prussia** invades **Bohemia** but is repelled by **Austrians** and **Saxons**.

1746 Russia and **Austria** ally against **Prussia**.

Southern and Western Europe

Praca de Commercio, Lisbon, rebuilt by **Pombal***

1755 Great earthquake kills tens of thousands and destroys **Lisbon, Portugal**.

1756 Alliances are formed between **Austria** and **France** and between **Britain** and **Prussia**.

1756-1763 Seven Years War: caused by rivalry between **Austria** and **Prussia** in **Europe** and between **Britain** and **France** in the colonies.

The participants of the **Seven Years War**.

Austria sided with her traditional enemy, France, in an attempt to win back **Silesia** from Prussia.

1759 Spain joins the **Franco-Austrian** alliance.

1761 Portugal is invaded by **Spain** for refusing to close its ports to **British** ships.

1762 Britain declares war on **Spain**.

1763 Peace of Paris ends the **Seven Years War**, leaving **Britain** as the major colonial power.

Peter the Great 1682-1725

Peter the Great was one of **Russia's** greatest rulers. He became joint **tsar** (emperor) in **1682**, at the age of ten, but from **1689-1725**, he was in effect sole ruler. He won brilliant victories against **Sweden** and **Turkey**, extending Russia's boundaries and making her stronger and safer. The wars with Sweden **(1700-1721)** marked the emergence of Russia as the main power in the **Baltic**.

St Petersburg became the capital in **1712**. It was designed on a grand scale, blending different European architectural styles, and was expanded and embellished under **Peter's** daughter, **Elizabeth**.

Peter the Great began **Russia's** rise to greatness. By the end of the century, it was the dominant power in **Eastern Europe**.

Peter wanted to make Russia a strong, westernized European power. In line with this policy, he built **St Petersburg**, a new city on the Baltic, in order to give himself a "window on the west". He introduced many reforms which helped to modernize and strengthen the country. He built new industries and a strong modern army, founded a navy and improved education. Despite all this, Russia remained an intensely conservative society, without a strong urban middle class. Many of the people were **serfs***, living under a **feudal system***.

Africa and India

1737 The **Marathas*** extend their power in **northern India**.

1737-1739 **Persians** occupy **western India**, attack **Delhi** and conquer the **Punjab**.

c.1740 The **Lunda** kingdom of **Kazembe** is established in **central Africa**.

1740-1756 **Bengal** becomes independent of the **Mogul Empire***.

1746 The **French** take **Madras**.

Town built on stilts in **Dahomey**.

1747-1748 **Yoruba*** conquer **Dahomey, Benin**.

1748 The **British** retake **Madras**: the beginning of intense **Anglo-French** rivalry in **India**.

1751 **Robert Clive*** defeats the **French** at **Arcot**: the end of French influence in **Madras**.

Asia

1751-1759 **China** overruns **Tibet, Dzungaria** and the **Tarim Basin**.

Battle between **Chinese** and **Tibetans**.

1752 The **Mons** people conquer **Upper Burma**. The Burmese leader, **Alaungpaya**, rebels and proclaims himself king. He gains control of most of Upper Burma.

1753 **Alaungpaya** takes the capital, **Ava**, and the **Shan states**.

1755 **Alaungpaya** seizes **Dagon** (renamed **Rangoon**) from the **Mons** in **Lower Burma**.

1755 War between the **Mataram Kingdom** in **Java** and the **Dutch** establishes the supremacy of the **Dutch East India Company*** in **Java**.

1756 **Alaungpaya** takes **Pegu** and now controls all **Burma**. His dynasty rules until 1885.

America and Australasia

1766 **Britain** occupies the **Falkland Islands**.

1767 New import taxes imposed by **Britain** on goods to the **North American colonies** upset the colonists.

1768-1779 **Captain Cook**, a **British** navigator, reaches **Australia** and **New Zealand**. He makes a scientific tour of **eastern Australia, New Caledonia, Tonga** and the **Sandwich Islands**.

Cook discovered species of animals and plants not yet known in **Europe**.

1770 **Captain Cook** claims **New Holland** (**New South Wales**) for **Britain**.

1770 The **Boston massacre**: **British** troops fire on a mob protesting against taxes.

Boston massacre

The American War of Independence 1775-1783

After the **Seven Years War* (1756-1763)** relations began to deteriorate between **Britain** and her **American** colonies. There were a number of causes: dislike of taxes, worries about growing British influence in **Canada** and desire for religious and political freedom. This led to the outbreak of rebellion in **April 1775**.

Battle of Lexington (April 1775): British troops were defeated by a group of settlers, led by **George Washington**.

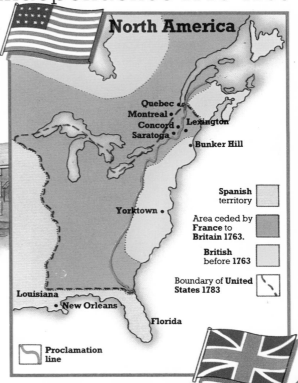

North America

- Quebec
- Montreal
- Concord — Lexington
- Saratoga
- Bunker Hill
- Yorktown
- Louisiana
- New Orleans
- Florida

Spanish territory

Area ceded by **France** to **Britain 1763**.

British before 1763

Boundary of **United States 1783**

Proclamation line

In **May 1775** representatives from all the colonies met at the **Philadelphia Congress** and set up an army, under **George Washington**. On **4 July 1776**, Congress signed the **Declaration of Independence**. After bitter fighting, the war ended in victory for the **Thirteen Colonies***. **Britain** recognized American independence at the **Treaty of Paris, September 1783**.

The growth of British power in India

During the **18th century**, **British** power in **India** grew impressively. The **Mogul Empire*** was in decline and local rulers asserted their independence. There were growing threats from warlike groups, such as the **Marathas*** in **central India** and the **Sikhs*** in the **Punjab**, and from hostile rulers in **Afghanistan** and **Persia**. This encouraged the **Europeans** to extend their settlements, partly as a protection against growing disturbances and unrest.

Calcutta, India's major port, in the 18th century.

In India, the **British East India Company** proved stronger than that of the **French**. In **1751** a young clerk, **Robert Clive**, also known as **Clive of India**, led a small force of 500 to victory against the French at **Arcot**. Between **1744-1763** there was fighting on the **Carnatic coast**, ending with the collapse of French power in India.

Portrait of the **Maratha** leader, **Sivaji**, with his warriors.

British domination was assured at the **Battle of Plassey (1757)**, when Clive's small force defeated the much larger army of the ruler of **Bengal**. The victory brought them effective control of Bengal, as well as **Bihar** and **Orissa**. The prosperity of the East India Company grew steadily, operating from its bases at **Calcutta**, **Madras** and **Bombay**. Lands and privileges were obtained from the wealthy native rulers in return for the Company's support and protection.

Clive obtained an edict from the **Mogul Emperor**, entitling the **British** to collect revenues for **Bengal**, **Bihar** and **Orissa**.

Northern and Eastern Europe

1747 **Sweden** allies with **Prussia** and **Russia** allies with **Britain**.

1757 **Russia** joins the **Franco-Austrian alliance** and invades **East Prussia**.

1758 **Russians** are defeated by **Prussians** at the **Battle of Zorndorf**.

1759 **Russians** and **Austrians** defeat the **Prussians** at the **Battle of Minden**.

1760 **Denmark** joins **Sweden** and **Russia** in a **Baltic alliance**.

1762 **Treaty of Hamburg** between **Sweden** and **Prussia**.

1762-1796 Reign of **Catherine II** ("the Great") of **Russia**. A **German** princess, she marries the heir to the throne, **Peter III**, and connives at his murder. Under her rule, Russia extends its boundaries, Russian culture develops and St Petersburg becomes a magnificent city. She introduces reforms in government and allows religious freedom.

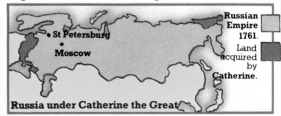

Russian Empire 1761.

Land acquired by Catherine.

• St Petersburg

• Moscow

Russia under Catherine the Great

Southern and Western Europe

1767 The **Spinning Jenny*** is invented by **James Hargreaves** (**British**).

1769 **Richard Arkwright** (**British**) invents the **water frame**, a water-powered spinning machine.

From c.1770s Great advances in **science and technology*** in **Europe**.

c.1770s Start of great age of **European** orchestral music: **Haydn** (1732-1809), **Mozart** (1756-1791) and **Beethoven** (1770-1827).

1778 **France** and **Holland** declare war on **Britain** in support of the **American*** colonists.

1779 **France** and **Spain** unsuccessfully beseige **Gibraltar**.

1781 **Joseph II** of **Austria** (1780-1790) introduces religious toleration and major reforms, including the abolition of **serfs***.

1782 **James Watt** (**Scottish**) invents the **rotary steam engine**.

18th century cellist.

One of **Watt's** steam engines.

The British gained the **Northern Sarkars** in **1768** and **Benares** and **Ghazipur** in **1775**. A series of wars brought more territory, as well as recognition of British **suzerainty*** by nearly all native rulers.

Map of India

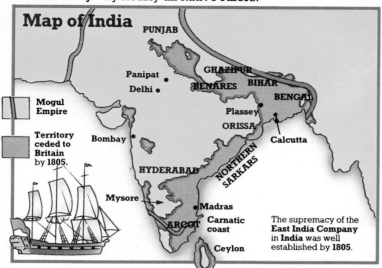

Mogul Empire

Territory ceded to Britain by 1805.

PUNJAB

Panipat
Delhi

GHAZIPUR
BENARES
BIHAR
BENGAL

Plassey
ORISSA
Calcutta

Bombay

HYDERABAD

NORTHERN SARKARS

Mysore

Madras
Carnatic coast

ARCOT

Ceylon

The supremacy of the **East India Company** in **India** was well established by **1805**.

The Indian possessions became so important that in **1784** the British government took control of their political administration. This was a major step towards **colonization***. In **1858**, after the **Indian Mutiny***, the government took over complete control and the East India Company lost all its governing powers.

Map of South East Asia

CHINA

BURMA

Ava
Pegu

Amarapura
Shan states

Dagon (Rangoon)

SIAM
Ayutthaya
Bangkok
Thonburi

Penang

MALAYA
Selangor
Johore

Sumatra

BORNEO

INDONESIA

Java

Mataram

Africa and India

1756 The Black Hole of Calcutta: the Nawab (ruler) of **Bengal** puts 146 **British** people into a tiny prison and many die.

Clive meeting the **Nawab of Bengal** after the **Battle of Plassey**.

1757 Battle of Plassey: the start of **British** supremacy in **India**.

1758 The Marathas* seize the **Punjab** and take **Lahore**.

1761 British capture **Pondicherry** and destroy **French** power in **India**.

1761 Battle of Panipat: the **Afghans** defeat the **Marathas***.

1761-1790 The rise of Sikh* power in **India**.

Asia

1757-1843 China reduces **European** influence by restricting foreign trade to **Canton**.

Foreign merchants at **Canton**.

1758 The Bugis people, who control **Johore**, recognize the **Dutch** tin trade **monopoly*** in **Malaya**.

1767 Burmese invade **Siam**, destroy the capital, **Ayutthaya**, and take control of most of the country.

1767-1769 China invades **Burma** and war breaks out between them. **Burma** becomes a **Chinese dependency***.

America and Australasia

1773 The Boston Tea Party. A gang of **Bostonians** throw chests of tea into the harbour, in protest against **British** taxes.

1775-1783 The American War of Independence*.

1775 Americans win the Battles of **Lexington** and **Concord**. The **British** win at **Bunker Hill**.

1776 American Declaration of Independence

1776 Spanish found **San Francisco**.

1777 British surrender at the **Battle of Saratoga**.

1778 France and **Spain** ally with the **Americans** against **Britain**.

1779 Captain Cook* is killed in **Hawaii**.

The **Boston Tea Party**

The death of **Captain Cook** in **Hawaii**.

Northern and Eastern Europe

1768-1774 War between **Russia** and **Turkey**.

1769 **Austria** seizes the **Polish** territories of **Lvov** and **Zips**.

1771 **Russia** conquers the **Crimea** and destroys the **Turkish** fleet.

1771-1792 Reign of **Gustavus III of Sweden**: a return to **autocratic*** rule.

The **Royal Palace, Stockholm**, at the time of **Gustavus III**.

1772 **First partition** of **Poland** by **Russia**, **Prussia** and **Austria**. Russia makes modest gains. Prussia **annexes*** most of the territory between **Pomerania** and **Eastern Prussia**. Austria annexes a large area north of **Hungary**.

1773-1775 Peasant uprisings in **Russia**, led by the **Cossack Pugachev**.

1774 Treaty of **Kuchuk-Kainarji** ends the **Russo-Turkish** war and increases Russian power. Russia gains ports on the **Black Sea** and the right to represent **Orthodox Christians** in the **Ottoman Empire***.

1781 **Austro-Russian** alliance against **Turkey**.

1783 **Russia** annexes the **Crimea**.

1787-1791 **Russia** goes to war with **Turkey** and gains the **Black Sea Steppes**.

1788 **Austria** declares war on **Turkey** and overruns **Moldavia**.

1788 **Gustav III of Sweden** declares war on **Russia**.

1791 The **King of Poland** adopts a new constitution to protect Poland from **Russian** interference. **Catherine II*** invades at the request of the nobles, destroys the constitution and divides large areas of Poland between **Russia** and **Prussia**.

1793 **Second partition** of **Poland**. Russia takes the eastern territory inhabited by **Ukrainians** and **White Russians**. **Prussia** gains **Danzig**, **Thorn** and **Posen** and expands its eastern frontier.

1795 **Third partition** of **Poland**. **Prussia** takes **Warsaw**. **Austria** takes **West Galicia** and **Russia** gains the remaining territory, including **Lithuania**.

Map of Polish partitions

Poland by the 17th century.

Poland after **First partition 1772**.

Poland after **Second partition 1793**.

Borders of **Russian**, **Austrian** and **Prussian** gains after **Third partition 1795**.

Southern and Western Europe

1784 **William Pitt the Younger** becomes **British** prime minister and dominates politics for 20 years.

1784 Power struggle in **Holland** between the **stadtholder***, the **Estates-General***, and the **Patriot** party, which aims at greater democracy.

1785 **Edmund Cartwright (British)** invents the **power loom**, which mechanizes weaving.

1787 Revolt in **Austrian Netherlands (Belgium)** against centralizing policy of **Joseph II***. Proclamation of a **Belgian Republic (1790)**, which is later reconquered by **Austria**.

1789 The storming of the **Bastille*** and the start of the **French Revolution***.

1791 **William Wilberforce's** motion for the abolition of **slavery*** is passed by the **British Parliament**.

Badge of the **Slave Emancipation Society**.

 Diagram of slave boat, showing the cramped conditions.

1792 **France** becomes a **republic*** and declares war on **Austria** and **Prussia**.

1793 Execution of **Louis XVI*** of **France** and his wife, **Marie Antoinette**. France declares war on **Britain**, the **Netherlands** and **Spain**.

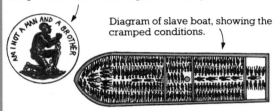

Louis XVI · Marie Antoinette

1793-1794 The **Reign of Terror*** in **France**.

1794 **France** invades and occupies the **Netherlands**. **William V of Holland** is deposed and the country declared the **Batavian Republic (1795-1806)**.

1795 A **coalition*** of **European** powers is formed against **France**.

1796 **Edward Jenner**, an **English** doctor, introduces **vaccination** against smallpox.

1796-1797 **French** troops, led by **Napoleon Bonaparte***, conquer much of **Italy**.

Napoleon leading his soldiers on his **Italian campaign**.

1798 **French** forces invade **Rome** and **Switzerland** and set up **Roman** and **Helvetic (Swiss) Republics**. Formation of a second **coalition*** against France.

1798 Unsuccessful rebellion by **Irishmen** seeking independence from **England**, led by **Wolfe Tone**.

1799 **Napoleon*** makes himself **First Consul**.

Africa and India

1764 Robert Clive* is appointed governor and commander-in-chief in Bengal (1764-1767).

1769-1772 James Bruce, a Scottish explorer, visits Ethiopia.

1774-1785 Warren Hastings becomes first governor-general of British India.

1775-1782 British and Marathas* at war in India.

c.1775 The Masai expand in East Africa, reaching the Ngong Hills.

1784 India Act: British government takes control of political affairs in British India.

1786 Turkish fleet is sent to restore control in Egypt, after a period of unrest.

1787 British establish a colony in Sierra Leone, West Africa.

c.1790 Buganda kingdom expands its frontiers and Luanda empire is at its height.

1795-1797 Mungo Park (British), reaches Segu and the River Niger.

Mungo Park travelling by boat.

1795 British take Cape of Good Hope, from the Dutch.

1796 The British take Ceylon from the Dutch.

1798-1799 Napoleon* invades Egypt. He is defeated by the British at the Battle of the Nile (1798), but defeats the Turks at Aboukir Bay (1799).

1799 British gain control over South India. Tippoo Sahib, ruler of Mysore (1750-1799), is killed fighting the British.

Tunis
Tripoli
EGYPT
GAMBIA
Upper Niger
Kano
Segu
Dahomey
Ashanti
Yoruba
Benin
Buganda
Masai
Luanda Empire
Zanzibar
Zimbabwe

Africa

Asia

1768 Taksin, a **Siamese** general, forms an army and drives out the **Burmese**. He defeats various local rulers and becomes the new **King of Siam**. His capital is at **Thonburi**.

1776 Siam regains independence.

18th century Siamese cloth.

1782 Taksin is deposed and executed after a rebellion. A leading general, **Prince Chakri**, seizes the throne. He becomes **Rama I**, first king of the **Chakri dynasty** and moves the capital to **Bangkok**. Under him **Siam** grows in prosperity, remaining the only **South East Asian** country uncolonized by **Europeans** in the **19th century**.

Grand palace, Bangkok.

1783-1823 The **Burmese** capital is moved to **Amarapura**.

1786 British East India Company* establishes a base in **Penang, Malaysia**: the first **British** settlement in **South East Asia**.

1787 Severe famine and rice riots in **Edo (Tokyo), Japan**.

Asia

East Turkestan
Mongolia
Dzungaria
Peking
Tarim Basin
Tibet
CHINA
JAPAN
Edo

1791-1792 War between **China** and **Tibet**.

1794 Aga Muhammed founds the Qaja dynasty in Persia, which lasts until **1925**.

America and Australasia

1780 British capture **Charleston**.

1780-1783 Tupac Amara, the last of the **Incas***, leads the **Peruvian Indians** in an unsuccessful revolt against the **Spanish**.

1781 The **British** surrender at **Yorktown**.

1783 Treaty of Paris: Britain recognizes the independence of the **Thirteen Colonies***, which become known as the **United States of America**. Britain gives **Florida** to **Spain**.

1787 A new constitution is drawn up in the **United States**, by **Thomas Jefferson**.

1788 Convicts are transported from **Britain** to **Sydney**, the first permanent British settlement in **Australia**.

1789 George Washington becomes first **President of the United States** (until 1797).

George Washington

1791 The Canada Act: Canada is divided into **English** and **French**-speaking territories.

1791 Slave* revolt in **Haiti** against the **French**, led by **Toussaint L'Ouverture**. He becomes lieutenant governor in **1796**.

1797 Britain takes **Trinidad** from **Spain**.

1798 Spanish found **Los Angeles**.

The Pacific

Bering Straits
Solomon Islands
Sandwich Islands
Samoa
Easter Island
Tonga

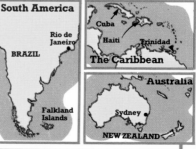

South America
Rio de Janeiro
BRAZIL
Falkland Islands

Cuba
Haiti
Trinidad
The Caribbean

Australia
Sydney
NEW ZEALAND

The Enlightenment

The **Enlightenment** or the **Age of Reason** are names used to describe a change in philosophy or outlook which came about in **Europe** between **c.1650-1750**. Its main centre was in **France**, although major contributions came from **Britain**, **Italy** and **Germany**. The Enlightenment contained many different elements. At its core was an optimistic belief in the powers of reason, or rational thought, and the possibility of human progress and development.

A meeting between the **French** writer, **Voltaire**, and **Frederick the Great***.

A **French** salon, the centre of intellectual life in the **18th century**.

The Enlightenment was an intellectual movement, characterized by a thirst for knowledge. There was a new respect for science and a curiosity about the societies, animals and plants of remote countries, many of which were just being discovered. One of the greatest achievements was the vast *Encyclopédie* **(1751-1777)**, which tried to record the total stock of knowledge at the time.

The *Encyclopédie* was compiled by the **French** philosopher, **Diderot**, and contained articles by many different scientists and philosophers. This engraving demonstrates canal locks.

The idea that people could themselves discover more about the world led to a rejection of authority. It posed an important challenge to the Church, who rightly felt threatened, even though most of the leading philosophers and scientists of the period were devout Christians. Some key figures, such as **Galileo***, were imprisoned. Others, like **Descartes**, had their books banned.

However, a number of Europe's **autocratic*** rulers, the so-called **enlightened despots***, supported the new trends. Universities, scientific societies and other institutions were set up and science and philosophy progressed rapidly. Humanitarian reforms were introduced, such as religious toleration.

Important people in the Enlightenment

1694-1778 Voltaire: French writer who criticized the Catholic Church.

1596-1650 René Descartes: French mathematician and philosopher who stressed the value of reason and logic.

1642-1727 Isaac Newton*: English scientist who discovered, among other things, the laws of gravity **(1666)**.

Scientific discoveries in the 18th century

The **Enlightenment** and the development of new **industries*** gave an impetus to scientific thought and many important inventions and discoveries were made.

1718 Gabriel Fahrenheit (German) invents the **mercury thermometer**.

1735 Carolus Linnaeus (Swedish) writes his **classification of nature**.

1742 Anders Celsius (Swedish) invents the **centigrade thermometer**.

1752 Benjamin Franklin (American) invents the **lightning conductor**.

1766 Henry Cavendish (English) identifies **hydrogen**.

1771 Karl Scheele (Swedish) discovers **oxygen**.

1772 Rutherford (English) discovers **nitrogen**.

1775 James Watt (Scottish) invents the **steam engine**.

1777 Antoine Lavoisier (French) shows that air consists of oxygen and nitrogen. He identifies the role of oxygen **(1782)** and produces the first **table of chemical elements (1890)**.

1790 Luigi Galvani (Italian) discovers **contact electricity**.

1783 Montgolfier brothers (French) make the first ascent in a hot-air balloon.

The **Montgolfier balloon**

The French Revolution

The storming of the
Bastille, 14 July 1789

On **5 May 1789**, faced with mounting debts and growing unrest, **Louis XVI** called a meeting of the **Estates-General**, a sort of national parliament, which had not met since **1614**. It consisted of representatives from the three **Estates: Nobility, Clergy** and **Commoners**. On **17 June** the Commoners decided to form their own **National Assembly**. This move marked the start of the **French Revolution**.

Rumours soon swept **Paris** that the King was about to dissolve the Assembly, and an angry mob stormed and destroyed the **Bastille** prison. Revolution now swept the country. There were peasant uprisings in rural areas.

The revolutionaries were known as **sans-culottes**, because they wore trousers, rather than knee breeches (which the nobles wore).

Execution of
**Louis XVI
21 June 1793**

The nobility were stripped of their titles and many fled abroad for safety. In **1790** the King had to accept a new constitution, based on the abolition of **feudal*** rights and a limited monarchy.

The King refused to co-operate and in **June 1791** tried to flee, but was discovered, taken back to Paris and forced to accept an even more **radical*** constitution. In **1792**, the Assembly was replaced by a **National Convention**, which declared **France** a **republic***. Power passed to a political group, the **Girondins**, and Louis XVI was executed for treason.

By **1793** the Girondins were superceded by a more extremist group, the **Jacobins**, led by **Maximilien Robespierre**. A period of terror and violence began. All those suspected of opposing the revolution, whether royalists or revolutionaries, were put to death. This continued until his fall and execution in **July 1794**.

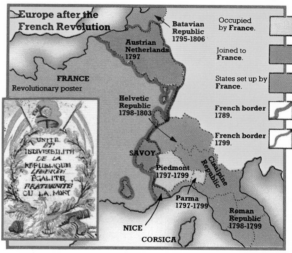

Europe after the French Revolution

FRANCE
Revolutionary poster

Occupied by **France**.

Joined to **France**.

States set up by **France**.

French border 1789.

French border 1799.

Batavian Republic 1795-1806

Austrian Netherlands 1797

Helvetic Republic 1798-1803

SAVOY

Piedmont 1797-1799

Cisalpine Republic

Parma 1797-1799

NICE

CORSICA

Roman Republic 1798-1799

From **1795-1799** France was ruled by a middle-class dominated government, the **Directory**, which became increasingly dependent on a brilliant young officer, **Napoleon Bonaparte***. From **1792-1815** France was almost continuously at war. Other **European** powers felt threatened, first by the spread of revolution, and later by Napoleon. By **1797** France had made great gains, taking the **Austrian Netherlands**, **Savoy** and **Nice** and establishing republics in **Italy** and the **Netherlands** (see map above). The revolution inspired **egalitarian*** movements everywhere. Some countries were forced to undertake internal reforms, and in others, new **nationalist*** forces were unleashed.

Napoleonic France

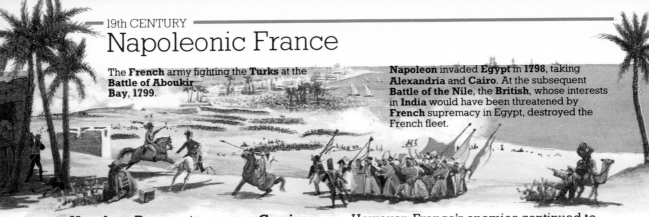

The **French** army fighting the **Turks** at the **Battle of Aboukir Bay, 1799.**

Napoleon invaded **Egypt** in **1798**, taking **Alexandria** and **Cairo**. At the subsequent **Battle of the Nile**, the **British**, whose interests in **India** would have been threatened by **French** supremacy in Egypt, destroyed the French fleet.

Napoleon Bonaparte, a young **Corsican** general, rose to political power in **France** after winning his reputation in the **Italian*** (1796) and **Egyptian campaigns*** (1798-1799). In **1799**, he made himself **First Consul** (effectively military **dictator***) and disbanded the by then corrupt and ineffective **Directory***.

In **1804**, **Napoleon** had himself crowned **Emperor Napoleon I.** He then crowned his wife, **Josephine**, Empress.

Napoleon proved successful as a statesman and administrator too. He introduced the *Code Napoléon* (**1804**), which confirmed the property rights granted to peasants during the **French Revolution***. In **1805**, a new coalition of **Britain**, **Austria**, **Russia** and **Sweden** allied against France. Napoleon won important victories, against Austria and Russia at **Austerlitz (1805)**, **Prussia** at **Jena (1806)** and Russia at **Friedland (1807)**. He forced **Francis II** of Austria to abandon the title of **Holy Roman Emperor*** and reorganized the **German** states.

A standard from one of the infantry divisions of **Napoleon's Grand Army.**

By **1812**, Napoleon controlled most of **Western Europe**. He installed members of his family as rulers in **Spain**, **Italy** and **Westphalia** (in **western Germany**). Taxes were levied and French institutions and laws introduced.

However, France's enemies continued to oppose his ambitions. Britain supported a resistance movement in **Spain** (the **Peninsular War 1808-1814**). In **1812**, Napoleon invaded Russia, with disastrous results.

Napoleon's army was under-equipped and ill-prepared for the harsh winter. Of 600,000 men only about 30,000 returned.

The retreat of the **Grand Army** from **Moscow**.

In **1813**, joint Austrian, Prussian and Russian forces won a series of major victories in Germany. This led to the collapse of the **Napoleonic system** in Germany, **Holland** and **Upper Italy**. Meanwhile the British defeated the French in Spain and invaded France itself. In **April 1814**, the allies reached **Paris**. Napoleon was exiled to **Elba** and replaced with a **Bourbon*** king, **Louis XVIII**.

At the **Battle of Waterloo**, Napoleon was defeated by the **Prussians**, led by **General Blücher**, and the **British**, led by the **Duke of Wellington.**

A year later, Napoleon made a dramatic escape from Elba and retook power for a brief period, known as the **Hundred Days**. He was finally defeated at **Waterloo** in **1815** and the threat of French domination of Europe was ended. British naval supremacy was assured, while Russia and Austria now became the major continental powers. Napoleon was exiled to **St Helena**, where he died in **1821**.

The Industrial Revolution

In the **mid 18th century**, **Britain** was already richer than most other **European** nations, with fertile and well-farmed land and a flourishing woollen cloth industry. From **c.1750-1850** her wealth grew rapidly, mainly due to the growth of new industries. These were transformed by new **inventions***, such as textile machinery and steam power. The series of changes which produced this growth is known as the **Industrial Revolution**.

The **Industrial Revolution** brought social changes, with the building of towns catering for large numbers of workers.

The **Spinning Jenny**, the first successful spinning machine, invented by **James Hargreaves (1767)**.

The Industrial Revolution was more than simply a collection of new inventions. Improved agriculture played a part and the development of banking, foreign trade and transport (road, canal and railway) made the movement of goods cheaper and more efficient.

The world's first iron bridge, near **Coalbrookdale**, built in **1777**.

During the **19th century**, more and more countries in **Europe** began building industries along similar lines. **Germany** expanded rapidly, encouraged by the development of railways from the **1840s** and the dismantling of internal customs barriers. The **United States** and, by the **20th century**, **Japan**, followed suit. As the industrialized countries became richer, a gap widened between them and the undeveloped areas of the **Third World***.

A gun made by the **German** company, **Krupps**, shown at the **Paris Exhibition** in **1867**.

Europe in 1810

- **France** under **Napoleon**
- Dependent states
- Areas ruled by **Napoleon's** family.

NORWAY
SWEDEN
DENMARK
BRITAIN
WESTPHALIA
IRELAND
London
RUSSIA
Friedland
Moscow
WARSAW
Waterloo
Jena
Confederation of the Rhine
Paris
Helvetic Republic
AUSTRIAN EMPIRE
Austerlitz
Vienna
FRANCE
ITALY
Illyrian provinces
Black Sea
Corsica
SPAIN
NAPLES
Elba
Sardinia
Sicily
Trafalgar

The Crimea

This map shows battles of the **Crimean War***.

Black Sea
Alma
Inkerman
Sevastopol
Balaclava

The Balkans

AUSTRIA-HUNGARY
ROMANIA
Black Sea
BOSNIA
SERBIA
BULGARIA
Adrianople
ALBANIA
GREECE
TURKEY
MONTENEGRO
Navarino

Crimean War, 95; **inventions**, 86; **Third World**, 114.

Asia

1800 **British** begin importing opium into **China**.

1801 **Russia** takes **Georgia**.

1801 **British East India Company*** takes **Tanjore** and the **Carnatic**.

1802 **Siam** annexes **Battambang, Cambodia**.

1802 Wars in the **Deccan** lead to the supremacy of the **British East India Company*** in **India**.

1802 **Ceylon** becomes a **Crown Colony***.

1809-1824 Reign of King **Rama II** of **Siam**. Start of contacts with **Europe** after a period of isolation.

1811-1813 **British** occupy **Dutch** colony of **Java**.

1811 War between **Russia** and **Persia**. Russia makes gains in the **Caucasus**.

1815-1816 **Britain** defeats the King of **Kandy** and **Ceylon** becomes British.

1817 Expansion of **Burmese** power in **Assam**.

1817-1818 War between **British East India Company*** and the **Marathas*** ends in Maratha defeat. The Company becomes effective ruler of **India**.

1818 **Java** is restored to the **Dutch**.

1819 **Singapore*** is founded by **Sir Stamford Raffles***, as a base for the **East India Company***.

South East Asia

Peking · Tientsin · CHINA · Kowloon · TONGKING · Hong Kong · Formosa · ANNAM · SIAM · CAMBODIA · COCHIN CHINA · PHILIPPINES · Indo-China

1821 **Siam** invades **Kedah**.

1824-1826 First **Anglo-Burmese War**. **British** take **Lower Burma** and **Assam**.

1825-1830 **Java War**: **Indonesians** revolt against the **Dutch**.

1826-1828 War between **Persia** and **Russia**. Russia gains **Armenian** provinces.

1830 **British East India Company*** takes **Mysore**.

1831-1840 **Syria** and **Lebanon** are occupied by **Egypt**.

1833 **British East India Company*** trade **monopoly*** with **India** and **China** is abolished.

A **clipper**, a ship developed in the **USA** in the **1820s**, for trade with the **East**.

1838 War between the **British** and **Afghans**.

1839 **Britain** takes **Aden**.

Africa and Oceania

1802-1803 The **Australian coast** is surveyed by **English** navigator, **Matthew Flinders**.

1802 **Trutor** and **Somerville** (**British**) explore **Bechuanaland**.

1804 **Hobart, Tasmania**, is founded.

1805-1848 **Mehemet Ali** is installed as **Pasha** (viceroy) of **Egypt**. His dynasty rules until **1952**.

Mehemet Ali at his palace in **Alexandria**. During his reign, **Egypt** was opened to **European** influences.

1806 The **Cape** becomes a **British** colony (recognized in **1814**).

1807 The **slave*** trade is abolished within the **British Empire**.

1807 **Sierra Leone** and **Gambia** become **British Crown Colonies***.

1808 Import of **slaves*** into the **USA** is prohibited.

1810 **Britain** takes **Mauritius** from **France**.

1810 **West Africa**: the **Yoruba*** kingdom breaks up.

1818 The **Mfecane**, or time of troubles, in **southern Africa**. **Shaka the Great** founds the **Zulu empire** and many local tribes are driven north.

1820-1821 **Egypt** conquers the **Sudan**.

1822 The **USA** founds **Liberia, West Africa**, as a colony for freed negro **slaves***.

1823-1831 War between the **British** and **Ashanti***.

1826 The **Black War** in **Tasmania** between settlers and **aborigines** (the native people).

1829 **Swan River Settlement** is founded in **Western Australia**.

1830 **French** forces conquer **Algiers**. The start of the French **colonization*** of **Algeria**.

1834 Settlement at **Port Phillip Bay** (**Melbourne**).

1835 **Tripoli** becomes an **Ottoman*** province.

1835-1837 The start of the **Great Trek** of **Boers** (**Dutch** settlers) from the **Cape**.

The **Dutch** trekkers set off north to find new lands, founding colonies in **Natal**, the **Orange Free State** and the **Transvaal**.

1838 **Boers** defeat the **Zulus** at the **Battle of Blood River**, **Natal**.

1839 **Dutch** settlers found the **Republic of Natal**.

1839 **New Zealand** is proclaimed a **British** colony.

1840 **Treaty of Waitangi**: **Maori** chiefs give **sovereignty*** over **New Zealand** to Britain.

Maoris.

Western Europe

1801 Act of Union unites **Britain** and **Ireland**.

1804 Richard Trevithick (English) builds the first **steam train**.

Trevithick's steam engine.

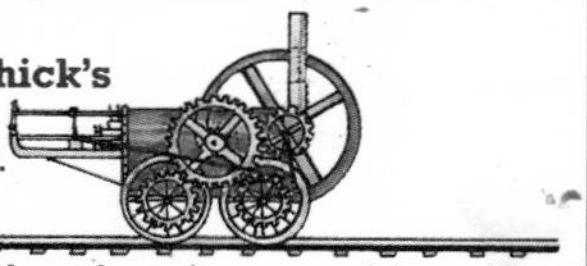

1804 Napoleon* crowns himself **Emperor of France**. The period of the **First Empire (1804-1815)**.

1805 Battle of Trafalgar.

The **British**, led by **Admiral Nelson**, defeat the **French** fleet.

1808 Napoleon* occupies **Spain** and installs his brother, **Joseph** as king. Spanish resistance leads to the **Peninsular War*** (1808-1814).

1810 Napoleon* marries **Princess Marie-Louise** of **Austria**. He is at the peak of his power and controls most of **Europe**.

1814 Napoleon* is forced to abdicate. **King Louis XVIII** is restored.

1815 The Hundred Days*, followed by the defeat of **Napoleon*** at **Waterloo***.

c.1820s Romantic movement in the **European** arts.

1820 Revolutions in **Spain** and **Portugal**.

1822 First fixed photographic image is produced by **French** inventor **J-N Niepce**.

The **Stockton** to **Darlington** railway.

1825 First passenger steam railway opens in **England** from **Stockton** to **Darlington**.

1830 Belgian uprising against **Dutch** rule leads to independence.

1830 July Revolution in **France** overthrows **King Charles X**, and installs **Louis Philippe**.

1832 Reform Act in **Britain** gives the middle classes the vote.

Eastern Europe (including Italy)

1800 Alessandro Volta, an **Italian**, invents the battery.

1804-1813 Serbs revolt against their **Ottoman*** rulers.

1806 Napoleon* dissolves the **Holy Roman Empire***.

Napoleon's troops entering **Vienna**.

1806-1812 War between **Russia** and **Turkey**.

1809 Russia gains **Finland** from **Sweden**.

1812 Napoleon* invades **Russia**.

Great fires break out in **Moscow** the day after **Napoleon's** troops arrive. The cause is still unclear.

1815 The Congress of Vienna meets to settle post-war boundaries and other problems, led by **Austrian** statesman, **Prince Metternich**.

1821-1829 Greek War of Independence* against **Turkey**.

1827 Battle of Navarino: **Greece's** allies destroy the **Turkish** fleet (see **Greek War of Independence***).

Battle of Navarino

1829 Treaty of Adrianople. Russia makes gains in the **Balkans**. **Turks** agree to **Greek** independence.

1848* The Year of Revolutions.

1849 Austria wins back her **Italian** possessions, after defeating **Sardinia-Piedmont**.

1849 Garibaldi* marches to **Rome** and deposes the **Pope** but the revolt is crushed.

The Americas

1803 The USA buys **Louisiana**.

American settlers moving to **Louisiana**.

1803 Britain acquires **British Guiana, Tobago** and **St Lucia**.

1808 Uprisings against the **Spanish** begin in **New Spain**.

1808-1825 Wars of independence from **Spanish** and **Portuguese** colonial rule in **South** and **Central America**. **Argentina** (Provinces of Rio de la Plata) declares independence in 1810, **Paraguay** and **Venezuela** in 1811, **Colombia** in 1813, **Uruguay** in 1814 and **Chile** in 1816.

South America

Map labels: NEW GRANADA, COLOMBIA, ECUADOR, PERU, CHILE, BRITISH GUIANA, VENEZUELA, BRAZIL, BOLIVIA, PARAGUAY, URUGUAY, ARGENTINA, Falkland Islands

Great Colombia

Provinces of the Rio de la Plata

1812 War between the **USA** and **Britain**, over trade.

1816 Argentina receives formal independence from **Spain**.

1818 A boundary is fixed between the **USA** and **Canada**.

1818 Chile becomes independent.

1819-1830 The state of Great Colombia is set up under **Simon Bolivar**. It achieves independence from **Spain** in 1822.

Simon Bolivar (1783-1830) was one of the great figures of the **Latin American** independence movement.

1819 Spain loses **Florida** to **United States**.

1848: Year of Revolutions

During **1848** a wave of revolutions swept **Europe**. The causes were many. In **France** and **Austria** there was opposition to conservative rulers, coupled with economic difficulties such as rising prices and food shortages. In **Italy** and **Hungary** there were **nationalist*** movements aimed at overthrowing foreign domination. And in **Germany** and Italy, there were calls for **unification*** and the founding of national states.

Uprising in **Paris**.

In **February 1848** an uprising in **Paris** forced **King Louis Philippe** to abdicate. The **Second Republic** was set up, with **Prince Louis Napoleon**, a nephew of **Napoleon***, as the first president. This caused fear and concern among Europe's **absolute*** rulers. It was followed by an uprising in **Vienna** in **March** and **Emperor Ferdinand** was forced to abdicate in favour of his nephew, **Francis Joseph**.

The inauguration of the **Second Republic** in **Paris**.

These events encouraged rebellions against Austrian rule in Italy (backed by **Sardinia**), **Bohemia** and **Poland**, and in **1849** in Hungary. There was revolt and disorder in many German states too. However, the **1848** rebellions were unsuccessful almost everywhere, except in France. After momentary panic, the old order managed to reassert itself. By **1849**, Austria had restored its position in Italy and **Eastern Europe** and attempts at unification in Germany had failed.

However, the events of **1848** had shaken the establishment severely, giving such forces as **liberalism*** and **nationalism*** a boost. **Socialism*** also dates from this time. **1848** was the year the *Communist Manifesto** was first published.

Scene from the **Berlin** uprising, **March 1848**.

1848 uprisings

12 Jan	Revolution in Sicily.
21-24 Feb	Revolution in Paris.
12 Mar	Revolution in Venice.
13-15 Mar	Revolution in Vienna.
18-19 Mar	Revolution in Berlin.
22 Mar	Revolution in Milan.
23 Apr	Polish uprising in Warsaw.
15 May	Communist* riot in Paris.
17 June	Czech revolt in Prague.

American Civil War

By the middle of the **19th century** the northern and southern states of the **USA** were growing further apart. The north was richer and more industrialized, while the south, with its economy based on cotton plantations, was increasingly dependent on **slavery***. As the movement for the abolition of slavery gained influence, bitter rows developed in **Congress***. The election in **1860** of an anti-slavery candidate, **Abraham Lincoln**, as president prompted seven southern states to break away and form the **Confederate States of America (1861)**. This led to civil war.

The United States

Canada

Unionist flag

California

Utah

New Mexico

Texas

Pennsylvania

Confederate flag

Georgia

Louisiana

Florida

Unionist states

Confederate states

Mexico

States that joined the **Confederacy**.

The **Northern Unionists** fought to preserve the unity of the USA. They defeated the **Southern Confederates**, after bitter fighting and great loss of life, and slavery was finally abolished.

Nationalism

Nationalism, the self-assertion of nations or groups of peoples with a common language or culture, was the major political force of the **19th century**. In many places it took the form of a struggle for independence from foreign rule. There were nationalist protests and uprisings in **Italy**, **Hungary**, **Poland**, **Belgium**, the **Balkans*** and **Norway**. It was often linked with another powerful force, **liberalism***, and so became associated with the desire for **parliamentary democracy***.

The revolt provoked cruel reprisals by the **Turks** and massacres by both sides.

Greek nationalist soldiers.

The first effective nationalist struggle broke out in **Greece** in **1821**. **Russia**, **Austria** and **Britain** intervened, since any possible break-up of the **Ottoman Empire*** would have involved changes to the balance of power. They forced **Turkey** to accept Greek independence in **1827**. In **1832**, **Prince Otto of Bavaria** became the first king of the new nation.

In 1867, the **Austrian Empire** was renamed the **Austro-Hungarian Empire**. This was known as the **Dual Monarchy**.

The **Austrian** Emperor being crowned **King of Hungary** in 1867.

The **1848*** rebellions shook the stability of the **Habsburg Empire***. In **1867**, the Hungarians demanded and were given self-government. In **Germany** and Italy, each made up of separate states, movements began which aimed at uniting them under single national states. However, their eventual **unification** owed less to national feeling than to the expansionist ambitions of two states, **Piedmont** and **Prussia***, and their chief ministers, **Cavour** and **Bismarck**.

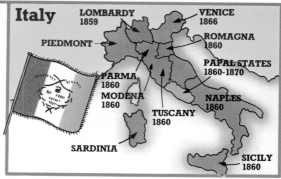

Italy
- LOMBARDY 1859
- VENICE 1866
- PIEDMONT
- ROMAGNA 1860
- PAPAL STATES 1860-1870
- PARMA 1860
- MODENA 1860
- NAPLES 1860
- TUSCANY 1860
- SARDINIA
- SICILY 1860

Cavour allied with **France** against Austria. Austria was beaten at **Magenta** and **Solferino (1859)** and lost most of her Italian possessions. Piedmont gained **Lombardy**. In **1860**, most of **northern Italy** was joined to Piedmont following a **plebiscite***. By the end of the year, **southern Italy**, which had been conquered by **Garibaldi**, was also absorbed. **Venice** followed in **1866** and **Rome** in **1870**.

Garibaldi, an **Italian** patriot, led an army of 1,000 volunteers and conquered **Naples** and **Sicily** in **1860**.

By the **1850s**, Prussia was the leading economic power in Germany. By a series of diplomatic and military manoeuvres, Bismarck ensured her political leadership as well. He defeated Austria over **Schleswig-Holstein (1866)** and incorporated the **Northern German states** into a **North German Confederation (1867)**. Prussia's victory over France **(1870)** convinced the **Southern Germans** that they should join. In **1871**, the King of Prussia became emperor of a united Germany.

Germany
- SCHLESWIG
- HOLSTEIN
- Friedland
- PRUSSIA
- Jena
- Berlin
- WESTPHALIA
- BAVARIA
- FRANCE
- Vienna
- SWITZERLAND

Boundaries of:
- German Empire 1871
- North German Confederation 1867

1848, 92; Balkans (see map, 89); Habsburg Empire (see Maria Theresa, 76), liberalism, 113; Ottoman Empire, 64-65; parliamentary democracy, 114; plebiscite, 114; Prussia, 77.

Asia

1839-1842 China's attempt to ban the **British** trade in **Indian** opium to China leads to the **Opium War.** As a result, China is opened to British trade and Britain acquires **Hong Kong.**

Canton harbour in **China** in the **19th century.**

1841 Egypt loses **Syria** to **Turkey.**

1842 Britain takes **Labuan, Borneo.**

1843 The **British** conquer and take **Sind.**

1845-1846 First Anglo-Sikh War. The **British** gain control of the **Punjab.**

1847 French expedition to **Cochin-China.**

1848-1849 Second Anglo-Sikh War. The **British** add the **Punjab** to their territory in **India.**

1850-1864 The Taiping Rebellion in **China** against the decaying **Manchu dynasty*.**

1852 Second Anglo-Burmese War. British take **Pegu.**

1853 United States gunboats force **Japan** to open its ports to foreign trade. **European** contacts with Japan increase after a long period of isolation. A time of growing unrest and weakness for the **Tokugawa dynasty*.**

Americans arriving in **Japan.**

1856 British East India Company* takes **Oudh.**

1857-1860 Anglo-French occupation of **Peking.**

1857 The outbreak of the **Indian Mutiny:** a series of uprisings against the **British** by **Bengali** soldiers, which soon spreads through **northern India.**

The rebels capture **Delhi** and besiege the **British residency*** at **Lucknow.**

1858 The **Indian Mutiny** is finally put down at the **Relief of Lucknow.** The **British** government takes over the powers of the **East India Company*** and administers **India** directly, through a **viceroy** (governor). The **Mogul*** emperor is deposed and the dynasty comes to an end.

Africa and Oceania

1840 Captain Wilkes, an **American** explorer, discovers the **Antarctic coast.**

1841 David Livingstone, a **Scottish** missionary, makes his first journey of exploration in **Africa.**

1842 Boers* establish the **Orange Free State.**

1842-1843 Wars between **Boers*** and **British** in **Natal.**

1844 War between **France** and **Morocco.**

1844-1848 Unsuccessful uprisings by **Maoris** (natives of **New Zealand**) against the **British.**

1844-1845 Charles Sturt, an **English** explorer, leads an expedition into **central Australia.**

1846-1847 British defeat **Bantus*** in **South Africa.**

1847 Liberia becomes independent.

1848 Otago, New Zealand, is founded.

1851 Gold is discovered at **Bathurst, Victoria.**

1853 Richard Burton (British) reaches **Mecca*.**

1853-1854 Gold rush in **Victoria, Australia.**

1854 Britain recognizes the independence of the **Transvaal.**

1855 Livingstone discovers the **Victoria Falls,** southern Africa.

1856 Pretoria becomes capital of **Transvaal. Natal** becomes a **British Crown Colony*.**

1858 John Speke, a **British** explorer reaches **Lake Victoria,** the source of the **River Nile.**

1858-1864 Livingstone explores the **River Zambezi.**

1859-1869 The **Suez Canal** in **Egypt** is built by a **French** company.

The first ships sailing down the **Suez Canal.**

1859 Queensland becomes a separate colony.

1860 The **French** begin expansion in **West Africa.**

1860-1861 Burke and **Wills,** British explorers, cross **Australia.**

1860-1864 War between **Maoris** (native peoples) and settlers in **New Zealand.**

1861 Australia becomes the first country to give women the vote.

1863 Gold rush in **New Zealand.**

1868 The end of the transportation of convicts (prisoners) from **Britain** to **Australia.**

1869 Diamond rush begins in **South Africa.**

1869 Tunisia is controlled by **Britain, France** and **Italy.**

Western Europe

1834 The **Tolpuddle Martyrs**, six **English** labourers, are sent to **Australia** for trying to set up a Trade Union.

1834-1839 **Carlist Wars** in Spain: **Don Carlos**, the **pretender***, attempts to gain the throne.

1836 **Chartist** movement in **England** demands the vote for all adult males.

1837-1901 Reign of **Queen Victoria** of **Great Britain**.

1837 The first **electric telegraph** is invented by **W. Cooke** and **C. Wheatstone** (**British**).

1838 The first **practical photographic process** is produced by a **French** inventor, **L. Daguerre**.

1840 First **postage stamp**, the **Penny Black**, issued in **Britain**.

1845-1848 **Great Famine** in **Ireland** leads to mass emigration to **USA**.

1847 Civil War in **Switzerland**.

1848* Revolutions affect most of **Europe**. The **Second Republic** is declared in **France** (1848-1851).

1848 *Communist Manifesto* is issued by **Karl Marx** (**1818-1883**) and **Friedrich Engels** (**1820-1895**).

1851 **Great Exhibition** in **London** of **British** culture and industry.

Crystal Palace, London, designed by **Joseph Paxton** to house the **Great Exhibition**.

1852 The **Second Republic** is overthrown and **Louis Napoleon** becomes **Emperor Napoleon III** of **France**. **Second Empire** (1852-1870).

1859 **Charles Darwin**, an **English** naturalist, outlines his theory of **evolution**.

1863 First **underground railway** is built in **Britain**.

1864 **Red Cross Society** is founded in **Geneva**, to provide medical care for war casualties.

Red Cross tents and ambulance.

Eastern Europe (including Italy)

1854-1856 **Crimean War**. **Russia** demands a protectorate over **Turkish Christians** and the use of the **Dardanelles** for Russian warships. **Britain**, **France** and **Turkey** declare war on her.

A scene from the **Crimean War**.

Russia suffers defeats at **Alma**, **Balaclava**, **Inkerman** and **Sevastopol** and is forced to make concessions at the **Treaty of Paris** (1856).

1859 **France** supports an **Italian** uprising against **Austria**, led by **Piedmont-Sardinia**.

1860 **Parma**, **Modena** and **Tuscany** unite with **Piedmont**. **Garibaldi*** leads a revolution in **Sicily** which joins it to the **Italian kingdom**. The **Papal States** are invaded and absorbed, but the **Pope** keeps **Rome**.

The opening of the first **Italian parliament** in **Turin** 1860.

1861 **Victor Emmanuel**, King of **Piedmont-Sardinia**, is proclaimed king of a united **Italy**.

1861 **Tsar Alexander II** of **Russia** emancipates the **serfs***.

Russian serfs.

1863-1864 **Polish** uprising against **Russia** is crushed.

1864 War between **Prussia** and **Denmark**. Denmark is forced to cede **Schleswig** and **Holstein** to **Prussia** and **Austria**.

1866 War between **Prussia** and **Austria** over **Schleswig-Holstein**.

1866 War between **Austria** and **Italy**. Italy gains **Venice**.

1866 **Mendel**, a **Bohemian** monk and botanist, publishes his **laws of inheritance**.

1867 **Prussia** forms the **North German Confederation***.

The Americas

1821 **Mexico** is proclaimed independent. **Agustin Iturbide** becomes **Emperor Agustin I** in 1822.

1822 **Haiti** is independent.

1822 **Brazil** declares independence and is ruled by **King Pedro I**.

1823 The **Monroe Doctrine**: **President Monroe** of the **USA** warns **European** powers not to interfere in **American** affairs.

1823 Formation of the **United Provinces of Central America**.

1823-1824 **Agustin I** is overthrown and **Mexico** becomes a **republic***.

1828 **Uruguay**, part of **Argentina** from 1816, becomes a separate **republic***.

1830s **American** settlers move West.

American Indian tribes, expelled from their homelands by settler expansion.

1830 **Great Colombia** breaks up: **Colombia**, **Ecuador** and **Venezuela** become independent **republics***.

1833 **Britain** takes possession of the **Falkland Islands**.

1836 **Texas** breaks away from **Mexico** and forms a **republic***.

1839-1840 Break-up of **United Provinces of Central America** into independent **republics*** of El **Salvador**, **Honduras**, **Nicaragua**, **Guatemala** and **Costa Rica**.

1840 **Upper** and **Lower Canada** are united and then given self-government in 1841.

1845 **Texas** and **Florida** become states of the **USA**.

1845-1848 War between **Mexico** and **USA**. Mexico loses **California**, **New Mexico**, **Arizona**, **Utah** and **Colorado**.

1848-1849 Gold is discovered in **California**.

1848, 92; **Garibaldi**, 93; **North German Confederation** (see map, 93); **pretender**, 114; **republic**, 114; **serfs**, 31.

The Scramble for Africa

At the beginning of the **19th century**, most of **Africa** was still unknown to **Europeans**. There was a handful of **British** and **French** settlements on the west coast, but these were mainly trading stations and strategic outposts necessary to protect trade. The only other established colonies were the **Portuguese** coastal colonies of **Angola** and **Mozambique**, the **Cape Colony** (which passed from **Dutch** to British control in **1814**) and from **1830**, the French colony in **Algeria**.

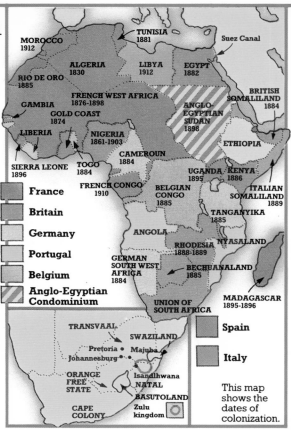

	France
	Britain
	Germany
	Portugal
	Belgium
	Anglo-Egyptian Condominium
	Spain
	Italy

This map shows the dates of colonization.

The first **Europeans** in **Africa** were explorers and missionaries, who came to convert the Africans to **Christianity**.

However, between **1877** and **1914** almost the entire continent was colonized by European powers. Existing settlements were enlarged and new colonies created. The process was so rapid that it has been called the **Scramble for Africa**.

Asia

1858 **Treaty of Tientsin**: 11 **Chinese** ports are opened to **European** trade.

1859-1860 **Anglo-Chinese** War. Anglo-French forces occupy **Peking**. China **cedes*** **Kowloon** to **Britain**.

1859-1865 **Mandalay** is the capital of **Burma**.

1861-1862 **France** goes to war with **Cochin-China** (S. Vietnam) and establishes a **protectorate*** over the province by **1867**.

1863 **France** establishes a **protectorate*** in **Cambodia**.

1868 The major clans in **Japan** organize opposition to the **Tokugawas***. The last **shogun***, **Kei-ki**, abdicates after a **coup d'état*** and the emperor's power is restored under a new government (the **Meiji Restoration** **1868-1912**). A period of growth and modernization.

Inside a **Japanese** silk factory.

During this period the Japanese built shipyards, cotton mills and arms factories. They adopted military conscription and set up railway and postal systems.

1873 Continued **Russian** expansion into **Asia**. Russia acquires **Khiva** and other provinces.

1874 **Annam** (Vietnam) is opened to **French** trade. **Tongking** is made a French **protectorate*** in **1883**.

1876 **Korea** is declared independent by **China**.

Africa and Oceania

1871 **Ujiji**, East Africa: Sir **Henry Stanley**, a **British** journalist and explorer, meets **David Livingstone***, who has been missing for four years.

The meeting of **Stanley** and **Livingstone**.

1872 **British** take over **Dutch** forts on **Gold Coast**.

1873-1874, 1893-1894, 1895-1896 Wars between the **British** and **Ashanti*** in **West Africa**.

1874-1877 **Stanley** explores the **Congo**.

1875 **British** Prime Minister, **Disraeli**, buys majority shares in the **Suez Canal Company**, thus ensuring control of the sea route to **India**.

The ceremony to mark the opening of the **Suez Canal**.

1876 **Britain** and **France** take control of **Egypt's** finances, to ensure repayment of her debts.

1877 **Transvaal** is **annexed*** by **Britain**.

1879 **Britain** and **France** control **Egypt**.

There were many reasons for the scramble. The French had long been trying to extend their influence in **North Africa** and on the west coast. **Industrialization*** in Europe and the expansion of world trade created a demand for new markets and materials. The activities of explorers and the development of railways opened up hitherto impenetrable regions.

Germans fighting **Herero** tribesmen in **South West Africa**. Despite fierce resistance, the only lasting **European** defeat was in **Ethiopia** (**1896**).

To a large extent the scramble came about because of land-grabbing by men on the spot. But it was also a question of rivalry between European nations and the prestige of having a colonial empire. Africa was the last great continent to be opened up and new nations such as **Germany** and **Italy** looked to it to provide them with an empire. Once the movement started, it took on a momentum of its own.

Raffles and Singapore

Singapore was founded in **1819** by **Sir Stamford Raffles**, then in charge of an **East India Company*** settlement in **Sumatra**. He dreamt of extending **British** power in **South East Asia** and sought a base to counter the **Dutch** port of **Malacca**, in order to safeguard the **India-China** trade. After negotiating with the island's ruler, he landed a small force and established a colony. This aroused the anger of the Dutch, but they came to an agreement in **1824**.

Strategically situated, but disease-ridden and almost uninhabited, Singapore soon grew to become the largest and most prosperous port in the region.

Western Europe

1865 Louis Pasteur, a French chemist, publishes his **germ theory of disease**.

1867 **Second Reform Act** extends the right to vote in **Britain**.

1867 **Karl Marx*** publishes *Das Kapital*, outlining his theories.

1867 The **Paris Exhibition**.

1870 **Irish Land Act** gives **Irish** tenants compensation for eviction by **English** landlords, but fails to stop unrest.

1870 War between **France** and **Prussia** ends in French defeat at the **Battle of Sedan**. Prussian forces besiege **Paris** and overthrow the **Second Empire***. A revolution establishes the **Third Republic** (**1870-1940**).

The siege of **Paris** by **Prussian** troops.

Eastern Europe (including Italy)

1867 The **Austrian Empire** is renamed the **Austro-Hungarian Empire** after **Hungary** is given equal status in the **Dual Monarchy***.

1870 **Rome** falls to the **Italian kingdom*** and becomes the capital of a united **Italy**. The **Pope** is guaranteed the **Vatican** (**1871**).

1871 **William I** of **Prussia** becomes **Kaiser** (Emperor) of a united **Germany***.

The proclamation of the **German Empire** at **Versailles 1871**.

1873 Alliance of three emperors: **Germany**, **Austria-Hungary** and **Russia**.

1874 **Iceland** becomes independent.

The Americas

1857 Civil war in **Mexico**.

1859 **Oil** is discovered in **Pennsylvania**.

The discovery of **oil** led to the start of the **modern oil industry**.

Pennsylvanian oil well.

1860s-1870s Great battles between **Indians** and settlers in **North America** lead to a reduction in the Indian population.

1860 **Abraham Lincoln** becomes President of the **USA**.

A battle between **Unionists** and **Confederates** in the **American Civil War**.

1861-1865 **American Civil War***.

1864 **France** installs **Archduke Maximilian** of **Austria** as **Emperor of Mexico**. He is shot in **1867** and the **French** withdraw.

American Civil War, 92; **Dual Monarchy, Germany, Italian kingdom,** (see **Nationalism,** 93); **East India Company,** 62; **industrialization,** 89; **Karl Marx,** 95; **Second Empire,** 95.

Asia

Queen Victoria

1877 Queen Victoria of **Britain** is proclaimed **Empress of India.**

1878-1880 War between **Britain** and **Afghanistan. British India** makes frontier gains and British influence in Afghanistan grows.

Middle East and Central Asia

1881 Further **Russian** expansion into **Turkestan.**

1883 Annam becomes a **French protectorate*.**

1883-1884 The **French** continue to expand in **South-East Asia.** War with **Tongking** and **China.**

1884 Cambodia is **annexed*** by **France.**

1885 Founding of **Indian National Congress,** the first national political party in **India.**

1885-1886 British attack and **annex* Ava** in **Burma.**

1887 France establishes an **Indo-Chinese Union.**

1890-1897 An **Armenian** revolutionary movement is formed against **Turkey.**

1894-1895 War between **Japan** and **China.** Japan gains **Formosa. Korea** becomes independent of China.

1896 Britain sets up the **Federated Malay States,** with **Kuala Lumpur** as the capital.

1896 Anglo-French agreement over spheres of influence in **Siam.**

1896 Rebellion in the **Philippines** against the **Spanish.**

1897 Anglo-Siamese agreements on boundaries between **Siam** and **Malaya.**

1898 War between **Spain** and the **USA** over the **Philippines.** Spain **cedes*** Philippines to the USA.

1898-1909 A period of reactionary and repressive rule in **China** under **Empress Tzu Hsi.** Attempts at liberal reforms are crushed.

Empress Tzu Hsi

Africa and Oceania

1879 Zulus* defeat **British** at the **Isandlhwana,** but are defeated the same year at **Ulundi.**

The **Battle of Isandlhwana.**

1881 The **Boers*** defeat the **British** at **Majuba Hill.** Britain recognizes **Transvaal** independence.

1881 Nationalist revolt in **Egypt.**

1882 British forces occupy **Egypt** and **Sudan,** in order to suppress **anti-European** riots.

1883 New Guinea is **annexed*** by **Queensland.**

1884 Uprising against the **British** in the **Sudan,** led by the **Mahdi,** a **Sudanese** religious leader. **General Gordon** is sent to **Khartoum.**

1885 The **Mahdi** takes **Khartoum** and **Gordon** is killed.

Gordon's residence, **Khartoum.**

1886 Gold is discovered in **Transvaal** and **Johannesburg** is founded.

1888-1889 Expansion of **British** influence in **Rhodesia** by the **British South Africa Company,** formed by **Cecil Rhodes. Salisbury** is founded.

1889 Italy claims a **protectorate*** over **Ethiopia.**

1891 Emperor Menelik of **Ethiopia** denounces the **Italian protectorate*.** Italians invade in **1895,** but are decisively beaten at **Adowa (1896)** and forced to recognize Ethiopian independence.

1895-1896 Jameson Raid in **South Africa:** a failed attempt by **Rhodes** to take over the **Transvaal.**

1898 The **Fashoda Crisis:** a confrontation at **Fashoda, Sudan** between **French** soldiers advancing north and **British** soldiers advancing south. It ends in French withdrawal.

1898 Battle of Omdurman: the **British,** led by **Lord Kitchener,** defeat **Sudanese** nationalists. **Sudan** comes under **Anglo-Egyptian** rule (**1899**).

Boer soldiers

1899-1902 Anglo-Boer* War in **South Africa.**

Australia

New Zealand

Western Europe

1871 **Paris** falls to the **German** forces. **France** loses **Alsace** and **Lorraine** and pays a large indemnity. A revolution led by a group called the **Paris Commune** is crushed by government forces.

The **Communards** (members of the **Commune**), after destroying the **Napoleon Column** in **Paris**.

1872-1874 Civil war in **Spain**.

1873 **Home Rule League** is founded to promote **Irish** self-government.

1874 **Impressionist** school of painting begins in **France**.

1880-1885 Period of unrest and **anti-British** agitation in **Ireland**.

1884 **Reform Act** in **Britain** gives the vote to all males over 21.

1888 **John Dunlop**, a **Scottish** surgeon, invents the **pneumatic tyre**.

The building of the **Eiffel Tower** for the **1889 Paris Exposition**.

1889 The **Eiffel Tower** is built for the **1889 Paris Exposition**.

1890 **Luxembourg** becomes independent from **Holland**.

1893 **Independent Labour Party** founded in **Britain** by **Keir Hardie**.

1893 **France** allies with **Russia**.

1894 **Dreyfus Affair** in **France**. Dreyfus, a **Jewish** army officer, is expelled for treason. Many are convinced of his innocence and it leads to a social and political battle. (He is cleared in **1906**.)

Dreyfus under arrest.

1898 **Pierre** and **Marie Curie**, **French** scientists, observe **radioactivity** and isolate **radium**.

Eastern Europe (including Italy)

1876 **Serbia** and **Montenegro** declare war on **Turkey**.

Turkish troops during the **Russo-Turkish** War.

1877-1878 **Russo-Turkish** War. **Romania**, **Montenegro** and **Serbia** gain independence from **Turkey**. **Bulgaria** becomes **autonomous***. **Russia** makes great gains, but these are reduced at the **Congress of Berlin** (1878).

The **Brandenburg Gate, Berlin**.

1879 **Dual Alliance** between **Germany** and **Austria-Hungary**. Joined by **Italy** (1882).

1881 **Tsar Alexander II** of **Russia** is assassinated. Repression follows under **Alexander III**.

1883 **Russian Marxist Party** is founded. Unrest follows.

1885 **Daimler** and **Benz**, **German** inventors, pioneer the **automobile**.

Karl Benz's first petrol-driven car 1885.

1888-1918 Rule of **Kaiser William II** of **Germany**, who encourages military expansion.

1892-1903 Modernization and industrial growth in **Russia** under **Sergei Witte** (finance minister).

1893 Alliance between **Russia** and **France**.

1894-1897 **Greeks** in **Crete** rise against the **Turks**. **Crete** is united with **Greece** in 1897.

1895 **Marconi**, an **Italian** physicist, invents the **wireless**.

1895 **Sigmund Freud**, an **Austrian** psychiatrist, publishes his first work on **psychoanalysis**.

The Americas

1864-1870 **Paraguay** fights a major war with her neighbours and her population falls by half.

1865 **American Civil War*** ends with the surrender of **Confederates*** to **Unionists***. **Slavery*** is abolished in the **United States**. **Abraham Lincoln** is assassinated.

1866 First successful **trans-Atlantic cable**.

1867 **United States** purchases **Alaska** from **Russia** for $7 million.

1867 **Canada** is given **dominion*** status.

1868-1878 **Cuba** loses war of independence against **Spain**.

1869 First **trans-continental railroad** is completed in the **USA**.

American railroad c.1860s.

1876 The **telephone** is patented in the **USA** by **Alexander Graham Bell**.

1877 **Thomas Edison**, an **American**, invents the **record player** (left) and the **electric light bulb** (1879).

1879 **Chile** is at war with **Bolivia** (to 1883) and **Peru** (to 1884). **Peru** and **Bolivia** lose territory to **Chile**.

1877-1911 Rule of **Porfirio Diaz**, **Mexican** dictator*. He establishes order, and wealth and industries grow.

1880 Start of the construction of the **Panama Canal**.

1889 **Pedro II** of **Brazil** is deposed and a **republic*** set up.

1890 **Battle of Wounded Knee**: last **Indian** uprising in the **USA**.

1893 **Hawaii** becomes a **US protectorate***.

1898 **Spanish-American War**. **Cuba** becomes independent under temporary **American** control.

American battleship c.1898.

Africa and the Middle East

1900 **British** win victories over the **Boers** and annex* the **Orange Free State** and **Transvaal**. The **Anglo-Boer War*** ends with the **Peace of Vereeniging** (1902).

1908 A revolution in **Turkey** by the **Young Turks**, an association of army officers, including **Mustafa Kemäl**. The **Sultan** introduces a liberal constitution and promises reforms. A period of instability follows. In **1909** the Sultan is deposed by the Young Turks.

A group of **Young Turks**.

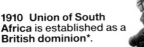

1910 **Union of South Africa** is established as a **British dominion***.

1911 **Italy** and **Turkey** are at war over **Tripoli**. **Libya** comes under Italian control in **1912**.

1914-1922 **Egypt** becomes a **British protectorate***.

1916 **Arab** nationalists in the **Hejaz** rise against **Turkey**. Further uprisings follow.

T.E.Lawrence (Lawrence of Arabia), a **British** soldier and writer, took part in the **Arab** revolt against the **Turks**.

Arab nationalists

1917 The **Balfour Declaration**: Britain announces support for a **Jewish*** national home in **Palestine**, on condition that **Arab** rights are respected.

1918 **Syria** proclaims independence. Not recognized by **France** (who claims Syria) or **Britain**. French forces take control in **1919**.

1918 The collapse of the **Ottoman Empire***. The **Allies*** control **Istanbul**.

1919 **German African** colonies are mandated* to the **Allied*** countries by the **League of Nations**.

1920 **Feisal I** becomes King of **Syria**. **Jordan** is separated from Syria.

Turkish flag.

1920 **Abdullah** is proclaimed King of **Iraq**.

1922 **Mustafa Kemäl (Atatürk)** (1881-1938) seizes power in **Turkey** and proclaims a **Turkish Republic**. A period of reform and modernization follows.

1922 **Britain** recognizes **Egyptian** independence.

1922 **League of Nations mandate*** over **Syria** is given to **France**.

1923 **Mandate*** over **Palestine** is given to **Britain**.

1923 **Southern Rhodesia** is formally annexed* as a **British** colony.

1924 Growth of **Moroccan** independence movement.

1926 **Ibn Saud** becomes King of **Hejaz** and **Nejd**. In **1932** they unite to form **Saudi Arabia**.

1926 A republic* is proclaimed in the **Lebanon**.

Asia

1900 **Boxer Rebellion** in **China** against foreign influence is crushed by an international force.

1901 A **British** company in **Persia** is given a 60 year oil concession giving it the right to search for oil. Oil is discovered in **1907**.

1904-1905 **Russia** and **Japan** at war over **Manchuria** and **Korea**.

1905 **Japanese** destroy **Russian** fleet at **Tsushima**. **Treaty of Portsmouth** gives Japan a **protectorate*** over **Korea** and territory in **China**.

Japanese soldiers (1904-1905).

1908-1909 **Sultan Ahmed Shah** seizes power in **Persia**.

1909 **Anglo-Siam Treaty**: Siam recognizes **British** control over **Malayan** states.

1909 **China** attacks **Tibet**. The Tibetan ruler, the **Dalai Lama**, flees to **India** (1909-1911).

1910-1945 **Korea** becomes a **Japanese** colony.

1910 **Malayan** states of **Trengganu** and **Perlis** accept **British** protection.

Map of Malaya

1910 **China**: uprising in **Yunnan** province.

1910 **Nationalist*** movement in **Burma** led by **Buddhist*** monks.

1911 **Chinese Revolution**: a revolutionary government is set up in **Nanking** under **Sun Yat-sen**. The **Manchu dynasty*** is overthrown in **1912** and a **republic*** is set up. This is followed by a period of great unrest and local rule by warlords.

Sun Yat-sen and soldiers.

1917 **China** and **Siam** join the **Allies*** in the **First World War***.

1919 **British** soldiers fire on a peaceful political meeting in **Amritsar**. This leads to a rise in **Indian** national feeling.

1920 **Mohandas (Mahatma) Gandhi** (1869-1948) forms the **Indian National Congress**: a non-violent campaign for independence in **India**.

1921 **Mao Zedong (Mao Tse-tung)** and **Li Ta-chao** form the **Chinese Communist Party** in **Peking**.

1923 An earthquake destroys much of **Tokyo**, **Japan**.

1924-1925 **Reza Shah** seizes power in **Persia**.

1925 Death of **Sun Yat-sen**. He is succeeded by **Chiang Kai-shek**, who campaigns against the warlords.

1926 **Hirohito** becomes **Emperor of Japan**.

Northern and Eastern Europe

1905 Unsuccessful revolts in **St Petersburg** and other **Russian** cities.

1905 **Norway** becomes independent from **Sweden**.

1907 Growing friendship between **Russia** and **Britain**.

1908 **Austria-Hungary** takes the **Turkish** provinces of **Bosnia** and **Herzegovina**. International tension follows.

Bosnian warrior

1912 First Balkan War: **Bulgaria, Greece, Serbia** and **Montenegro** unite and defeat **Turkey**.

1913 Second Balkan War: **Turkey, Romania, Serbia** and **Greece** defeat **Bulgaria**.

1914 Murder of the **Archduke Franz Ferdinand** in **Sarajevo** triggers the **First World War*** (1914-1918).

Archduke Franz Ferdinand driving in **Sarajevo**.

1917 The **Russian Revolution***.

March 1918 Treaty of Brest-Litovsk: **Russia** is defeated and makes a separate peace with **Germany**. Germany surrenders to the **Allies*** in **November**.

1918 New nations become independent: the **Baltic republics** (**Latvia, Estonia** and **Lithuania**), **Czechoslovakia** and **Yugoslavia**.

1918 Revolution in **Berlin**. The **Kaiser*** flees and the **Weimar Republic** is set up (**July 1919**).

1918 **Emperor Charles** of **Austria-Hungary** abdicates.

1919 **Finland** is proclaimed a **republic***.

Map of new nations

FINLAND
ESTONIA
New nations
LITHUANIA LATVIA
POLAND
CZECHOSLOVAKIA
AUSTRIA HUNGARY
YUGOSLAVIA

1923 Unsuccessful rising of the **Nazis** (**National Socialists**), a **German Fascist*** party, led by **Adolf Hitler** (1889-1945).

Southern and Western Europe

1901 Death of **Queen Victoria of Great Britain** (1837-1901) and the accession of **King Edward VII**.

1902 **Britain** makes an alliance with **Japan**, marking the end of a long period of isolation.

1903 **Delcassé, French Foreign Minister**, visits **London**. Growing **Anglo-French** friendship.

1904 **Entente Cordiale**: a pact of friendship between **Britain** and **France**.

1907 Growing **British** friendship with **Russia**.

1910 Revolution in **Portugal**; the king is deposed. A **republic*** is declared in **1911**.

1914-1918 **First World War***.

1914 **Germans** advance through **Luxembourg** and **Belgium**. Start of trench warfare on the **western front***.

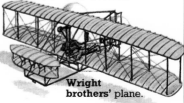

German cavalry officer (**First World War**).

1915 **Italy** joins the **Allies***.

1916 **Easter Rising** in **Dublin**: **Irish** rise against the **British**.

1916 **British** use tanks for the first time.

British tank **1917**.

1916 Battles of **Verdun** and the **Somme**: stalemate on the **western front***.

1917 Battle of **Passchendaele**: stalemate continues.

1918 **Britain**: the vote is given to women over 30.

1919 **Mussolini** establishes the **Fascist*** movement in **Italy**.

1919 **Paris Conference** sets up the **League of Nations**, to help preserve world peace.

1919-1921 Period of disorder and terrorism in **Ireland**.

1920 The six northern counties separate from the rest of **Ireland**, and set up parliament in **Belfast**.

1921 The **Irish Free State** (**Eire**) is recognized as a **dominion*** within the **British Empire**.

America and Australasia

1900 **New Zealand** takes the **Cook Islands**.

1900 **Papua** is transferred from **Britain** to **Australia**.

1901 The **Commonwealth*** of **Australia** is established.

1903 Revolution in **Panama**. It gains independence from **Colombia** as a **US protectorate***.

1903 First wireless transmission from **USA** to **England**.

1903 **Wright brothers** (**USA**) make the first successful flight in a petrol-powered aircraft.

Wright brothers' plane.

1904 Construction of **Panama Canal** is begun.

1907 **New Zealand** is given **dominion*** status.

1908-18 Period of unrest and lawlessness in **Haiti**.

1911 A revolution in **Mexico** overthrows **Porfirio Diaz***. Followed by a time of disorder and the rise of local **dictators***.

Mexican revolutionaries.

1912 **Amundsen**, a **Norwegian**, is the first to reach the **South Pole**.

1912 **Henry Ford** (**USA**) begins mass-production of motor cars.

1914 Opening of **Panama Canal**.

1917 **American** ships are sunk by **German** submarines. Tension grows. **USA** declares war. **South American** states and **Cuba** join the **Allies***.

1919 First aircraft is flown between **England** and **Australia**.

1919 **Australia** acquires former **German** colonies in the **Pacific**.

1920 **USA** decides not to join **League of Nations** (see left). **Prohibition** (an act prohibiting alcohol) is introduced.

1921 The end of unrestricted immigration into the **USA**.

1927 **Canberra** becomes the **federal*** capital of **Australia**.

1927 **The Jazz Singer**, the first talking picture, or **movie**.

The First World War 1914-1918

The **First World War**, or **Great War**, was largely a **European** war, fought in Europe to solve European disputes. Nevertheless, it affected most of the world, in one way or another. Many **non-European** countries, particularly the colonies of the European powers, were directly involved.

Initially, there was a wave of patriotism and enthusiasm for the war, which most people believed would be a short one. This dulled as the war stretched into a series of horrific and inconclusive battles.

French pro-war poster.

The Central Powers:
Germany, Austria-Hungary.

The Allies: Britain, France, Russia.

Countries who later joined the **Central Powers**.

Countries who later joined the **Allies**.

RUSSIA
Eastern front

Brest-Litovsk

GERMANY

Passchendaele

BRITAIN

The Somme
Verdun
The Marne

AUSTRIA-HUNGARY

Western front
FRANCE

Sarajevo

ROMANIA

ITALY

BULGARIA

Gallipoli
GREECE

OTTOMAN EMPIRE

Europe 1914-1918

Since the **1870s** various alliances had been concluded among the great powers to preserve the balance of power. By **1914** there were two armed camps: on one side, **Germany** and **Austria-Hungary**, and on the other, **France** and **Russia**, supported by **Britain**. There were many issues which might have led to conflict. The danger was that the alliances were so delicately balanced that an attack on one country would automatically involve its allies.

German warships

German flag c.1914.

The fundamental problem of the background to the war was the rise of Germany. Her increase in wealth and military strength threatened the balance of power.

The incident which triggered the war was the assassination by a **Serbian** of **Archduke Franz Ferdinand**, the heir to the Austrian throne, at **Sarajevo** in **June 1914**. Austria had long been troubled by **nationalist*** rebels among her **Slav** subjects, who were assisted by Serbia. Austria decided to strike back, giving Serbia an **ultimatum***. It ran out without satisfactory reply and on **28 July** Austria declared war. The Great War had started.

Initially, the Germans made advances in France, but they were soon checked by the **Allies** in northern France. Both sides dug trenches and fortified their positions. By **1915** there was stalemate on both the **western** and the **eastern fronts**. The ill-equipped and often half-starved Russians suffered enormous casualties. The resulting loss of morale contributed to the **Russian Revolution***.

For four years, fighting on the **western front** consisted of attempts by one side to gain a little territory from the other, often at a huge cost in lives, only to lose the territory again in a bloody counterattack.

In the **German** trenches.

Important battles

April 1915 British, French and Australians land at Gallipoli, but are repulsed by Turks.

Feb-June 1916 Battle of Verdun: stalemate.

July-Nov 1916 Battle of the Somme: stalemate.

July-Nov 1916 Battle of Passchendaele: British offensive fails.

March-April 1918 German Spring Offensive, led by General Ludendorff, breaks through Allied lines in **northern France**.

July-Aug 1918 Battle of the Marne: The German Spring Offensive is broken.

In **April 1917**, the **USA** entered the war on the Allied side. This made a crucial difference and by **1918**, Germany was becoming exhausted. Final surrender came on **11 November 1918**. The war had involved destruction on a scale never seen before. Yet the terms placed on Germany at the **Peace of Versailles (1919)** – loss of territory, no armies in the **Rhine** area, and crippling reparation payments – left problems which would take another major war to settle. The outcome of the war changed Europe; the old empires broke up and new nations emerged.

The Russian Revolution 1917

Growing unrest against the oppressive and **autocratic*** rule of the **Russian tsars*** came to a head in **1917**. The **First World War*** brought defeats and enormous loss of life and there was widespread suffering and starvation at home. Both the army and the people turned against the Tsar. Riots broke out in **March 1917** (known as the **February Revolution** because the Russians followed a different calendar). The Tsar was overthrown and a provisional **democratic*** government set up.

Lenin addressing a crowd. After the **Second World War**, **Communist** control extended over most of **Eastern Europe**.

The new government acted through a **Congress of Soviets** (workers councils). It centralized control of land and confiscated church property. There was powerful opposition, which led to a vicious civil war (**1918-1920**). Despite anti-Communist invasions by foreign powers, the **Soviet Red Army** emerged victorious.

Nicholas II, the last **Tsar**.

The storming of the **Winter Palace**, Petrograd in **March 1917**.

The provisional government, led by the **Menshevik Party**, wanted to stay in the war, but most Russians wanted peace. The **Bolshevik Party**, led by **Vladimir Illich Ulyanov** (**Lenin**) (**1870-1924**), also opposed the war. In **November 1917** (the **October Revolution**) they seized power and set up a **Communist*** government.

Important dates

Revolutionary poster

1900 Lenin goes into exile and develops the philosophy of **Marxism-Leninism**. In **1903** he leads a breakaway movement, the **Bolsheviks**.

13 March 1917 Tsar Nicholas II abdicates and a provisional government is set up. Real power is held by the **Soviet** in **Petrograd**.

8 November 1917 Lenin and **Trotsky** take control of the **Petrograd Soviet** and overthrow the government.

Summer 1918 The **Tsar** and his family are murdered by the **Communists**.

1919 The **Comintern** (a **Communist International** organization) is formed.

1921 New Economic Policy (NEP) introduced. It stimulates private trade and industrial growth.

1923 Russia is renamed the **Union of Soviet Socialist Republics (USSR)**.

The Great Depression

From **1929** until the **mid-1930s**, nearly every country in the world experienced an economic crisis, which has become known as the **Great Depression**. There was falling production, declining incomes and mass unemployment. **Germany**, the **USA**, **Eastern Europe**, and many primary producing countries in **Africa**, **Asia** and **Latin America** were the worst affected. Many countries tried to improve the situation through new economic policies. Some tried to become self-sufficient by cutting imports and investing in home industries.

The Depression had three main causes. Firstly, the **Great War*** had left much poverty. In place of the old empires were new, weak and unstable states, who borrowed money they could not easily repay. Secondly, a fall in prices for raw materials and agricultural goods hit countries, such as **Australia**, that depended on them. A third factor was the weakness of the US economy, on which many countries depended as a market for their exports and a source for borrowing money. The collapse of the **New York** stock market (the **Wall Street Crash**) in **October 1929** sparked a slump in America and a chain reaction throughout the world.

Fascism* became a powerful force in many **European** countries in the **1930s**, led by **Germany**, under **Hitler** (right) and **Italy**, under **Mussolini**. The Fascist parties promised radical solutions to the economic problems.

Africa and the Middle East

1927 The independence of **Saudi Arabia** and **Iraq** is recognized by **Britain**.

TURKEY **SYRIA**
LEBANON **IRAQ** **IRAN**
JORDAN
EGYPT **ISRAEL** **SAUDI ARABIA**

Middle East

YEMEN

1930 A revolution in **Ethiopia** establishes **Haile Selassie I** (1892-1975) as Emperor.

1935 **Italy** invades **Ethiopia**, using poison gas.

1936 **Ethiopia** is **annexed*** by **Italy**.

1936 **Arab** revolt in **Palestine** against **Jewish** immigrants.

1940 **Italy** invades **Egypt**, but is driven back by the **British**, who occupy **Libya**.

1940 Many **French African** colonies declare support for **General de Gaulle's Free French Forces**.

1941 **German** counter-offensive against the **Allies*** in **North Africa**, led by **General Rommel**.

1941 The **Allies*** defeat the **Italians** in **Ethiopia**.

1942 **Rommel** is defeated by the **British**, led by **General Montgomery** at the **Battle of El Alamein**.

The **Battle of El Alamein, Egypt (1942)**.

1943 **Germans** surrender in **Tunisia**: the end of German involvement in **Africa**.

1945 Formation of the **Arab League** in **Cairo**.

1945 A rising against the **French** in **Algeria**.

1946 **Transjordan** is declared independent by **Britain** and renamed **Jordan**.

1947 The partition of **Palestine** into **Arab** and **Jewish*** states is agreed by the **United Nations***, but opposed by Arabs. This leads to battles between Arabs and Jews in Palestine, after the **British** withdrawal.

Israeli flag

1948 The **Afrikaner Nationalist Party** wins an election in **South Africa** on a programme of **apartheid***.

1948-1949 **Arab League** goes to war with **Israel**, but fails to stop the establishment of the state.

1952 Revolution in **Egypt**: **King Farouk** abdicates. A **republic*** is proclaimed in 1953.

1952-1955 Risings by the **Mau Mau** in **Kenya**, a secret society opposed to **British** rule.

1953 The **Federation of North and South Rhodesia and Nyasaland** is established.

1954 **Nasser** (1918-1970) comes to power in **Egypt**.

Asia

1927 **Chiang Kai-shek**, leader of the **Kuomintang (Chinese Nationalist Party)**, breaks with the **Communist Party*** and civil war follows. The Communists set up small bases in remote areas.

1928 **Chiang Kai-shek** becomes **President of China**.

1929 **Gandhi*** demands the independence of **India** and begins a campaign of **civil disobedience**. A period of unrest follows.

1931 **Japanese** occupy **Manchuria**. In 1932 they proclaim the **Republic of Manchukuo**, under complete Japanese control.

1934 Rapid military and naval rearmament in **Japan**.

1934 The start of the **Long March** by **Communists*** to **North China**, led by **Mao Zedong***. Starting from **Kiangsi**, they reach **Yenan** in 1935, where they set up government.

The **Long March** through the mountains of **China**.

Mao Zedong (Mao Tse Tung)

1935 **Persia** is renamed **Iran**.

1937 **Burma** is separated from **British India** and ruled as an individual colony.

1937-1945 **Japanese** attack on **China** leads to war. The Japanese take **Shanghai** and **Nanking** (1937), **Canton** and **Hankow** (1938).

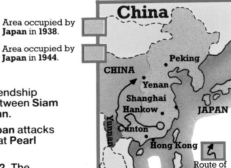

China

Area occupied by **Japan** in 1938.

Area occupied by **Japan** in 1944.

CHINA
Peking
Yenan
Shanghai
Hankow
Canton
JAPAN
Hong Kong
Yunnan

Route of the **Long March**.

1940 Friendship treaty between **Siam** and **Japan**.

1941 **Japan** attacks **US** fleet at **Pearl Harbor**.

1941-1942 The **Japanese** occupy much of **South East Asia** and the **Pacific**.

1944 **US** forces occupy **Guam** and inflict heavy defeats on the **Japanese** navy.

1944 The **USA** seizes **Saigon** and launches bombing raids against **Japan**.

1945 **US** forces destroy **Japanese** fleet at the **Battle of Okinawa**. **Atomic bombs** dropped on Japan lead to surrender on **14 August**.

1945 **Korea** is administered by the **USSR** and **USA**.

1945 **Ho Chi Minh*** forms a government in **Hanoi**. **French** attempts to reassert control (1946) lead to a war of independence in **Indo-China** (1946-1954).

1945-1951 **Allies*** occupy and administer **Japan**.

Northern and Eastern Europe

1924 **Lenin*** dies and is replaced as **Russian** leader by **Joseph Stalin** (1879-1953).

Joseph Stalin

1924 The **Greek** monarchy is replaced by a **republic***.

1924 **Ahmad Zogu** seizes power in **Albania**, becoming king in **1928**.

1925 **Treaty of Locarno**: agreement on frontiers and **demilitarization** of the **German Rhineland**.

1925 **Hitler*** publishes his ideas in his book *Mein Kampf*.

1926 **Pilsudski** takes control of the government in **Poland** and is virtual **dictator*** until **1935**.

1929 **Russia**: **Trotsky*** is exiled. The first **Five Year Plan** is launched; a period of rapid growth and industrialization.

1930 A period of terror begins in **Russia**. **Stalin** enforces the **collectivization*** of agriculture. Millions of *kulaks*, peasant farm owners who oppose this, are crushed and murdered.

1932 The **Nazi Party**, led by **Adolf Hitler***, makes large gains in the **German** elections.

A **Nazi rally** (1932).

1933 **Adolf Hitler*** becomes **Chancellor of Germany**. In **1934** he is appointed *Fuhrer* (leader) and becomes **dictator***. **Germany** becomes a **one-party state***.

1934 The **Austrian Chancellor** is assassinated. Growing disorder and fighting between **socialists*** and **fascists***.

1934-1939 **Stalinist Purges** in **Russia**: **Stalin** crushes all political opposition.

1935 The **Saar** territory, under **League of Nations*** control, votes to join **Germany**. **Germany** increases her military strength.

1935 **Nuremberg Laws**: start of persecution of **German Jews**.

1936 **German** troops occupy the **Rhineland** in defiance of the **Treaty of Locarno**.

Southern and Western Europe

1922 **Mussolini*** marches on **Rome**. He is appointed Prime Minister and forms a **Fascist*** government.

Benito Mussolini (1883-1945), the **Italian Fascist** dictator.

1923 Revolution in **Spain**. **De Rivera** becomes **dictator***.

1925 **Mussolini*** bans all political parties in **Italy** but the **Fascists***.

1926 9 day **General Strike** in **Britain**.

Buses being driven by students during the **General Strike (1926)**.

1928 **Alexander Fleming** (Scottish) discovers **penicillin**, the first **antibiotic**.

1931 Growth of **republican*** sentiment in **Spain**. **King Alfonso XIII** leaves the country and a republic is set up. A period of disorder follows.

1931 **Statute of Westminster**: an important step in the founding of the **British Commonwealth***. The rights of **dominions*** are defined.

1932 **Salazar** becomes **Prime Minister** and virtual **dictator*** of **Portugal** until **1968**.

1936 **King Edward VIII** of **Britain** abdicates to marry **Mrs Simpson**.

1936 **General Franco**, leader of the **Spanish Nationalists** (a **fascist*** party), rebels against the **Republican** government. The start of the **Spanish Civil War (1936-1939)**. **Germany** and **Italy** give military aid to **Franco's** government. **Russia** supports the **Republicans**. **Franco** is proclaimed **Head of State**.

1938 **Franco** wins major victories against the **Republicans** in **Spain**.

1939 **Franco** takes **Barcelona** and **Madrid** and is **dictator*** of **Spain** until his death in **1975**.

1939-1945 **Second World War***.

1940-1945 A **coalition*** government in **Britain**, led by **Sir Winston Churchill**.

America and Australasia

1927 **Charles Lindbergh** (USA) makes the first solo flight across the **Atlantic**.

1929 The **Wall Street Crash**: **US** stock market collapses. The beginning of the **Depression***.

1932-1935 War between **Paraguay** and **Bolivia** over the disputed **Chaco** region.

1933-1945 **F.D. Roosevelt** is **US President**. He introduces the **New Deal** policies to deal with the **Depression***. End of **Prohibition***.

1938 Unsuccessful **Nazi*** plots in **Chile** and **Brazil**.

1941 **Japanese** attack **US** naval base at **Pearl Harbor, Hawaii**. The **USA** enters the **Second World War***.

The attack on **Pearl Harbor (1941)**.

1942 The first **nuclear reactor** is built by **Fermi** in the **USA**.

1942 **Mexico** and **Brazil** declare war on **Germany** and **Japan**. All other **American republics***, except **Argentina**, cut off diplomatic relations with **Germany** and **Japan**.

1943 A revolution in **Argentina** brings **Juan Peron** to power as virtual military **dictator***.

1945 **Harry Truman** becomes **US President**.

1945 The **USA** explodes the first **atom bomb** in **New Mexico**.

1945 **San Francisco Conference**: the **United Nations** is founded. 48 nations sign **UN Charter**.

1946 **Trygve Lie** becomes first **Secretary General** of the **United Nations**.

The **United Nations** flag and headquarters, **New York**.

1946 **Juan Peron** becomes **President of Argentina**.

1946 **USA** announces the **Marshall Plan** for giving aid to help reconstruct **European** countries. It gives $12,000 million in **Marshall Aid** between **1948-1951**.

The Second World War 1939-1945

The **Second World War** broke out on **3 September 1939**. **German** military strength and ambition had grown greatly during the **1930s** under **Adolf Hitler***, and threatened to establish German domination of **Europe**. Hitler took **Austria (1938)** and **Czechoslovakia (1939)**. On **1 September 1939** he invaded **Poland**. Two days later **Britain** and **France** declared war.

German soldiers occupying **Paris (June 1940)**.

By **June 1940**, the Germans had conquered **Poland, Norway, Denmark, Belgium, Holland, Luxembourg** and France. During the **Battle of Britain (Aug-Dec 1940)**, the German *Luftwaffe* attacked airports, factories and cities, but the **Royal Air Force** won a decisive victory.

British

German

Planes used during the **Battle of Britain**.

German involvement in **eastern Europe** aroused **Russian** concern. Fearing a sudden attack, Hitler invaded Russia in **June 1941**. The invasion was at first a great success, but it committed large numbers of troops to a war on the **eastern front**.

The **Blitz** (bombing) in **London**.

In **September 1940**, **Japan**, which had colonial ambitions, signed a pact with Germany and **Italy**. The Japanese attack on the **US** fleet at **Pearl Harbor, Hawaii (7 December 1941)** brought the **Americans** into the war. By **April 1942** Japan controlled much of **South East Asia** and the **Pacific**.

South East Asia

Japanese territory.

Allied territory

USSR

JAPAN

CHINA

Hiroshima
Nagasaki

Midway

Hong Kong

PHILIPPINES

Pearl Harbor, Hawaii

Japanese flag

Singapore

BORNEO

NEW GUINEA

SUMATRA

From **1942**, the superior resources of the **Allies** began to reverse the earlier successes of the **Axis**. There were important victories at **El Alamein** in **Egypt (1942)** and **Stalingrad (1943)**. In **May 1944**

American tanks on a **Pacific** beach.

the German lines in Italy were broken. After **D-Day (6 June)**, they were driven out of France. In **April 1945**, Russian and Allied troops, pushing from opposite directions, arrived in **Berlin**. Faced with defeat, Hitler committed suicide on **30 April**, and on **8 May** the new leaders surrendered. In early **1945** the Japanese suffered defeats in the **Far East**. On **6 August** and **9 August**, atomic bombs devastated **Hiroshima** and **Nagasaki**. Final surrender came on **2 September**.

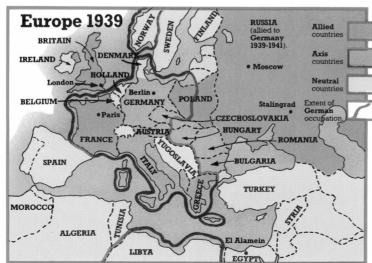

Europe 1939

BRITAIN

IRELAND

NORWAY

SWEDEN

FINLAND

RUSSIA (allied to Germany 1939-1941).

Allied countries

Axis countries

Neutral countries

Extent of German occupation.

DENMARK

HOLLAND

London

BELGIUM

Berlin
GERMANY

POLAND

• Moscow

Stalingrad

• Paris

CZECHOSLOVAKIA

FRANCE

AUSTRIA

HUNGARY

SPAIN

YUGOSLAVIA

ITALY

ROMANIA

BULGARIA

TURKEY

GREECE

SYRIA

MOROCCO

TUNISIA

ALGERIA

LIBYA

El Alamein

EGYPT

Decolonization

In **1939**, **European** countries still had widespread colonial empires – including most of **Africa***, the **Pacific** and **Caribbean** and much of **Asia**. However, between **1947** and **1975** almost the entire fabric of colonies crumbled. The colonial powers were weakened by the **Second World War***. Many of the Asian colonies had been occupied by **Japan**, and struggles against the Japanese led naturally to independence movements. Public opinion was also changing; it was no longer seen as justifiable that a country should dominate peoples in another continent.

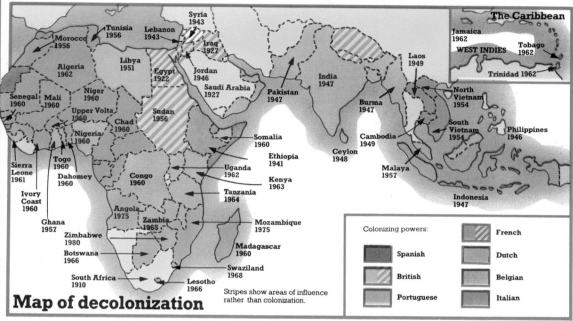

Map of decolonization

Stripes show areas of influence rather than colonization.

Colonizing powers: Spanish, British, Portuguese, French, Dutch, Belgian, Italian

The independence of **India*** in **1947** was a significant landmark, starting the break-up of the largest empire, the **British Empire**. Once some countries had obtained independence, it became increasingly difficult to resist demands from elsewhere. In **1949**, the **Dutch** were forced to recognize the independence of **Indonesia** and in **1954**, the **French** had to leave **Indo-China***.

In **1957** the **Gold Coast (Ghana)** became the first of many **black African** countries to gain independence. In **1960**, British Prime Minister **Harold Macmillan** spoke of a **"wind of change"** blowing throughout the continent.

Indian flag

Ghanaian flag

Algerian flag

In **Rhodesia (Zimbabwe)**, a white minority government broke away from British rule in **1965** under **UDI** (the **Unilateral Declaration of Independence**). After a fierce civil war, power was handed over to a black majority government in **1980**.

Decolonization was neither quick nor easy. There were many terrible wars, both against colonial powers and civil wars, to decide who should rule in their place. Especially bad were the wars in **Algeria (1954-1962)**, **Indo-China* (1946-1954)** and **Angola** and **Mozambique (1961-1975)**. Despite the establishment of **democratic*** governments at the start of independence, many countries have been subject to **dictatorships*** and **coups***. However, most former colonies have maintained close ties with their ex-rulers. Most former British colonies, for instance, have become members of the **Commonwealth***, of which the Queen is the head.

Africa and the Middle East

1954-1962 War against **French** rule in **Algeria** ends with independence.

1956 Oil is discovered in **Nigeria**.

1956 President Nasser* of Egypt nationalizes the **Suez Canal***. This is opposed by **Britain** and **France**. **Israel** invades Egypt, and Britain and France occupy the **Canal Zone**. **US** opposition and world opinion force Britain and France to withdraw.

1957 **Gold Coast** (renamed **Ghana**) becomes independent under **Kwame Nkrumah**. An important step in the **decolonization*** of **Africa***.

Ghanaian flag

1957 **King Feisal** of **Iraq** is assassinated and a **republic*** is proclaimed.

1958 **United Arab Republic (UAR)** is set up between **Egypt** and **Syria**, later joined by **Yemen**. Syria leaves in **1960**.

1960 A meeting of oil-producing countries in **Baghdad** sets up **OPEC (Organization of Petroleum Exporting Countries)**.

1960 The **Sharpeville massacre** in **South Africa**. 67 black **Africans** are killed when troops open fire on a demonstration.

1960 **Congo** becomes independent from **Belgium**. Chaos and civil war follow. **Katanga** province declares independence. A military **coup*** in the Congo brings **President Mobuto** to power.

1961 **South Africa** leaves the **Commonwealth***.

1963 **OAU (Organization for African Unity)** is formed in **Addis Ababa** by 30 African countries.

1964 **Tanganyika** and **Zanzibar** unite to become **Tanzania**.

1964 Rebel activity against the **Portuguese** increases in **Mozambique**.

1965 **UDI (Unilateral Declaration of Independence)**: **Rhodesia** (formerly **Southern Rhodesia**) is declared independent under white **minority rule*** by **Ian Smith**, leader of the **Rhodesian Front Party**. This leads to civil war.

1966 **Jean Bokassa** seizes power in the **Central African Republic**.

1966 **Milton Obote** seizes power in **Uganda**.

1966 Revolution in **Ghana** overthrows **Nkrumah**.

1966 **Dr Verwoerd**, Prime Minister of **South Africa**, is assassinated.

1966 Revolution in **Nigeria**.

1967 **Six Days' War** between **Israel** and the **Arab** states. Israel makes gains and occupies **Sinai**.

Israeli missile base during the **Six Days' War**.

1967-1970 **Nigerian Civil War**: Eastern Nigeria breaks away and declares independence as **Biafra**. By **1970** the central government restores control.

Asia

Government House, New Delhi.

1947 **India** becomes independent and is divided into the **Hindu*** state of India and **Muslim*** Pakistan. This leads to a bloody civil war. They fight over **Kashmir**, which is awarded to India.

1946-1949 Civil war between **Nationalists** and **Communists*** in **China** ends in Communist victory. Nationalists set up the state of **Nationalist China** in **Formosa (Taiwan)**.

1948 **Communist*** terrorism leads to a **state of emergency*** in **Malaya**.

1948 Two **republics*** are declared in **Korea**: a **pro-Communist** regime in **North Korea** and a **pro-Western** regime in **South Korea**.

1949 **Siam** is renamed **Thailand**.

1949 The **US** occupying administration launches a programme to improve the **Japanese** economy. Japan becomes important as a bulwark against **Communism***.

1950-1953 **The Korean War**: **North Korea**, backed by **Russia**, invades **South Korea**. **United Nations*** forces (mainly **American**) support South Korea. **China** supports North Korea. The **Communists*** make advances at first, but in **1951**, UN forces counter-attack. The **Treaty of Panmunjon (1953)** fixes the border between North and South Korea.

Border fixed by the **Treaty of Panmunjon**.

CHINA

NORTH KOREA

• Pyongyang

North Korean flag.

• Seoul

SOUTH KOREA

South Korean flag.

1950 **China** invades **Tibet**.

1951 **Mussadeq**, Prime Minister of **Iran**, nationalizes the **Anglo-Iranian Oil Company**. Tension with **Britain** follows.

1951 A peace treaty with the **Allies*** gives **Japan** full independence. A period of rapid economic growth begins. The **US** occupation ends in **1952**.

1953 **Edmund Hillary (New Zealand)** and **Sherpa Tensing (Nepal)** reach the summit of **Mount Everest**, the world's highest mountain.

1954 Major **French** defeat at **Dien Bien Phu***.

1954 **South-East Asia Treaty Organization (SEATO)** is set up to check the spread of **Communism***. It is signed by **Australia**, **France**, **New Zealand**, **Britain**, **Pakistan**, **Philippines**, **Thailand** and the **USA**.

1954-1973 **Vietnam War***.

1957 Unsuccessful uprising in **Tibet** against the **Chinese**. The **Dalai Llama** (ruler) flees to **India**.

1960 War between **China** and **India** over disputed border claims.

1960 Worsening relations between **China** and **USSR**.

1964 Increasing **American** involvement in **Vietnam***.

Northern and Eastern Europe

1937 Axis Pact formed by **Germany** and **Italy**.

1938 **Germany** takes **Austria**.

1938 Growing **German** demands for control of the **Sudetenland** (German-speaking **Czech** territory).

1938 **Munich Agreement** gives **Germany** the **Sudetenland**.

1939 **Hahn** and **Strassman** (**German**) discover nuclear fission.

1939 **Hitler** occupies **Czechoslovakia**.

1939 **Mussolini*** seizes **Albania**.

August 1939 **Nazi-Soviet Pact**. **Hitler*** and **Stalin*** agree to co-operate against **Poland**.

September 1939 **Germany** and **Russia** attack **Poland**. This leads to the **Second World War*** (1939-1945).

June 1941 **Germany** invades **Russia**.

1943 **German** defeat at **Stalingrad**.

1944 **Allies*** take **Athens**.

1944-1949 Civil war in **Greece**.

1945 **Germany** surrenders and is split into **French**, **British**, **US** and **Russian** occupation zones.

1945-1946 War trials of **Nazi*** leaders at **Nuremberg**.

1946 **Hungary**, **Bulgaria** and **Albania** become republics*, followed by **Romania** in 1947.

1948 **Communists*** seize power in **Czechoslovakia**, **Hungary**, **Romania**, **Bulgaria** and **Poland**.

1948-1949 **Berlin Blockade**: **Russians** cut off **West Berlin** in an attempt to force the **West*** to let **Berlin** become part of the **Eastern Bloc***. The blockade is broken by an **Anglo-American** airlift of supplies.

Supplies arriving during the **Berlin Airlift**.

1949 **West** and **East Germany** established as separate states.

1953 Death of **Stalin***. **Khrushchev** becomes Party leader in **USSR**.

1953 Anti-**Communist** unrest in **East Germany** and **Poland**.

Southern and Western Europe

1940 **France** falls to **Germany**. General **de Gaulle** establishes **Free French Forces (FFL)** to continue fighting the **Germans**.

1943 Fall of **Mussolini*** and the surrender of **Italy**. **Germany** occupies **North Italy** and **Rome**.

1944 Continued **Allied*** advances on all fronts. Allies take **Rome** and liberate **France**. **De Gaulle** sets up government in **Paris**.

British parachutes landing in **France** on **D-Day** (**June 1944**).

1945 **Labour Party** under **Attlee** comes to power in **Great Britain**.

1945 General **de Gaulle** heads government in **France**.

1946 Growing tension between **USSR** and the **West***.

1946 **King of Italy** abdicates and a republic* is proclaimed.

1947-1958 **French Fourth Republic**.

1947 **Belgium**, **Netherlands** and **Luxembourg** form a **Customs Union**. The beginning of movement for **European** unity.

1947-1948 Unrest in **France**. Frequent changes of government.

1948 First computer, **Mark I**, is built in **Manchester, England**.

1948 **OEEC** (**Organization for European Economic Co-operation**) is established.

1949 **Eire** leaves the **Commonwealth**.

1951 **European Coal and Steel Treaty** between **Belgium**, **France**, **Holland**, **Italy**, **Luxembourg** and **West Germany**. An important step towards European unity.

1952 **Elizabeth II** becomes **Queen of Great Britain**.

1953 The structure of **DNA** is worked out by **Crick** (**English**) and **Watson** (**American**).

1957 **Treaty of Rome** establishes the **EEC** (**Common Market**).

Flags of the original **EEC** countries.

1958 **De Gaulle** becomes **French Prime Minister**. A new constitution establishes the **Fifth Republic**. **De Gaulle** is **President**.

America and Australasia

1949 **Western*** powers form the **North Atlantic Treaty Organization (NATO)**. Members: **Belgium**, **Canada**, **Denmark**, **Great Britain**, **France**, **Holland**, **Iceland**, **Italy**, **Norway**, **USA**.

1950 **US President Truman** authorizes the development of the **hydrogen bomb**.

1950-1954 Senator **McCarthy** (**USA**) leads a drive against **Communists***. Exaggerated fears result in excessive policies.

1952 **Cuban Revolution**: General **Batista** seizes power. His regime is opposed by **Communists***, led by **Fidel Castro**. A period of unrest and civil war follows.

1955 A revolution in **Argentina** overthrows **President Peron***.

1958 The silicon chip is patented in the **USA** by **Texas Instruments**. Early **silicon chip**.

1958 **Alaska** becomes the 49th state of the **USA**.

1958 Revolution in **Cuba**: **Castro** overthrows **Batista**.

1958-1967 Demands in **USA** for civil rights* for black people.

1959 Growing tension between **USA** and **Cuba**.

1959 **Hawaii** becomes the 50th state of the **USA**.

1960 **Brasilia** becomes the new capital of **Brazil**.

1961 **Bay of Pigs**: an invasion of **Cuba**, backed by the **USA** to overthrow **Castro**, fails.

1962 **Jamaica**, **Trinidad** and **Tobago** gain independence.

1962 **Cuban missile crisis**: **Russia** establishes **nuclear bases** in **Cuba**. The **USA** threatens war unless they are dismantled. **Russia** gives in.

FLORIDA — **American blockade zone**. Missile bases. CUBA, HAITI, BARBADOS, JAMAICA, GRENADA, TOBAGO, TRINIDAD.

1963 **US President Kennedy** is assassinated in **Dallas, Texas**.

1965 **US** spacecraft lands on the **Moon**.

1966 **British Guiana** (**Guyana**) and **Barbados** become independent.

Africa and the Middle East

1968 Guerrilla* warfare increases in **Rhodesia.**

1969 A revolution in **Libya** overthrows **King Idris I** and puts **Colonel Gadaffi** in power.

1970 Military **coup*** in **Uganda** brings **Idi Amin** to power.

1970 Israel and **Egypt** fight over **Sinai.**

1972 Amin expels many of the 40,000 **Asians** living in **Uganda.**

1973 Yom Kippur War between **Israel** and the **Arab** states, who achieve some success. **Israel** is attacked by **Egypt** and **Syria.** OPEC* restricts oil supplies. This leads to huge increases in oil prices and a worldwide economic crisis.

1974 Civil war begins between rival religious (**Christian** and **Muslim***) and political groups in the **Lebanon.** By 1985, over 40,000 people have been killed in **Beirut** and other cities during the fighting.

1974 Haile Selassie* is deposed by a **Marxist junta*.**

1975 Angola and **Mozambique** become independent.

1976 Serious rioting among black **Africans** in **Soweto, South Africa.**

1977 President Sadat of **Egypt** visits **Israel** to discuss peace. Ends with the **Camp David Agreement (1978).**

1978 United Nations* force is sent to try to keep the peace on the **Israel-Lebanon** border.

A soldier from the **United Nations Peace-keeping Force** in the **Lebanon.**

1979 Peace treaty between **Israel** and **Egypt** is signed. Israel agrees to withdraw from **Sinai.**

1979 Uganda: civil war and military invasion by **Tanzania** leads to the overthrow of **Idi Amin.**

1979 The Lancaster House Conference in **London** draws up a new constitution for **Rhodesia.**

1980 Rhodesia becomes independent and is renamed **Zimbabwe. Robert Mugabe** becomes Prime Minister.

1980 Beginning of war between **Iran** and **Iraq.**

1981 President Sadat of **Egypt** is assassinated.

1982 Israel invades **Lebanon,** attempting to drive out the **PLO (Palestinian Liberation Organization),** and to establish a strong **Christian** government in **Beirut. Syria** opposes Israel. A period of civil war and terrorism follows.

1983-1985 Israeli forces withdraw from **Lebanon.**

1983 War between **Iran** and **Iraq** intensifies.

1984 A ten-year drought leads to terrible famine in **Ethiopia, Sudan** and **Chad.** Thousands die.

1985 Riots by black people in the **Eastern Cape, South Africa.**

1986 USA bombs **Libya,** in retaliation for **terrorist*** activities in **Europe.**

Asia

1965 India and **Pakistan** fight over **Kashmir.**

1965 Singapore becomes independent from **Malaya.**

1966 Mao Zedong starts the **Cultural Revolution** in **China:** a two year period of terror in which supposedly **capitalist*** influences are crushed.

1967 China explodes its first **H-bomb.**

1970 The Khmer Republic is set up in **Cambodia.**

1971 Pakistan attacks **India** but is defeated.

1972 Pakistan is forced to give up **East Pakistan,** which forms the independent state of **Bangladesh.**

1973 Ceylon changes its name to **Sri Lanka.**

1973 The last **American** troops leave **Vietnam*.**

1973 King of **Afghanistan** is overthrown.

1975 Vietnam is united under **Communist*** rule.

1975 Communists* seize power in **Cambodia** and **Laos.**

1976 Death of **Mao Zedong*.**

1977 A military coup* in **Pakistan** by **General Zia al-Haq.** Former president, **Bhutto,** is overthrown.

1978 Vietnam (pro-Russian) invades **Cambodia** to support rebels who overthrow the **pro-Chinese Khmer** government. A pro-Vietnamese regime is set up.

Ayatollah Khomeini

1979 The Shah of Iran is overthrown. An **Islamic*** Republic led by **Ayatollah Khomeini** is proclaimed.

1979 Civil war against the **socialist*** regime in **Afghanistan. Russian** troops invade in support of the **pro-Soviet government.** A period of guerrilla* war against the Russians follows.

1980 War between **Iran** and **Iraq** begins.

1983 Unrest between **Tamil separatists*** and **Singhalese** in **Sri Lanka.**

1984 Britain and **China** agree on terms for the independence of **Hong Kong.**

Hong Kong

1984 Assassination of Prime Minister **Indira Gandhi** of **India.** This follows repressive action to put down **Sikh*** unrest in the **Punjab.**

1985 Cambodia: Vietnam* launches an offensive against the last rebel strongholds near **Thai** border.

1985 War between **Iran** and **Iraq** intensifies.

Northern and Eastern Europe

1954 EOKA movement in **Cyprus** for union with **Greece**. A period of **anti-British** unrest until **1959**.

1955 Soviet Union signs the **Warsaw Pact**, an East European (**Communist***) defence treaty.

1956 Anti-Communist* uprising in **Hungary** is crushed by **USSR**.

1957 Russia launches the first space satellite, **Sputnik I**.

1960 Cyprus gains independence from **Britain**, **Greece** and **Turkey**.

1961 Yuri Gagarin (**USSR**) makes the first manned spaceflight.

A **Russian** stamp commemorating **Gagarin's** spaceflight.

1961 East German Communists* and **Russians** build the **Berlin Wall** to stop East Germans fleeing to the **West***.

1964 Fighting between **Greeks** and **Turks** in **Cyprus**.

1967 King of **Greece** is deposed.

1968 A liberal* movement within the **Czechoslovak Communist Party** is crushed by **USSR**.

Russian tanks invading **Prague**.

1973 Denmark joins the **EEC***.

1973 Greece becomes a **republic***.

1980 Death of **President Tito** (1892-1980), ruler in **Yugoslavia** since **1945**.

1980 Serious unrest in **Poland** as the independent trade union movement **Solidarity**, led by **Lech Walesa**, gains support. Polish government declares **martial law***, bans Solidarity and imprisons many of its leaders.

Solidarity poster

1985 President Gorbachev becomes leader of the **USSR**.

1986 Nuclear reactor disaster at **Chernobyl, USSR**.

Southern and Western Europe

1962 Britain applies to join the **EEC***, but is rejected by **France**.

1965 Death of **Sir Winston Churchill***.

Student protesters in **Paris**.

1968 Student unrest and strikes in **Europe**, especially in **France**.

1968 Civil rights* riots in **Northern Ireland**. The beginning of a period of violence and clashes between **Protestant Unionists** (who want to maintain union with **Britain**) and **Catholics** (who want separation).

1969 Resignation of **General de Gaulle*** as **President of France**.

North Sea oil rig.

1970 British find oil in **North Sea**.

1970 Death of **de Gaulle***.

1970 Spain: serious unrest among **Basque separatists** (people from the Basque region who want separation from Spain).

1971 Decimal currency is adopted in **Britain**.

1971 Women are given the vote in **Switzerland**.

1972 The situation in **Northern Ireland** worsens. **Britain** imposes direct rule from **Westminster**.

1973 Denmark, **Eire** and **UK** join the **EEC***.

1974 Revolution in **Portugal**.

1975 Death of **Franco**. The monarchy is restored in **Spain** under **Juan Carlos**, who reintroduces **democracy*** in **1977**.

1976 Concorde, the first supersonic passenger aeroplane, begins a transatlantic service.

Concorde, invented by **Britain** and **France**.

1980s Increase in anti-nuclear demonstrations in **Europe**.

1981 Mitterand becomes the first **Socialist*** President of **France**.

America and Australasia

1967 Peace riots in many cities of the **USA**.

1967 Che Guevara, leader of **left-wing*** guerrillas* in **Bolivia**, is killed.

1968 Martin Luther King, a **Black American** civil rights* leader, is assassinated.

1969 July 21: US astronaut, **Neil Armstrong**, becomes the first man to step on to the Moon.

Neil Armstrong on the Moon.

1969 Growing demonstrations in **USA** against the **Vietnam War***.

1973 Revolution in **Chile**, supported by **USA**, overthrows **Marxist*** President Allende.

1973 The end of **US** military involvement in **Vietnam***.

1973 Juan Peron* becomes **President of Argentina** again.

1973-1974 Watergate scandal in **USA**. President Nixon resigns.

1978 USA establishes diplomatic relations with **China**.

1979 President Somoza of **Nicaragua** is overthrown. The **left-wing*** Sandanista government comes to power.

1981 The first reuseable **shuttle** spaceflight is made.

1981 Ronald Reagan becomes **President** of the **USA**.

1982 British Honduras becomes independent, as **Belize**.

1982 Falklands War: Argentina invades the **British Falkland Islands**. **Britain** sends a naval taskforce and retakes the islands by force.

1983 Left-wing* coup* in **Grenada** is put down by **US** intervention.

1983 Democracy* is restored in **Argentina**.

1985 Democracy* is restored in **Brazil** and **Uruguay**.

The Cold War

After the **Second World War***, a split developed between the **Eastern Bloc** (the **USSR** and her **Communist*** allies) and the **Western Bloc** (the **USA** and her non-Communist allies). The **Cold War** is the name used to decribe the state of hostility and tension between them, which reached its peak from **1948-1962**.

Flag of the **USSR**.
Flag of the **USA**.

Even before the end of the War, differences among the **Allies*** had become apparent. Failure to agree on a settlement for **Germany** led to the **Berlin Blockade* (1948-1949)** and the division of the country. Increased tension led to rearmament and the formation of military alliances: **NATO* (1949)** and the **Warsaw Pact* (1955)**. The two camps supported opposing sides in conflicts such as the **Korean War* (1950-1953)**.

Europe

NORWAY, SWEDEN, FINLAND, DENMARK, BRITAIN, EAST GERMANY, WEST GERMANY, POLAND, FRANCE, CZECHOSLOVAKIA, AUSTRIA, HUNGARY, USSR, SWITZERLAND, ROMANIA, YUGOSLAVIA, SPAIN, ITALY, BULGARIA, GREECE, TURKEY

The line dividing **Eastern Europe** from non-Communist **Western Europe** became known as the **Iron Curtain**.

Warsaw Pact
NATO
Neutral countries

Hostility reached a dangerous point with the **Cuban Missile Crisis* (1962)**. Since the early **1970s**, there has been an easing of tension, known as *détente*, although the build-up of powerful, particularly nuclear, weapons has continued unchecked.

The Vietnam War

The three ancient kingdoms of **Vietnam**, **Laos** and **Cambodia** were colonized by the **French** between **1860-1900** and were known as **French Indo-China**. During the **Second World War***, they were occupied by **Japan**. In **Northern Vietnam** a **pro-Communist*** independence movement grew up, known as the **Vietminh**, led by **Ho Chi Minh**. In **1945**, he set up a government in **Hanoi**. French resistance to this led to a war of independence **(1946-1954)**, ending in French defeat at **Dien Bien Phu** in **1954**.

French Indo-China
Dien Bien Phu
Hanoi
LAOS
NORTH VIETNAM
Vientiane
CAMBODIA
SOUTH VIETNAM
Phnom Penh
Saigon

North Vietnam won independence. **South Vietnam** also became independent, under an anti-Communist government. North Vietnam did not accept the division of the country and civil war broke out for control of South Vietnam.

North Vietnam helped the pro-Communist rebels in the South (the **Viet Cong**). The South Vietnamese government in **Saigon** was backed by the **USA**, who, from **1961**, became more and more actively involved. In **1965**, American aircraft began bombing North Vietnam. Depite a huge American presence (half a million troops by **1968**), as well as contingents from other nations, the Viet Cong proved to be masters of jungle warfare and won victory after victory.

American helicopters flying over the **Vietnamese** jungle.

The Americans withdrew by the end of **1973**. A cease-fire was declared, but the Communists were determined to control South Vietnam. Saigon fell in **1975**, and Vietnam was united under Communist rule. Laos also fell under Vietnamese control, followed by Cambodia in **1978**.

Glossary

amnesty
A general pardon given by a government for crimes committed. Sometimes granted in an attempt to reach a peaceful settlement during a civil war.

annex
To join a territory to a larger territory by conquering or occupying it.

apartheid
The **South African** policy of the separation of races.

aristocracy
Government by nobles or a privileged class.

autocracy
Government by a person or group, with unrestricted authority, that does not allow opposition. Government of this kind is described as **autocratic**.

autonomy
Self-government, often of a limited nature, granted to a nation or people, by a more powerful nation.

Bantu
A group of **African** languages or peoples found between the **equator** and the **Cape of Good Hope**.

caliphate
The office or state of a **caliph***.

canonize
To declare a person a **saint**.

capitalism
The system where the means of production (industries, business, etc.) are owned by a relatively small group, who provide the investment and take a major share of the profits.

cede
To give up or surrender a territory, often as part of the terms of a peace treaty following a war.

charter
A document issued by a government, granting certain rights, such as the right to found a colony.

Christendom
All the peoples, or nations, who belong to the **Christian Church**.

civil rights
Equality in social, economic and political matters.

coalition
A temporary alliance between different groups or political parties, for instance in a government.

collectivization
The organization of the ownership of the means of production (industries, agriculture and business) by the state into groups, or **collectives**.

colonization
To establish a **colony** (or **colonies**) – settlement in a country distant from the homeland. A **Crown colony** is a colony whose administration is controlled by the **Crown** (the King or Queen).

Commonwealth
The organization formed by former member countries of the **British Empire**, with the aim of mutual co-operation and assistance.

Communism
An ideology mainly based on the ideas of **Karl Marx***, which advocates a society without social classes, in which private ownership has been abolished. A system where the means of production (industries and businesses) are owned by the state.

Congress
The government of the **USA**, made up of two houses: the **Senate** and the **House of Representatives**.

coup d'état
The sudden overthrow of an existing government by a small group, often made up of army officers.

demilitarization
The removal of any military presence (soldiers, weapons, etc) from an area.

democracy
An ideology originating in **Ancient Greece***, meaning rule by the people.

dependency
A territory subject to a nation, to which it is not usually linked geographically.

despot
An **absolute*** or autocratic ruler, or **tyrant***. An **enlightened despot** is one who tries to govern in the interests of the people, according to the ideals of the **Enlightenment***.

dictator
A non-royal **autocratic** ruler, who imposes his rule by force. The government is called a **dictatorship**.

dominion
The name formerly used for a self-governing colony within the **British Empire**, such as **Canada**.

ecclesiastical
Relating to the **Christian Church** or clergy.

egalitarian
A system that promotes equality.

excommunicate
To expel a person from the **Christian Church**.

Fascism
An ideology first developed by **Mussolini***. A form of government which allows no rival political parties and which controls the lives of its citizens. **Nazism*** is a form of Fascism.

federal
Relating to a type of government in which power is shared between central government and several regional governments.

guerrilla
A fighter operating in secret, usually against the government. From the **Spanish** *guerra*, meaning war.

hegemony
The domination of one power or state within a league or federation.

homage
A public display of respect or honour to someone, such as a **feudal*** lord.

infallibility
Being incapable of error. A principle applied to certain pronouncements of the **papacy***.

junta
Government by a group of military officers, often after a **coup d'état**.

left-wing
A phrase used to describe any ideology that tends towards **socialism*** or **Communism***.

liberalism
An ideology which advocates individual freedom and maintains that governments should interfere as little as possible with people's lives.

mandate
The authority given to a country by the **League of Nations***to administer another country under its trusteeship.

martial law
The rule of law established by military courts, and maintained by soldiers, in the absence of civil (non-military) authority.

Marxist
A person or government following the teachings of **Karl Marx***. The belief that actions and institutions are determined by economics, that the class struggle is the instrument of change and that **capitalism** will eventually be overcome by **Communism**.

medieval
Relating to the **Middle Ages**, a period in **European** history dating loosely from **c.500-1500**.

minority rule
Government by a group of people who are different, politically or racially, from a larger group over whom they rule.

monopoly
The sole right to sell or trade in a specific product or a specific area.

nepotism
The granting of an official position, or other privilege, to a member of the family, or friend.

nomads
People who move continually from place to place. They are described as **nomadic**.

one-party-state
A nation that is dominated by the one and only party that is allowed to exist.

papal bull
A formal document issued by the **Pope**.

parliamentary democracy
A modern form of **democracy***, in which representatives elected by the people make decisions on their behalf.

patent
A document issued by a government, granting specified rights.

plebiscite
A direct vote by the people of a state on an issue of particular importance, such as **unification*** with another state.

pretender
Someone who makes a claim to a throne or a title.

privateer
A privately-employed soldier, sailor (or vessel) commissioned for service by a government.

Protector
Someone who exercises royal authority during the reign of a minor (a child) or the incapacity of the monarch.

protectorate
A territory largely controlled by, but not **annexed*** to, a more powerful nation.

radical
Tending towards extreme or fundamental social, political or economic changes.

regent
The ruler of a country during the reign of a minor (a child) or the absence or incapacity of the monarch.

republic
A state governed by the representatives of the people, without a king or queen.

residency
The official house of a **British** governor at the court of an **Indian** prince.

sack
The plunder or destruction of a place by an army or mob.

secular
Relating to worldly, as opposed to religious or **ecclesiastical***, things.

separatist
A person or organization that advocates separation from a larger unit, such as a nation.

socialism
An ideology that stresses equality of income and wealth, and believes in public (state) ownership of industries (the means of production).

sovereignty
The supreme authority or power of a sovereign (monarch) or state.

state of emergency
A crisis during which a government temporarily suspends all the usual rights and liberties of a people.

sultan
The supreme ruler (sovereign) of a **Muslim*** country, such as the **Ottoman Empire***.

suzerainty
The position of a state exercising a degree of domination over a **dependent** state (see **dependency***).

temporal
Relating to worldly or **secular**, as opposed to religious or spiritual, matters.

terrorist
Someone who uses terror (bombing attacks, assassinations, etc.) as a means of political persuasion.

Third World
The relatively underdeveloped, unindustrialized countries of **Africa**, **Asia** and **South America**, which remain outside the **Eastern*** and **Western Blocs***.

tribute
Payment made by one nation or peoples to another, more dominant nation or ruler, usually acknowledging submission.

triumvirate
A **coalition*** of three officials, such as **Caesar***, **Crassus*** and **Pompey***, ruling jointly.

tyranny
Oppressive and unjust government by a **despotic*** ruler or rulers.

ultimatum
A final offer by a government or party, in which it insists on certain conditions.

Index

Page numbers printed in **bold** type indicate a feature, or the place where a main definition or explanation of the word can be found. Page numbers in *italics* indicate maps. These show routes of explorers and kingdoms, as well as place names.

Country entries are broken down into periods, shown by feature headings or dates. The dates show the earliest and latest date relating to the subject on a page or double-page spread. For example: **Turkey, 1876-1894, 98, 99;** ... (You may sometimes find the earlier date occuring on the right rather than on the left-hand page.)

39 Articles, 58
1848, Year of Revolutions, 91, *92,* 95

A

Aachen (Aix-la-Chapelle), Germany, 22; chapel, 23
Abbasids, 23, *24,* 24, 25, 27, 42
Abbas the Great, Shah of Persia, 61, 67
Abdullah, King of Iraq, 100
aborigines, 90
Aboukir Bay, Battle of, 1799, 85, 88
absenteeism, 56
absolutism, 72
Abu Bakr, caliph, 23
Abu Simbel, Upper Egypt, *10;* temple, 11
Abydos, Upper Egypt, *10*
Acamapitzin, King of the Aztecs, 37
Achaemenid dynasty, 16
Acre, Palestine, *32,* 33, 37, 41
acropolis, 13
Actium, Battle of, 30BC, 14, 15
Act of Supremacy, 1534, 58
Acts of Uniformity, 1549, 1552, 58
Act of Union, 1801, 91
Adana people, 5, 11
Adowa, Battle of, 1896, 98
Adrianople, Turkey, *43, 44*
  Battle of, 378, 14, 19; *812,* 26
Aegean, 4, *12,* 13
Aelia Capitolina, Judaea, 16
Afghanistan, *13;* **997, 1447-1494,** 45; **1504,** 51; **1581,** 55; and Moguls, 59, *59,* 82; **1709-1737,** 79; **1761,** 83; **1838,** 90; **1878,** 98, *98;* **1973-1979,** 110
Afonso, King of the Kongo, 51
Africa, *17, 33;* in 16th, **58-59,** *59;* slaves, 62; *85;* colonization, **96-97;** decolonization, *107; see also* individual countries
Afrikaner Nationalist Party, 104
Aga Muhammed, ruler of Persia, 85
Agincourt, Battle of, 1415, *38,* 39, 40
agriculture, earliest: Fertile Crescent, 9000BC, 4
Agung, Sultan of Mataram, Java, 67
Ahmed Bey, ruler of Tripoli, 79
Ahmed Shah, Sultan of Persia, 100
Ahuizotl, Aztec Emperor, 51
Ain Jalut, Battle of, 1260-1261, 37, 42, *45*
aircraft, 101, 105, 111
Aix-la-Chapelle, Germany; *see also* Aachen
  Peace of, 1748, 78
  Treaty of, 1668, 70, 77
Akbar, Prince of India, 75
Akbar the Great of India, 55, 59, *59,* 61, 65, 71
Akhenaten, Pharaoh of Egypt, 9
Akkad, Akkadians, 4, 5, 6, *6,* 7
Alans, 16
Alaska, USA, 99, 109, *111*
Alaungpaya, leader of Burma, 81
al Badr, Battle of, 624, 24

Albania, *89;* **1924,** 105; **1939-1946,** 109
Albert of Hohenzollern, 50
Albert I, Habsburg, 43
Albert II of Habsburg, 44
Alberti, 47
Albigensians, 34, 36
Alemanni, *19,* 22, *22*
Aleppo, Syria, 33
Aleutian islands, 79
Allende, President of Chile, 111
Alexander II, Tsar of Russia, 95, 99
Alexander III, Tsar of Russia, 99
Alexander VI, Pope, 41
Alexander of Novgorod (Nevsky), 43
Alexander the Great, 7, 10, 11, **13,** *13,* 14, 15, 16, 17
Alexandria, central Asia, *13*
Alexandria, Egypt, *13,* 15, 17, 19, *19, 21,* 88
Alexandria Oxiana, India, 13
Alexius Comnenus, Byzantine Emperor, 32
Alfonso XIII, King of Spain, 105
Alfonso of Aragon, 40
Alfred the Great, King of England, 26, 28
Algarve, Portugal, 45
Algeria, 16th, 59, *59;* **1830,** 90; colonization, 96, *96;* **1945,** 104, *106;* decolonization, 107, *107;* **1954,** 108
Algiers, Algeria, 90
Alhambra palace, 44
Ali, caliph, 24
Allies: First World War, 100, 101, 102, *102;* Second World War, 104, 106, *106,* 108, 109, 112
Alma, Battle of, 1854, *89,* 95
Almohads, *24,* 32, *32, 45*
Almoravids, *24,* 31, *33*
Alodia, north Africa, 21
alphabets, 13, 26, 29
Alsace, *38,* 99
Altai region, Mongolia, 19
Altan-Khan, Mongol leader, 55
Altranstadt, Treaty of, 1706, 78
Alva, Duke of, 60
Alyattes, King of Lydia, 14
Amarapura, Burma, *83,* 85
Amboyna Massacre, 1623, 67
Ambuila, Battle of, 1662, 73
American Civil War, 1861-1865, 92, *92,* 97, 99
American Declaration of Independence, 1776, 81, 83
American War of Independence, 1775-1783, 81, 83
Amin, Idi, President of Uganda, 110
Ammonites, 17, *17*
Amorites, 6, 7
Amritsar, Golden Temple, 75, 100
Amsterdam, Netherlands, 69, *69*
Amundsen, 101
Anabaptists, 54
Anasazi people, 23, 27, *31*
Anatolia, 6000BC, 4, *4;* **5000BC-AD200,** *6;* **200BC,** *7;* Greek colonies in, 13; **1071,** 25; *see also* Turkey
Andreas II, King of Hungary, 36
Angevin Empire, 32, *38*
Angkor kingdom, 27, *31,* 33
Angkor Wat, 33
Angles, 16, 19: *see also* Anglo-Saxons
Anglican Church, *57,* 58
Anglo-Boer War, 1899-1902, 98, 100
Anglo-Burmese Wars, 1824-1852, 90, 94
Anglo-Chinese War, 1859-1860, 96
Anglo-Dutch Trade Wars, 1652-1674, 66, 69, 70
Anglo-Egyptian Condominium, 96
Anglo-Iranian Oil Company, 108
Anglo-Portuguese Treaty, 1373, 40
Anglo-Saxons, 16, *19,* 22; *see also* Angles, Saxons
Anglo-Siam Treaty, 1909, 100
Anglo-Sikh Wars, 1845-1849, 94
Angola, 96, *96,* 107, *107,* 110
Ani, Armenia, 37
Anjou, France, 35, 38, *38,* 44

Ankara, Turkey, 43
Annam, Indo-China, 51, *53,* 61, *90,* 96, 98
Anne Boleyn, 58
Anne of Brittany, 38
Anne, Queen of England, 74
Anne, wife of Ferdinand I, Holy Roman Emperor, 52
Antarctic, 94
Antigonid dynasty, 10
Antigua, 63
Antioch, Anatolia, 19, *19,* 23, *32, 32,* 41
Antwerp, Southern Netherlands, *57,* 60
Apulia, Italy, 30
Aquinas, Thomas, 36
Aquitaine, France, 19
Arabic: language, 5; numerals, 36
Arab League, 104
Arabs, *5;* **543,** 21; **632,** 20; **632-700,** 23; **674-771,** 22; and the Franks, 23; rise of Islam, *24,* 24; kingdoms in Spain, 24, 36, 44, 45; **976-1054,** 26; **700s-909,** 27; **1212,** 36; **1352-1400,** 41; in Africa, 59; nationalists, 100; **1936-1948,** 104; **1973,** 110
Aragon, Spain, 36, 44, *45,* 52, *52*
Aramaeans, *5,* 7
Ararat, Armenia, 8
archons, 8
Arcot, Battle of, 1751, 81, 82, *83*
Arctic Circle, 67
Ardashir I, Sassanid king, 16
Argentina, 1808-1816, 91, *91;* **1828,** 95; **1942-1946,** 105; **1955,** 109; **1973-1983,** 111, *111*
Argos, Greece, 10
aristocracy, 13
Arizona, USA, 23, *92,* 95
Arkwright, Richard, 82
Armagnacs, 40
Armenians, Armenia: language, 5; **976,** 26; **1239,** 37; **1375,** 41; **1514,** 51; **1826,** 90; **1890,** 98, *98*
Armstrong, Neil, 111
Arpad dynasty, 25, 26, 40
Arras, Peace of, 1482, 38, *38;* **1578,** 60, *60*
Arthur, King of the Britons, 20
Artois, France, 38, *38*
Aryans, 5
Ashanti kingdom, 71, 79, 85, 90, 96
Ashurbanipal, King of Assyria, 10
Asia Minor, *6;* **550-304BC,** 14; **535BC,** 16; and Byzantines, 21, 23; **1030,** 31; **1071,** 32; **1250,** 43; *see also* Anatolia
Askia David, King of Songhai, 55
Asoka, India, 11, 17
Assam, India, 90
Assassins, 31
Assur, Mesopotamia, 6, 7
Assyria, 6, *7;* **9000BC,** *4;* **1814-835BC,** 6, 8; **745-615BC,** 10
Astrakhan, Russia, 55
Asturias, Spain, 22
Astyages, King of Media, 16
Athabascan Indians, 37, *41*
Athens, Greece, 8, 10, *12,* 13, *43,* 109
Atlantic, North, 55
atomic bombs, 104, 105
Attlee, Prime Minister of Britain, 109
Augsburg, Germany, 52
  League of, 1686, 72, 73
  Peace of, 1554, 54, 56, *57*
Augustin I, Emperor of Mexico, 95
Augustus II, Elector of Saxony and King of Poland, 78, 80
Augustus III of Poland, 80
Augustus, Roman Emperor, 14, 18
Aurangzeb, Mogul Emperor, 59, *59,* 71, 73, 79
Austerlitz, Battle of, 1805, 88, *89*
Australia, *62;* **1614,** 67; **1644,** 71; **1688,** 75; **1768,** 81; **1788,** 85, *85;* **1802-1829,** 90; **1844-1868,** 94; **1834,** 95, *98;* **1900-1927,** 101; First World War, 102; **1954,** 108

First published in 1987 by Usborne Publishing Ltd, 20 Garrick Street, London WC2E 9BJ.
Copyright © 1987 Usborne Publishing Ltd. All rights reserved. No part of this publication may be reproduced, stored in a retrieval system, or transmitted by any means, electronic, mechanical, photocopying, recording, or otherwise, without the prior permission of the publisher. The name Usborne and the device 🐝 are Trade Marks of Usborne Publishing Ltd. Printed in Scotland.